THE EVERYTHING

BEDTIME STORY BOOK

Familiar favorites
and brand-new
classics that
will enchant
the whole family

Mark Binder

An Everything® Series Book.
Everything® is a registered trademark of Adams Media Corporation.

Published by Adams Media Corporation
260 Center Street, Holbrook, MA 02343

ISBN: 1-58062-147-3

Printed in the United States of America.

J   I   H   G   F   E   D

Library of Congress Cataloging-in-Publication Data
Binder, Mark.
The everything bedtime story book / Mark Binder.
p.   cm.
Summary: A collection of 100 stories and poems for bedtime.
ISBN 1-58062-147-3
1. Children's literature. [1. Literature—Collections.] I. Title.
PZ7.B51165Ev   1999   98-47668
                                        CIP
                                        AC

Illustrations by Barry Littmann

*This book is available at quantity discounts for bulk purchases.
For information, call 1-800-872-5627.*

See the entire Everything® series at everything.com.

For Max and the players to be named later

Thanks to Debbie and Emily, Mom and Dad, Pam Liflander,
and of course Alicia

Contents

x

Introduction

*O*nce upon a time, my editor said, "Bring me a collection of bedtime stories. Find the best stories and poems from around the world, and retell them so that they'll be suitable for young kids." Piece of cake, I thought. No, it was much harder than that.

We didn't want to focus just on the standards. Yes, we've included many of them—Grimm's, the *Arabian Nights*, Aesop, and Hans Christian Andersen—but we've also tried to find tales of diversity from around the world. We included classic stories by Mark Twain, Nathaniel Hawthorne, and Washington Irving. Plus, we've collected a number of bedtime stories in poem form, and dug up a few oldies that have slipped from the public eye.

Almost all of these stories have been altered. Some are shorter, some are longer, and some of the language has been modernized. (I didn't touch a word of "Casey at the Bat" or "The Ballad of East and West.") A few stories have been drastically rewritten in the name of fun. (Take my version of the "Three Bears" or "The Two Monks and the Gross Slimy Monster.") And I've edited out all of the explicit sex scenes from the *Arabian Nights*.

Still, many of these tales are not politically correct. It would have been easy to bowdlerize, cutting the social or political elements that we don't agree with (this year), but far too many story books already do that. Some stories are violent, and some are sexist. I've tried to include warning notes when a story contains a particularly nasty bit.

There was also the question of what to do when we discovered that in the original version of "Chicken Little," Foxy Loxy eats the hero and all the other animals. We fixed that one. Fortunately, most of the stories in this book already came with happy endings, but we have left intact a few important stories that don't end with the famous "and they lived happily ever after."

As a parent, you can pick and choose what you want to expose your child to. Storytelling is a flexible art. Edit out parts that you don't like in the same way that you might fast-forward past a scary segment of a videotape. Elaborate on other stories when the children beg for more.

Throughout the book we also offer glimpses into history, hints, and suggestions that will make your bedtime storytelling more engaging and more fun for everyone involved.

Not every story will be appropriate for every child. Some will go right over the heads of the younger ones. Others will be boring for the older ones. Still, it's our hope that years later when your youngsters stumble across "Tom Sawyer," they'll say, "Hey, I remember this. This is a great story!"

This story book will give your boys and girls windows into the wide world of literature and storytelling. Oh, and don't forget to finish with the most important words in any bedtime story: "Good night."

Mark Binder
Chelmsford, Massachusetts

1. The Three Bears

There are as many stories about Goldilocks and the three bears as there are storytellers. The ending in this one is a little bit happier than it is in some.

READER TIP: Kids love exaggeration and enthusiasm. In this story, Baby Bear's chair doesn't just break, it breaks into a million billion trillion pieces. You can keep going (gazillion, etc.) or raise your voice enthusiastically. Also, when Goldilocks reads the magazine, feel free to personalize it—select the child's favorite magazine, or change the magazine to a television.

*O*nce upon a time, there were three little bears, a mama bear, a papa bear, and a baby bear. These bears lived in a house in the woods, which is very unusual for bears.

One day Mama Bear was making porridge for breakfast, but the porridge was too hot. The bears decided to go for a walk.

While they were out, a little girl with long golden curls came to the door of their house and knocked. Her name was Goldilocks. She knocked and knocked, but no one answered. Goldilocks was lost and tired and very hungry.

Finally, she opened the door and peeked inside. "Hello?" she said, but no one answered. Goldilocks went into the dining room, where she found three bowls of porridge on the table.

She tasted Papa Bear's porridge, but it was too hot. She tasted Mama Bear's porridge, but it was too cold. She tasted Baby Bear's porridge, and it was just right! So, she ate it all up.

Then she decided to sit down in the living room and read a magazine. First she sat in Papa Bear's chair, but it was too hard. Then she sat in Mama Bear's chair, but it was too soft. Finally, she sat in Baby Bear's chair, and it was just right! She started reading her magazine, but then Baby Bear's chair broke—CRACK—into a million billion trillion pieces!

Goldilocks was very tired now, so she went upstairs to look for a bed to lie down in. First she tried Papa Bear's bed, but it was too hard. Then she lay in Mama Bear's bed, but it was too soft. Finally, she lay in Baby Bear's bed, and it was just right! She fell fast asleep.

A little while later, the three bears came home from their walk. They went into the dining room and sat down to eat their breakfast.

"Somebody's been eating my porridge," said Papa Bear.

"Somebody's been eating my porridge," said Mama Bear.

"And somebody's been eating my porridge," said Baby Bear. "And they ate it all up. Boo hoo!"

The Bear family went into the living room to discuss what should be done.

"Somebody's been sitting in my chair," said Papa Bear.

"Somebody's been sitting in my chair," said Mama Bear.

"Somebody's been sitting in my chair, too," said Baby Bear. "And they broke it into a million billion trillion pieces. Boo hoo!"

By now the Bear family was quite upset. They went upstairs to check the rest of the house.

"Somebody's been sleeping in my bed," said Papa Bear.

"Somebody's been sleeping in my bed," said Mama Bear.

"Somebody's been sleeping in my bed," said Baby Bear. "And there she is!"

"GROWL!" said all the bears.

Goldilocks woke up with a start, and the bears chased her all around the house, until everyone was quite exhausted.

Goldilocks explained that she was lost and hungry and that she was very, very sorry. Baby Bear was still very upset.

Finally, they all came up with an answer. Goldilocks helped Papa Bear fix the chair. She helped Mama Bear cook more porridge And she taught Baby Bear how to make his bed. Then Goldilocks washed up all the dishes, and the bears told her how to get home from the forest.

And they all lived happily ever after.

— *The End* —

2. How Tom Sawyer Painted a Fence

Mark Twain, The Adventures of Tom Sawyer

Mark Twain's story of how Tom Sawyer painted his fence is a classic. I've tried to change it as little as possible, mostly just editing it down. When your child finally gets old enough to read the original, he or she will already be familiar with the characters.

READER TIP: Have fun with Tom and Ben's language and accent.

Saturday morning was come, and all the summer world was bright and fresh and brimming with life.

Tom Sawyer appeared on the sidewalk with a bucket of whitewash and a long-handled brush. He surveyed the fence, and all gladness left him. Thirty yards of board fence nine feet high to paint.

Sighing, he dipped his brush and passed it along the top plank. He did it again and compared the insignificant whitewashed streak with the continent of unwhitewashed fence and sat down on a tree-box discouraged. . . .

At this dark and hopeless moment an inspiration burst upon him! Nothing less than a great, magnificent inspiration.

He took up his brush and went tranquilly to work.

Ben Rogers hove in sight presently—the very boy whose ridicule he had been dreading. Ben's gait was a hop-skip-and-jump. He was eating an apple and giving a long, melodious whoop, followed by a deep-toned ding-dong-dong, ding-dong-dong, for he was impersonating a steamboat.

"Stop her, sir! Ting-a-ling-ling!" He drew up slowly toward the sidewalk.

Tom went on whitewashing—paying no attention to the steamboat.

Ben stared a moment and then said: "Hi-yi! You're up a stump, ain't you!"

No answer. Tom surveyed his last touch with the eye of an artist, then he gave his brush another gentle sweep.

Ben ranged up alongside him. Tom's mouth watered for the apple, but he stuck to his work.

Ben said: "Hello, old chap, you got to work, hey?"

Tom wheeled suddenly and said: "Why, it's you, Ben! I warn't noticing."

"Say," said Ben, "I'm going a-swimming. Don't you wish you could? But of course you'd druther work—wouldn't you? Course you would!"

Tom contemplated the boy a bit and said: "What do you call work?"

"Why, ain't that work?"

Tom resumed his whitewashing, and answered carelessly: "Well, maybe it is, and maybe it ain't. All I know, is, it suits Tom Sawyer."

"Oh come, now, you don't mean that you like it?"

The brush continued to move.

"Like it? Well, I don't see why I oughtn't to like it. Does a boy get a chance to whitewash a fence every day?"

That put the thing in a new light. Ben stopped nibbling his apple. Tom swept his brush daintily back and forth—stepped back to note the effect—added a touch here and there—criticized the effect again—Ben watching every move and getting more and more interested, more and more absorbed. Presently he said: "Say, Tom, let me whitewash a little."

Tom considered, was about to consent; but he altered his mind: "No—no—I reckon it wouldn't hardly do, Ben. You see, Aunt Polly's awful particular about this fence—right here on the street, you know. If it was the back fence I wouldn't mind and she wouldn't. Yes, she's awful particular about this fence. I reckon there ain't one boy in a thousand, maybe two thousand, that can do it the way it's got to be done."

"No—is that so? Oh come, now—lemme just try. Only just a little—I'd let you, if you was me, Tom."

"Ben, I'd like to, honest injun; but Aunt Polly—well, Jim wanted to do it, but she wouldn't let him; Sid wanted to do it, and she wouldn't let Sid. Now don't you see how I'm fixed? If you was to tackle this fence and anything was to happen to it. . . ."

"Oh, shucks, I'll be just as careful. Now lemme try. Say, I'll give you the core of my apple."

"Well, here—No, Ben, now don't. I'm afeard. . ."

"I'll give you all of it!"

Tom gave up the brush with reluctance in his face, but alacrity in his heart. And while Ben worked and sweated in the sun, Tom sat on a barrel in the shade close by, dangled his legs, munched his apple, and planned the slaughter of more innocents.

There was no lack of material; boys happened along every little while; they came to jeer, but remained to whitewash. By the time Ben was fagged out, Tom had traded the next chance to Billy Fisher for a kite, in good repair; and when he played out, Johnny Miller bought in for a dead rat and a string to swing it with—and so on, and so on, hour after hour. And when the middle of the afternoon came, from being a poor poverty-stricken boy in the morning, Tom was literally rolling in wealth. He had, besides the things before mentioned, twelve marbles, part of a jew's harp, a piece of blue bottle glass to look through, a spool cannon, a key that wouldn't unlock anything, a fragment of chalk, a glass stopper of a decanter, a tin soldier, a couple of tadpoles, six fire-crackers, a kitten with only one eye, a brass door knob, a dog collar—but no dog— the handle of a knife, four pieces of orange peel, and a dilapidated old window sash.

He had had a nice, good, idle time all the while, plenty of company, and the fence had three coats of whitewash on it! If he hadn't run out of whitewash he would have bankrupted every boy in the village.

Tom had discovered a great law of human action, without knowing it—namely, that in order to make a man or a boy covet a thing, it is only necessary to make the thing difficult to attain.

— *The End* —

3. *The Three Little Pigs*

*O*nce upon a time, there were three little pigs who lived near a forest. They were all brothers. They liked to eat and play all day and sleep all night. Winter was coming soon, so they decided to build themselves some houses.

The first little pig built a house made out of straw. The second little pig built his house out of twigs. The third little pig built his house out of bricks.

One day, a hungry wolf wandered out of the forest, and came to the straw house. BANG, BANG, BANG. He knocked on the door of the straw house.

"Who is it?" asked the little pig, who was inside.

"I'm a big bad wolf!"

"Go away!" said the little pig. "We don't want any wolves."

"Little pig, little pig, let me in." said the wolf.

"Not by the hair of my chinny chin chin," said the pig.

"Then I'll huff. And I'll puff. And I'll blow your house in."

"Go ahead," said the pig. "Give it a try."

The wolf huffed. And he puffed. And he blew.

The straw house blew apart into a million billion trillion pieces.

"Eeek!" said the first little pig, and he ran, ran, ran to the house made out of sticks.

"What's wrong?" said the second pig.

"There's a wolf coming!" panted the first pig. "Lock the door!"

Just then, there was a knock. BANG, BANG, BANG!

"Who is it?" said the two little pigs, who were inside.

"I'm a big bad wolf!"

"Go away," the pigs said. "There's nobody home."

"Little pigs, little pigs, let me in."

"Not by the hair of our chinny chin chins."

"Then I'll huff. And I'll puff. And I'll blow your house in."

"Go ahead," said the pigs. "Give it a try."

The wolf huffed. And he puffed. And he blew.

The house made of sticks blew apart into a million billion trillion pieces.

"Eeek!" said the first and the second little pig, and they both ran, ran, ran to the house made out of bricks.

"What's wrong?" said the third pig.

"There's a wolf coming!" panted the first pig.

"He's mean!" gasped the second pig.

"Lock the door!" they both shouted.

Just then, there was a knock. BANG, BANG, BANG!

"Who is it?" said the three little pigs, who were inside.

"I'm a big bad wolf!"

"Go away," the pigs said. "We don't like big bad wolves."

"Little pigs, little pigs, let me in."

"Not by the hair of our chinny chin chins."

"Then I'll huff. And I'll puff. And I'll blow your house in."

"Go ahead," said the pigs. "Give it a try."

The wolf huffed. And he puffed. And he blew.

But nothing happened.

So he huffed. And he puffed. And he blew.

But still nothing happened.

The wolf kept huffing and puffing and blowing until suddenly, GASP, he died of a heart attack.

The three little pigs came out of the house made of bricks.

"Who's afraid of the big bad wolf?" the three pigs sang and danced.

And they lived together happily ever after—in the house made of bricks.

— *The End* —

4. The Walrus and the Carpenter

Lewis Carroll, Through the Looking-Glass and What Alice
Found There

The sun was shining on the sea,
Shining with all his might
He did his very best to make
The billows smooth and bright—
And this was odd, because it was
The middle of the night.

The moon was shining sulkily,
Because she thought the sun
Had got no business to be there
After the day was done—
"It's very rude of him," she said
"To come and spoil the fun!"

The sea was wet as wet could
*   be,*
The sands were dry as dry.
You could not see a cloud,
*   because*
No cloud was in the sky:
No birds were flying overhead—
There were no birds to fly.

The Walrus and the Carpenter
Were walking close at hand:
They wept like anything to see
Such quantities of sand.
"If this were only cleared away,"
They said, "it would be grand!"

"If seven maids with sevens mops
Swept for half a year,
Do you suppose," the walrus said,
That they could get it clear?"
"I doubt it," said the Carpenter,
And shed a bitter tear.

"O Oysters, come walk with us!"
The Walrus did beseech."
"A pleasant talk, a pleasant walk,
Along the briny beach:
We cannot do with more than four,
To give a hand to each."

The eldest Oyster looked at him,
But never a word he said:

The eldest Oyster winked his eye,
And shook his heavy head—
Meaning to say he did not choose
To leave the oyster-bed.

But four young Oysters hurried up,
All eager for the treat:
Their coats were brushed, their faces
    washed,
Their shoes were clean and neat—
And this was odd, because, you know,
They hadn't any feet.

Four other Oysters followed them,
And yet another four;
And thick and fast they came at last,
And more, and more, and more—
All hopping through the frothy waves,
And scrambling to the shore.

The Walrus and the Carpenter
Walked on a mile or so,
And they rested on a rock
Conveniently low:
And all the little Oysters stood
And waited in a row.

"The time has come," the Walrus said,
"To talk of many things:
Of shoes—and ships—and sealing wax—
Of cabbages—and kings—
And why the sea is boiling hot—
And whether pigs have wings."

"But wait a bit," the Oysters cried,
"Before we have our chat;
For some of us are out of breath,
And all of us are fat!"
"No hurry!" said the Carpenter.
They thanked him much for that.

"A loaf of bread," the Walrus said,
"Is what we chiefly need:
Pepper and vinegar besides
Are very good indeed—
Now, if you're ready, Oysters dear,
We can begin to feed."

"But not on us!" the Oysters cried!,
Turning a little blue.
"After such kindness, that would be
A dismal thing to do!"
"The night is fine," the Walrus said.
"Do you admire the view?"

"It was so kind of you to come!
And you are very nice!"
The Carpenter said nothing but
"Cut us another slice.
I wish you were not quite so deaf—
I've had to ask you twice!"

"It seems a shame," the Walrus said,
"To play them such a trick,
After we've brought them out so far,
And made them trot so quick!"
The Carpenter said nothing but
"The butter's spread too thick!"

"I weep for you," the Walrus said:
"I deeply sympathize."
With sobs and tears he sorted out
Those of the largest size,
Holding his pocket-handkerchief.
Before his streaming eyes.

"O Oysters," said the Carpenter,
"You've had a pleasant run!
Shall we be trotting home again?"
But answer came there none—
And this was scarcely odd, because
They'd eaten every one.

— *The End* —

13

5. *The Gingerbread Man*

READER TIP: A note about voices: Funny voices are a wonderful part of storytelling. The trick is to come up with a funny voice that you can remember and that won't strain your vocal cords. Try giving the Gingerbread boy a high-pitched voice. The old woman and old man can sound creaky. The cow and horse can moo and whinny. Of course the fox should bark or yip from time to time. When you feel comfortable with voices, you'll find that any story can become a lot of fun.

*O*nce upon a time, there was a little old woman and a little old man who lived all alone in a little old house. They didn't have any children. So one day, the little old woman made a boy out of gingerbread.

His eyes were fine, fat raisins, and his mouth was rose-colored sugar. He had a gay little cap of orange candy and a chocolate jacket. She put him in the oven and shut the door.

"Now," she thought, "I shall have a little boy of my own." When the timer went off, she opened the oven. Out jumped the little Gingerbread Boy, and away he ran, out the door and down the street!

The little old woman and the little old man ran after him as fast as they could, but he just laughed, and shouted: "Run! run! as fast as you can! You can't catch me, I'm the Gingerbread Man!"

The Gingerbread Boy ran on and on, until he came to a cow, by the roadside. "Stop, little Gingerbread Boy," said the cow; "I want to eat you."

The little Gingerbread Boy laughed, and said: "I have run away from a little old woman and a little old man, and I can run away from you, I can!"

And, as the cow chased him, he looked over his shoulder and cried: "Run! run! as fast as you can! You can't catch me, I'm the Gingerbread Man!"

A horse in a pastures said, "You look very good to eat." But the little Gingerbread Boy laughed out loud. "Hee hee" he said: "I have run away from a little old woman, a little old man, a cow, and I can run away from you, I can!"

And, as the horse chased him, he looked over his shoulder and cried: "Run! run! as fast as you can! You can't catch me, I'm the Gingerbread Man!"

Soon the little Gingerbread Boy came to a town. He smelled so good that every one in the town tried to pick him up. They said, "Don't run so fast, little Gingerbread Boy; you look very good to eat."

But the little Gingerbread Boy ran harder than ever, and as he ran he cried out: "I have run away from a little old woman, a little old man, a cow, a horse, and I can run away from you, I can!"

And then he ran right past every one in the town. He turned and shouted back to them: "Run! run! as fast as you can! You can't catch me, I'm the Gingerbread Man!"

By this time the little Gingerbread Boy was so proud that he didn't think anybody could catch him.

Soon he saw a fox coming across a field. The fox looked at him and began to run. But the little Gingerbread Boy shouted across to him, "You can't catch me!" The fox began to run faster, and the little Gingerbread Boy ran even faster, and, as he ran, he laughed: "I have run away from a little old woman, a little old

15

man, a cow, a horse, an entire town, and I can run away from you, I can! Run! run! as fast as you can! You can't catch me, I'm the Gingerbread Man!"

"Why," said the fox, "I would not catch you if I could. I would not think of disturbing you."

Just then, the little Gingerbread Boy came to a river. He could not swim across, and he wanted to keep running away from the cow and the horse and all the people.

"Jump on my tail, and I will take you across," said the fox.

So the little Gingerbread Boy jumped on the fox's tail, and the fox swam into the river.

When he was a little way from shore he turned his head, and said, "You are too heavy on my tail, little Gingerbread Boy, I fear I shall let you get wet. Jump on my back."

The little Gingerbread Boy jumped on his back.

A little farther out, the fox said, "I am afraid the water will cover you there. Jump on my shoulder."

The little Gingerbread Boy jumped on his shoulder.

In the middle of the stream the fox said, "Oh, dear! little Gingerbread Boy, my shoulder is sinking; jump on my nose, and I can hold you out of water."

So the little Gingerbread Boy jumped on his nose.

The minute the fox got on shore he threw back his head and gave a snap!

"Dear me!" said the little Gingerbread Boy, "I am a quarter gone!" The next minute he said, "Why, I am half gone!" The next minute he said, "My goodness gracious, I am three quarters gone!"

And after that, the little Gingerbread Boy never said anything more at all.

— *The End* —

16

6. The Little Red Hen

READER TIP: This is a quick, but fun, story, especially if you add in noises for the barnyard animals. If your child has a favorite animal (perhaps a pig or a cat), feel free to substitute, but try to remember to use the same animals the next time.

*T*he Little Red Hen was in the farmyard with her chicks, when she found a grain of wheat.

"Who will help me plant this wheat?" she said.

"Not I," said the Goose.

"Not I," said the Duck.

"Not I," said the Cow.

"Not I," said the Horse.

"Then I will," said the Little Red Hen, and she planted the grain of wheat.

When the wheat was ripe she said, "Who will help me harvest this wheat?"

"Not I," said the Goose.

"Not I," said the Duck.

"Not I," said the Cow.

"Not I," said the Horse.

"Then I will," said the Little Red Hen, and she harvested the wheat.

"Now," said the Little Red Hen, "who will help me take this wheat to the mill?"

"Not I," said the Goose.

"Not I," said the Duck.

"Not I," said the Cow.

"Not I," said the Horse.

"Then I will," said the Little Red Hen, and she took the wheat to the mill.

When she brought the flour home she said, "Who will help me make some bread with this flour?"

"Not I," said the Goose.

"Not I," said the Duck.

"Not I," said the Cow.

"Not I," said the Horse.

"Then I will," said the Little Red Hen.

When the bread was baked (it smelled so good, warm, and fresh), the Little Red Hen said, "Who will help me eat this bread?"

"I will," said the Goose

"I will," said the Duck

"I will," said the Cow.

"I will," said the Horse.

"No, you won't," said the Little Red Hen. "I shall eat it myself. Cluck! Cluck!" And she called her chicks to help her.

And they ate it all up. Yum.

— *The End* —

7. I Have a Little Shadow

Robert Louis Stevenson

I have a little shadow that goes in and out with me
And what can be the use of him is more than I can see.
He is very very like me from the heels up to the head;
And I see him jump before me, when I jump into my bed.

The funniest thing about him is the way he likes to grow,
Not at all like proper children, which is always very slow.
For he sometimes shoots up taller, like an India-rubber ball,
And he sometimes gets so little that there's none of him at all.

He hasn't got a notion of how children ought to play.
And can only make a fool of me in every sort of way.
He stays so close beside me, he's a coward you can see;
I'd think shame to stick to nursie as that
shadow sticks to me.

One morning very early, before the
sun was up
I rose and found the shining
dew in every buttercup;
But my lazy little shadow, like
an arrant sleepy-head
Had stayed at home behind me and was
fast asleep in bed.

— *The End* —

19

8. For Want of a Nail

For want of a nail, the shoe was lost;
For want of the shoe, the horse was lost;
For want of the horse, the rider was lost;
For want of the rider, the battle was lost;
For want of the battle, the kingdom was lost,
And all for the want of a nail.

— *The End* —

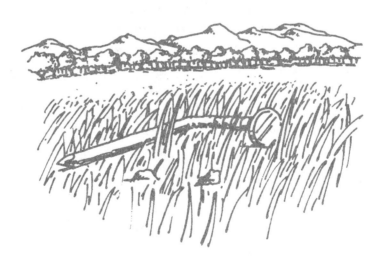

9. Three Little Kittens

The following classic Mother Goose poems are favorites of our family because their simple rhythms can lull children right to sleep. And they sound so sweet when the youngsters repeat them back to you! In this one, it's fun to take on the voices of the kittens and the mother cat: all children respond well to copying the animal noises.

Three little kittens,
They lost their mittens,
And they began to cry,
Oh, mother dear, we sadly fear
Our mittens we have lost.

What! Lost your mittens,
You silly kittens!
Then you shall have no pie.
Mee-ow, mee-ow, mee-ow.
No, you shall have no pie.

The three little kittens,
They found their mittens,
And they began to cry,
Oh, mother dear, see here, see here,
Our mittens we have found.

Put on your mittens,
You happy kittens,
And you shall have some pie.
Purr-r, purr-r, purr-r,
Oh, let us have some pie.

The three little kittens
Put on their mittens,
And soon ate up the pie;
Oh, mother dear, we greatly fear
Our mittens we have soiled.

What! Soiled your mittens,
You silly kittens!
Then they began to sigh,
Mee-ow, mee-ow, mee-ow.
Then they began to sigh.

The three little kittens,
They washed their mittens,
And hung them out to dry;
Oh, mother dear, do you not hear
Our mittens we have washed?

What! Washed your mittens,
Then you're good kittens!
Now it's time for bed, bye-bye.
Purr-r, Purr-r, Purr-r,
It's time for bed, bye-bye.

— *The End* —

10. Sing a Royal Song

Sing a song of sixpence,
A pocket full of rye;
Four and twenty blackbirds
Baked in a pie!

When the pie was opened,
The birds, began to sing;
Wasn't that a dainty dish
To set before the king?

The king was in his counting-house,
Counting out his money;
The queen was in the parlor,
Eating bread and honey.

The maid was in the garden,
Hanging out the clothes;
There came a little blackbird,
And snapped off her nose!

— The End —

11. Little Boy Blue

Little Boy Blue come blow your horn
The sheep's in the meadow,
The cow's in the corn.

Where is the boy who looks after the sheep?
He's under a hay stack
Fast asleep.

Will you wake him? No, not I.
For if I do,
He's sure to cry.

— *The End* —

12. The Rain Poems

READER TIP: Read on a rainy afternoon or eve, these rhymes are sure to please, although even after years of telling, I don't really understand the subtleties of the first poem.

It's raining
It's pouring
The old man is snoring
Went to bed with a bump on his head
And he didn't get up in the morning.

Rain rain
Go away
Come again
Some other day
Little children want to play!

• • •

Three young rats with black felt hats,
Three young ducks with white straw flats,
Three young dogs with curling tails,
Three young cats with demi-veils,

Went out to walk with two young pigs
In satin vests and sorrel wigs.
But suddenly it began to rain
And so they all went home again.

— *The End* —

13. Pussy Cat, Pussy Cat

Pussy cat, pussy cat
Where have you been?
I've been to London
To look at the Queen

Pussy cat, pussy cat
What did you there?
I frightened a little mouse
Under her chair.

— The End —

14. Hey Diddle Diddle

Hey diddle diddle
The pussycat and the fiddle
The cow she jumped, she jumped right
    over the moon

The little dog laughed
To see such a sport
And the dish ran away with the spoon

Yes the dish ran away with it
What can you say
But the dish ran away with the spoon.

— *The End*—

15. *Hansel and Gretel*

Like many fairy tales, Hansel and Gretel, is not politically correct. The stepmother is wicked, the father is heartless, and the witch assumes that Gretel knows how to cook. Still, the clever way the children outfox the grown-ups makes it an old favorite. Not to mention the idea of eating an entire house!

READER TIP: Feel free to elaborate on the house's ingredients—chocolate pudding flowers, vanilla cookie doorsteps, whatever will please your child the most.

If you want to omit the nasty parents, begin the story with "Once upon a time, Hansel and Gretel were lost in the woods when up ahead in a clearing they saw the strangest little house. . . ."

*O*nce upon a time, Hansel and Gretel lived deep in the forest with their father, a poor woodcutter, and their stepmother.

The winter was hard, and there wasn't enough food to eat. The wicked stepmother told the father that he must take the two children into the forest and leave them behind.

"How can I do that to my poor children?" the woodcutter asked.

"You fool!" said the stepmother. "If you do not, then all four of us shall starve."

Hansel and Gretel were not asleep, and when they overheard this conversation, Gretel began to cry.

"Don't worry," Hansel said, "I will find a way."

The moon shone brightly that night, and Hansel crept downstairs and sneaked outside to collect a pocketful of pebbles that shone bright white.

When day dawned, the wicked stepmother woke up the children, gave them each a piece of bread for dinner, and told them to hurry up and get dressed. Together, all four went into the forest.

Their father built a large fire. Then he kissed Hansel and Gretel gently on their foreheads and bade them a tearful good-bye.

As soon as they were gone, Gretel began to cry, but Hansel told her to shush. He had dropped pebbles from out of his pocket, all along the way. They stayed close to the fire all day, and when the full moon rose high in the sky, Hansel took his little sister by the hand and followed the pebbles, which shone like bright silver coins. They walked all night, and as the sun began to come up, found the door to their father's house.

When they knocked on the door, their stepmother opened and said, "You naughty children, we thought you were never coming back at all."

Their father smiled and hugged his two children close.

Not long after, food once again ran out, and Hansel and Gretel once again heard their stepmother order their father to leave the children in the forest. That evening, when the old folks were asleep, Hansel crept downstairs to collect more pebbles, but found that the old woman had locked the door to the house. Gretel began to cry, but Hansel hushed her, and said "Don't worry, I will find a way."

When day dawned, the wicked stepmother woke up the children, gave them each a piece of bread for dinner, and told them to hurry up and get dressed. Together, all four went into the forest.

All along the way, Hansel broke off pieces of bread and dropped the crumbs on the ground to make a trail leading home.

Their father built a large fire. Then he kissed the children gently on their foreheads and bade them a tearful good-bye.

They stayed close to the fire all day, and when the full moon rose high in the sky, Hansel took his little sister by the hand and looked for the white pieces of bread crumbs that he had dropped.

But they found no bread crumbs, because the thousands of birds that live in the forest had eaten them all up. Gretel once again began to cry, and Hansel took her hand.

"Come with me, Sister, I think I remember the way."

Off they went, deeper into the forest. They were very lost and very hungry and about to give up when up ahead in a clearing they saw the strangest little house.

Its walls were built of brown gingerbread, and its roof was made of frosted cake. Even the windows were made of clear sugar.

"I'm going to eat it all!" Hansel said. "I'm going to eat it all!" They both ran to the house and began breaking off pieces.

Then, a soft voice from inside said,
"Nibble nibble like a mouse
Who is nibbling on my house?"
The children answered,
"Only the wind, only the wind
Blowing out and blowing in."
And they went on eating heartily.

Suddenly, the door opened, and a woman as old as the hills hobbled out on crutches.

Hansel and Gretel were terribly frightened. The old woman smiled and said, "Do come in and stay with me." She led them inside and fed them pancakes and apples and sugar and nuts. Afterwards, she showed them to two pretty little beds, where they immediately fell asleep.

The old woman, who was really a wicked witch, had only pretended to be so kind. While they were sleeping, she seized Hansel and locked him in a little stable behind a grated door. Then she shook Gretel until she woke and told her to fetch water and cook something good for Hansel.

"When he is fat," the witch said, "I will eat him!"

Gretel cried and cried, but she was forced to do what the wicked witch commanded. She cooked all the best food in the house for poor Hansel, but was given nothing to eat but crab shells.

Every morning, the old woman crept to the little stable and told Hansel to stretch out his finger to see if he would soon be fat enough to be eaten.

Hansel, however, was very smart. He stretched out a little chicken bone to her, and the old woman, who could not see well, thought it was his finger. Week after week went by, and she was astonished that he ate and ate without gaining a single pound.

When a month had gone by, and Hansel still remained thin, the witch told Gretel she could not wait any longer.

"Whether Hansel is fat or lean, tomorrow I will kill him and cook him!" the witch laughed.

The next morning, the witch woke up Gretel and told her that it was time to bake some bread to eat with Hansel.

"The oven is warming, and the dough is ready," the witch said. "Creep inside the oven and see if it is hot enough to put the bread in."

Gretel was smart, too, and she knew that the witch intended to lock her up in the oven, bake her, and eat her, too.

"I don't understand," Gretel said, "How can I get in?"

"Silly goose," said the old woman, "that door is big enough. Look, I can fit in myself."

The old witch crept up and thrust her head into the oven.

Then Gretel gave her a big push and shoved her all the way in. She shut the iron door and fastened the bolt.

The witch began to howl and scream, but Gretel would not let her out.

Gretel ran like lightning to Hansel, set him free, and cried, "Hansel, we are saved! The old witch is dead."

They hugged and kissed and danced. In the witch's house they found chests filled with pearls and jewels. They filled their pockets with the booty.

"But how will we get home?" Gretel asked.

"Don't worry," Hansel said, "I will find a way."

Fortunately for the children, the witch's house was not far from the woodcutter's cabin, and soon they were home.

They rushed into the parlor and threw their arms around their father's neck. Their father had not known one happy hour since he had left his children in the forest. The stepmother, however, was dead. Hansel and Gretel emptied their pockets of pearls and precious stones, and from that day until this they lived together in perfect happiness.

— *The End* —

16. Gilgamesh and Enkidu

The Epic of Gilgamesh *is known as the oldest written story in the world. It was written on clay tablets more than four thousand years old. This is just a portion of the story. The complete adult story is rich and filled with topics that are best not discussed with young children. By the way, Enkidu is typically pronounced "Anky-doo."*

*I*n ancient times Gilgamesh was the founder of the great city of Urak, but he was at times a cruel and wicked king, and his people prayed to the gods and begged for help.

The gods heard their prayers and created a wild man named Enkidu in the harsh and wild forest. Enkidu was stronger than dozens of wild animals. He ran with the gazelles and lurked with the beasts.

Gilgamesh heard of Enkidu, and he sent a woman from the city to meet the wild man and steal away his power. When Enkidu met the woman, he lost his desire to stay with the animals, and she fell in love with him and realized that he was very wise.

"Come to Urak," she told him, "and meet Gilgamesh."

Enkidu agreed, and together they traveled to the great walled city.

When they arrived a wedding celebration was in progress, but the groom was very sad.

"What's the matter?" Enkidu asked.

"Gilgamesh, the king, is inside the long hall, stealing my bride," the groom said.

With that, Enkidu burst into the long hall, and stood in Gilgamesh's way.

The two great ones stared at each other. Gilgamesh was taller, but Enkidu was wider. Both were strong.

Immediately, they began to fight. They wrestled and rolled around for what seemed like hours. At last, Gilgamesh threw Enkidu down. The two men laughed, and they became good friends. The wedding celebration continued with joy and dancing.

Years passed and the two friends grew bored with living in the city. Gilgamesh suggested that they travel to the Land of the Cedar Trees. Together, he bragged, they would cut down the trees and kill the ferocious giant Humbaba, whose name meant "Hugeness."

Enkidu was afraid. He knew of Humbaba from his days running wild in the forest. He tried to convince Gilgamesh that the trip was foolish, but the king would not listen. Together they set off.

They crossed seven deserts and seven mountains before they came to a gate that led into the Land of the Cedar Trees.

"Do not touch that gate!" Enkidu warned. "When I touched it, I lost the strength of my right hand."

Gilgamesh just laughed. "Do you want people to think me a coward?"

Gilgamesh opened the gate, and they walked into the great Cedar Forest. The trees were tall and beautiful, the mountains were fragrant and green. Gilgamesh took his great ax and began cutting down trees.

"Who is cutting down my beautiful Cedar trees?" Humbaba screamed. The demon appeared before them, huge and enraged.

"We two are stronger than you," Enkidu said. "Be gone!"

"Do you, a king, take orders from this animal man?" Humbaba laughed.

The monster began to approach, and Gilgamesh was greatly afraid.

Then Enkidu shouted, "Gilgamesh, forward! Together we will attack. Together we have nothing to fear."

The battle raged wide and furious. One at a time, Gilgamesh and Enkidu cut down seven cedar trees, and with the falling of each tree, Humbaba grew weaker.

At last Humbaba begged for his life. "Spare me, and I will become your servant."

But Enkidu urged Gilgamesh to kill the demon, and with one stroke, Gilgamesh sliced off Humbaba's head.

Together, the heroes returned to Urak in triumph.

— *The End* —

17. The Mouse Kingdom

A Japanese Folk Tale Retold by John Gardner

*O*nce there was a kind old man who loved all sorts of animals and even most of the people he met. One day while he was working in his storehouse he stopped to lunch on some rice balls.

As he ate he noticed a mousehole. He broke off a big chunk of rice ball and tossed it down the hole. Then he finished the rest of the rice and went back to work.

After a bit the old man heard someone call. He looked around and saw a mouse waving from the hole.

"Thank you very much for the rice ball," the mouse said. "We are all very grateful."

"It was nothing, really," said the old man.

"My master has sent me to tell you how much we appreciate your kindness."

"Please don't mention it. It was nothing."

"My master wishes to thank you personally. Please join us for a meal this evening."

Of course the old man didn't know the mouse at all and was embarrassed at the thought of imposing on his hospitality. But the messenger insisted and insisted, finally the old man agreed.

"How shall I get there?" he asked. "I can hardly join you in the hole."

"Please cover your eyes and grab my tail. There will be no problem. But don't open your eyes—that is very important."

The old man did as he was told and was soon walking through a cool, dark tunnel. In a few minutes, after many twists and turns on the way, the man felt the sunshine on his back just as the mouse told him to open his eyes. They were standing in a sunny meadow filled with flowers.

The young mouse led the old man across the meadow to a mansion where the entire household and servants were waiting to greet him.

A prosperous-looking old mouse bowed and thanked the old man, then led him into a large hall where a banquet was set. The food was not the coarse grains he had expected mice to eat, but a large variety of fresh and pickled vegetables, and even a few fish and meat dishes.

The old man was ashamed to have said that his bit of rice ball "was nothing" now that he realized how nearly true that was.

After the meal, the mice sang and danced for the old man.

Yoi, yoi, yoi yoi.
Hyaku ni nattemo, ni hyaku ni nattemo,
Neko no koe wa, kikitakunai ja.

Which means something like

"Yeah, yeah, yeah, yeah
If I live to be a hundred,
If I live to be two hundred,
I'll never want to hear
The voice of a cat."

The old man clapped and sang along, even though he liked cats himself.

Finally the mice gave the old man a beautiful finely woven basket filled with pearls and he was led back to the storehouse with his eyes closed.

Now, the kind old man had a greedy neighbor. Once the greedy neighbor man saw the basket filled with pearls, he wouldn't rest until he had heard the whole story.

And so, the next day the greedy neighbor was in the storehouse, tossing grains of millet down the mousehole. After a while, a young mouse came out to offer his thanks. He agreed to lead the greedy neighbor down to the mouse kingdom, warning him first to keep his eyes closed till they reached the meadow.

After dinner the greedy neighbor listened to a few songs, including the one about cats. That gave him an idea on how to get more than one basket of pearls.

When the mice showed him the baskets of pearls, the greedy neighbor covered his mouth and made a loud "Niaao."

All the mice immediately stopped whatever they were doing. "Niaaoo."

As the greedy neighbor had hoped, all the mice turned and ran. But he had not expected them to blow out all the lights to help them hide from the cat.

The greedy neighbor was now free to take as many baskets as he could carry, but he was lost and alone in the kingdom of the mice, with no one to lead him back to his own country.

And as far as I know, he is still there today.

— *The End* —

18. The Monkey-Crab War

A Japanese Folk Tale Translated by John Gardner

Once a crab was walking along sideways when she found a rice ball someone had dropped. Rice balls were her favorite food. She picked up her find with her large pincer to take home to her family. As she did, a monkey high on top of a persimmon tree noticed the crab down below. When he saw the happy crab, he wanted her rice ball, even though he had already filled up on persimmons.

"Kani, Kani!" the monkey called, "Do you want to trade your rice ball for a persimmon?"

"Okay," the crab replied.

That surprised the monkey. "I'm almost out of persimmons," he said. "Will you take a persimmon seed instead?"

"Okay," the crab replied.

Thinking that the crab was too stupid to be any fun, the monkey slid down the tree and picked off a persimmon seed that was stuck in his hair. He dropped it in front of the crab, stuffed her rice ball in his mouth, then ran to sit on a rock and play.

"Thank you, Saru-don," the crab called to him. She took the seed back to her hole and planted it out in front. Every day the crab watered and weeded the spot. Before long a sprout popped up, and it grew taller and stronger every week.

One spring after the sprout had become a tree, it was covered with blossoms, and a bee pollinated them on an afternoon when he wasn't busy. When the blossoms fell they left behind the start of fruit that grew into shiny green balls, and by late fall many of them had become delicious orange persimmons.

It was time to start picking, and the crab realized she had a problem—the fruit was far beyond the reach of her pincers. Fortunately the monkey came by just them.

"Saru-don, Saru-don," the crab called. "Do you remember the seed you traded for a rice ball? It's grown now, and the fruit is ripe. Will you pick some for me?"

The monkey quickly scampered up the tree, and stuffed a juicy red persimmon in his mouth.

"Almost ready," he called down, and stuffed in two or three more. "These aren't bad," he said as he moved up to the next branch—"Delicious, in fact." He said everything except "Thank you," but it was hard to hear his words through the mush of persimmons.

As the monkey moved over to the left side of the tree, the crab called up to him, "Saru-don, please save me one!"

"Don't nag so much," the monkey growled back. He reached up for a hard, shiny, green persimmon, and threw it down so straight and fast that it cracked the poor crab's shell.

The bee found the crab at the foot of the persimmon tree. He helped her back to her home, then flew off to find the rice flour mortar.

"Usu-don, Usu-don! The monkey has injured the crab!" the bee said.

The mortar, who had been cut from a tree stump years before, rolled out of the kitchen, and they hurried back to the crab's home, but on the way they met the chestnut.

"Kuri-don, Kuri-don!" the mortar said. "The monkey has injured the crab!"

When the three friends arrived, the crab told them the whole story. The mortar advised her not to get too excited and brought another cool cloth to help her get to sleep.

The friends talked as they watched over the crab, and they became angrier and angrier.

"This monkey is a real threat, Usu-don," the chestnut said. "Someone has to do something."

"There is no one to do it but us, Kuri-don," the mortar replied.

"He runs fast and is clever in a way," the bee said.

"That's right, Hachi-don. We will have to find him when he is not expecting anything."

The bee flew off a little before dawn, leaving the others to watch over the crab. He returned late in the morning and reported that the monkey had awakened and left his house. The three left the crab in the care of her three sons and hurried to the monkey's home.

"I'll wait here in the back of the firepit," the chestnut said. "Perhaps you could wait in the water barrel, Hachi-don."

The bee flew into the water barrel, and the mortar silently climbed up into the eaves.

Finally, late in the afternoon, the monkey returned. He picked up the fire tube and puffed on the coals until they began to glow. The chestnut found himself growing hotter and hotter as he thought about the monkey's coarseness, and finally he burst with rage and flew out of the firepit, striking the monkey in the eye with great force and great heat.

Howling with pain, the monkey leaped to the water barrel to cool his burn. As soon as he removed the lid, the bee buzzed out and stung his nose. The monkey, clever as he was, realized that something unusual was happening and rushed to the door to escape.

Just then, the heavy mortar dropped from the eaves and pinned the monkey to the dirt floor of the entryway. They remained there while the chestnut explained, calmly but at great length, how angry everyone was about the monkey's wild deeds.

In the end, the monkey went with the others back to the crab's home. They stopped by the persimmon tree and the monkey, accompanied by the bee, climbed up and selected four shiny, ripe, orange persimmons.

Once inside the crab's home, the monkey pushed the fruit forward as he bowed and apologized. "Kani-san, Kani-san. I'm sorry for the inconvenience I have caused you, and I will make certain that nothing of the kind happens again."

After that, the monkey visited several times each fall to pick persimmons for the crab and her family. The rest of the year he stayed far away.

— *The End* —

19. Johnny Appleseed

No one knows if the story of Johnny Appleseed is true or not. Some sources say he is as real as George Washington, while others imply that he was closely related to Paul Bunyan.

In 1775, just one year before America declared its independence, John Chapman was born in Springfield, Massachusetts. As a boy, he loved to roam in the forests and fields, listen to the birds singing, collect flowers and plants, and gaze at the stars. Wherever he went, he planted apple seeds and cultivated nurseries for apple trees. Over the years, folks started to call him "Appleseed John," and finally "Johnny Appleseed."

In the early days of the United States, he traveled everywhere. Once he was spotted poling his way up the Ohio river in a strange contraption. Instead of a normal boat, he'd taken two canoes and lashed them together. Over each arm was slung a sack of apple seeds.

Whenever he struck land, he'd settle down for a while and plant apple trees, or sell young saplings to farmers he met for a few pennies. If the farmers couldn't pay, Johnny Appleseed would take some old clothes, or a new pair of shoes in trade.

Johnny Appleseed was known as a polite and frugal man. He wore a flour sack for a shirt, and went barefooted year-round. He was almost six feet tall and had blue eyes and lanky long arms.

Sometimes, new settlers would stake out a plot of land near a stream or river, and find a small orchard, complete with a low fence to keep out critters, just waiting for them.

While he traveled, Johnny Appleseed camped outside. He never killed any animals, not even for food. Instead, he'd make himself a batch of apple mush mixed with cornmeal in an old tin cooking pot, which he sometimes wore on his head as a hat.

Even the Indians, who lived wild throughout the land, regarded Johnny Appleseed as a medicine man, so they never troubled him.

During the War of 1812, Johnny Appleseed frequently warned settlers when the British were coming.

Once, the town of Mansfield was surrounded by the British. There were no American troops nearby to protect them. The people asked for volunteers to travel to a fort nearly thirty miles away.

Night was falling, the entire trip to the fort and back again needed to be made before dawn.

A tall, thin volunteer shyly raised his hand. "I'll go," Johnny Appleseed said.

And off he set, barefoot and unarmed. He raced silently through the woods, slipping past the sleeping animals and the British soldiers, stopping only to knock on settlers' cabin doors to warn them about the danger.

He made it to the fort on time and returned with the troops. The town was saved.

Johnny Appleseed lived to a ripe old age and died happily among his trees.

The only memorial to this brave man are the many apple orchards scattered here and there throughout the United States. Apple cider, apple pie, apple turnovers, apple tarts. Oh, my what a tasty memorial.

— *The End* —

20. David and Goliath

David was a young shepherd boy who cared for his father's sheep. All day long he would stay with his flock, making sure that they got enough grass to eat, water to drink, and didn't get lost or taken away by wild animals.

One day, David came home from the fields and learned that his country was at war with the Philistines. All the strong men of Israel, David's country, had been summoned to fight for their king. Already, David's three older brothers had gone to the battlefield, but since David was just a boy, he was told to stay home and take care of the sheep.

A short time later, David's father sent David to the battlefield to bring his brothers bread and cheese for them to eat and share with their captain. When David reached the camp of Israel, he found the army of Israel standing on one mountain and the army of the Philistines on another mountain.

In between was a valley, and in the valley stood Goliath, a giant of a man and the champion of the Philistines.

"Choose your champion," Goliath shouted in challenge. "If he can kill me in a fair fight, we will become your slaves. But if I prove too strong for him, and kill him, you shall be our slaves and serve us."

The king and all the Israelites were very afraid, because they knew that no one among their ranks was strong enough to defeat the giant.

As David made his way through the camp, he heard rumors that Saul, the king of the Israelites, had promised to make whomever killed Goliath rich, to give the brave soldier his daughter in marriage, and make his family free.

David's oldest brother, Eliab, overheard David talking with the men, and he became angry. "What are you doing here? Shouldn't you be taking care of the sheep?"

"I'm just asking some questions," David replied. "I was just wondering why there is no one brave enough to challenge this man."

King Saul heard what David had said and ordered the boy to be brought before him.

David said, "Don't worry, sire. I will go and fight this Philistine."

Saul laughed. "You can't fight him. You're just a boy, and he is a soldier."

David stood tall and said, "Sire, I am my father's shepherd. When a bear or a lion tries to take a sheep from the flock, I chase it and rescue the victim from its jaws. If it attacks me, I will kill it with my own hands. I have killed lions and bears, and this Philistine will fare no better."

"Go," said Saul, "and may God be with you."

Then Saul gave David his own armor and weapons. He put a brass helmet on David's head, and gave him a coat of mail and a sword to wear.

The young boy found all this new equipment uncomfortable. He said to Saul, "I cannot go with these, because I'm not used to them." And he took off all the fancy armor and weapons.

Instead, he picked up his stick, and chose five stones from a brook, and put them in his shepherd's bag. Then, with his sling in his

hand, he walked
down the mountain into the valley to meet the Philistine.

Goliath was huge, more than nine feet tall. He wore brass armor that shone in the sun, and he had a brass helmet on his head. His spear was as long as a tall tree, and his shield was so heavy that it took two normal men to carry it.

When Goliath looked up and saw David, he scowled, because David was just a boy with ruddy cheeks and bright eyes.

"Am I a dog that you'll attack with a stick?" Goliath bellowed. "Come closer, and I'll feed your body to the birds of the sky and the beasts of the fields."

David looked up at the giant and answered, "You come to me with a sword and a spear and a shield, but I come to you in the name of God and the armies of Israel that you have challenged. Today, God will deliver you into my hand, and I will kill you and take your head. I will give your body to the birds of the sky and the beasts of the field. Everyone here today will know that there is a God in Israel, and he will give you into our hands."

Then Goliath stood up to his full height and charged toward David.

David also ran toward Goliath, but he stopped while the Giant was still far away. He reached his hand in his bag and took out a stone. He put the stone into his sling. Then he spun the sling around his head, and let the stone fly. It flew out straight and true and hit Goliath in the forehead. The giant fell flat on his face in the earth, dead.

David ran to the fallen giant, drew Goliath's sword, and cut his head right off.

When the army of the Philistines saw that their champion was dead, they fled. But the army of Israel chased them and defeated them.

After the battle, David was brought to King Saul as a hero, and given command of an army. Eventually he became king himself. He went home only briefly to say good-bye to his father and to his flock of sheep.

— *The End* —

21. Sleeping Beauty

$\mathcal{O}$nce upon a time, the king learned that the queen was about to have a baby girl. All the fairies in the land were invited to be godmothers, and after the baptism, a banquet was planned. Seven places of honor were set with golden dishes and diamond goblets.

The great day came, and the baby girl was born. At the banquet, one by one the seven fairy godmothers began to give their gifts and blessings. One fairy gave the baby great beauty. Another gave her wit, and the third gave her graciousness. The next two made her a wonderful singer and dancer. The sixth gave her great skills with musical instruments.

Just then an old and withered fairy appeared at the banquet.

"Is there no place setting for me?" the old fairy asked, looking at the seven gold and diamond places.

Well, no one had invited the old fairy because they all thought she was dead. The king and queen quickly tried to make a place for her, but she scowled.

"I'll give her a gift," the old fairy said. "When she turns sixteen, the princess will cut her finger on a spindle, and die." Then the old fairy vanished in a puff of smoke.

Everyone was horrified, but the seventh good fairy godmother spoke up. "Your majesty, I can't completely undo this curse, but I can temper it. Instead of dying, when the princess cuts her finger, she will fall asleep for a hundred years and be awakened by a prince."

Nevertheless the king tried to prevent the curse by making a law forbidding spindles in his kingdom.

On the princess's sixteenth birthday, she was exploring the topmost turret of the castle, where she found an old woman smiling and spinning thread.

"What is that?" she asked, because she had never seen a spinning wheel.

"A spindle," said the old woman. "Would you like to see it?"

The princess reached her hand out and cut her finger on the spindle. She immediately fell asleep on the floor. The old lady, who was really the wicked old fairy, vanished in a puff of smoke.

When the king finally found his daughter, he knew that the curse had come true at last. His daughter was asleep and would not wake for a hundred years.

The fairy that had saved the girl's life came to the castle, and the king explained that he was worried about his daughter. "She'll be so sad and afraid if she wakes up a hundred years from now all alone."

The good fairy waved her wand, and everyone in the castle, from the animals in the stables to the maids and cooks, fell asleep.

The king and queen thanked the good fairy and went off to live in another palace.

A hundred years went quickly by, and the old castle had become forgotten, lost in an overgrown forest.

One day, a prince was lost in the forest. He was far from his own kingdom, hungry and tired. He was just about to give up all hope when he noticed that the thicket seemed to part off to one direction. He followed the path and was amazed to notice that it closed up behind him.

In a short while he came to the castle, which was quite magnificent despite the vines creeping up along its walls and the huge lawn at had grown up in its moat.

He made his way inside and marveled at the inhabitants of the castle, who had all fallen asleep. Guards stood at their posts asleep, and seamstresses sat on their stools, as if dozing in mid-stitch.

The prince climbed the stairs and found his way to the topmost turret where the beautiful princess slept. There on a high bed was the most beautiful girl he had ever seen. She was so lovely that the sunlight seemed to cast a golden shadow all around her body.

The prince leaned forward and kissed the sleeping girl on her forehead.

Just then, the princess's eyes fluttered open, and she looked at the prince as if she'd known him always.

"Is that you, my prince?" she whispered. "I've waited so long."

The prince's hand closed around her's. He told her that he had loved her from the first moment he'd laid eyes on her.

One by one the servants awoke, and they prepared a great feast.

The prince and princess were married that very afternoon, and they lived in the castle happily ever after.

— *The End* —

22. King Midas and the Golden Touch

*O*nce upon a time, there was a king named Midas, who loved gold more than anything else in the world, except perhaps his little daughter called Marygold.

If he happened to gaze at the gold-tinted clouds of sunset, he wished that they were real gold, that he could squeeze safely into his strong box. When little Marygold ran to meet him, with a bunch of buttercups and dandelions, he used to say, "Poh, poh, child! If these flowers were as golden as they look, they would be worth the plucking!"

One day, Midas was in his treasure-room, when he saw a stranger, standing in the bright and narrow sunbeam! It was a young man, with a cheerful and golden face.

"You are a wealthy man, friend Midas!" the stranger observed. "I doubt whether any other four walls on earth contain this much gold."

"I have done pretty well," answered Midas, in a discontented tone. "But, this isn't much when you consider that it has taken me my whole life to get it together."

"What would satisfy you?" asked the stranger. "I'm just curious."

Raising his head, Midas said, "I wish that everything that I touch could be changed to gold!"

The stranger's smile grew broad and brighter, "The Golden Touch! And will you never regret the possession of it?"

"What could induce me?" asked Midas. "I ask nothing else, to render me perfectly happy."

"Be it as you wish," replied the stranger, waving his hand in token of farewell. "Tomorrow, at sunrise, you will find yourself gifted with the Golden Touch."

The figure of the stranger then became exceedingly bright, and then he vanished.

The next morning, when a streak of golden sunlight touched Midas on the forehead, he awoke to discover that his very bed sheets had been transmuted into a woven texture of the purest and brightest gold!

Midas ran about the room, touching everything. His bed-post, became a fluted golden pillar. A book on a table turned gold, and as he ran his fingers through the pages, behold! it was a bundle of thin golden plates, in which all the wisdom of the book had grown illegible.

He put on his clothes, which immediately became a magnificent suit of gold cloth, flexible and soft, although a little heavy. Even the handkerchief that little Marygold had hemmed for him had turned gold!

Somehow or other, this last transformation did not quite please King Midas. He would rather that his little daughter's gift should have remained just the same as when she climbed his knee and put it into his hand.

When Midas put on his glasses, they too turned to gold, and it struck him as rather inconvenient that, with all his wealth, he could never again be rich enough to own a pair of serviceable spectacles.

"It is no great matter, nevertheless," he said to himself.

So he went down to breakfast, watching in awe and amazement as the staircase and bannister became gold as he walked. In the garden, he reached down to pick up a fragrant rose, and it too became gilded solid.

He sat down at the table to eat his breakfast and was about to eat when his daughter ran into the room, crying.

"What's the matter?" cried Midas.

Marygold held out one of the roses that Midas had so recently transmuted.

"This is the ugliest flower that ever grew!" sobbed the child. "All the beautiful red roses, that smelled so sweetly, are blighted and spoilt! They are quite yellow, as you see this one, and have no longer any fragrance!"

"Pooh, my dear little girl, don't cry about it!" said Midas. "Come here and give me a kiss."

Marygold ran to her father, and he threw his arms around her. He leaned down and kissed her. He felt that his little daughter's love was worth a thousand times more than he had gained by the Golden Touch.

"My precious, precious Marygold!" cried he.

But Marygold made no answer.

Alas, what had he done? The moment the lips of Midas touched Marygold's forehead, her sweet, rosy face, so full of affection as it had been, assumed a glittering yellow color, with yellow tear-drops congealing on her cheeks. Little Marygold was a human child no longer, but a golden statue!

Suddenly, the stranger from the treasure-room appeared.

"Well, friend Midas," said the stranger, "how do you succeed with the Golden Touch?"

"I am very miserable," Midas shook his head. "Gold is not everything. And I have lost all that my heart really cared for."

"Ah! So you have made a discovery, since yesterday?" observed the stranger. "Let us see, then. Which of these two things do you think is really worth the most, the gift of the Golden Touch, or your own little Marygold, warm, soft, and loving as she was an hour ago?"

"Oh my child, my dear child!" cried poor Midas wringing

his hands. "I would not have given that one small dimple in her chin for the power of changing this whole big earth into a solid lump of gold!"

"You are wiser than you were, King Midas!" said the stranger. "Go and plunge into the river that glides past the bottom of your garden. Take a vase of the water, and sprinkle it over any object that you may desire to change back again from gold into its former substance."

King Midas ran to the river and plunged into the water. He dipped a golden pitcher into the water, and he smiled as it changed from gold back to pottery. The curse of the Golden Touch had really been removed.

He ran back to the castle, and began throwing water by handfuls over the golden figure of little Marygold. No sooner did it fall on her than the rosy color came back to the dear child's cheek and she began to sneeze and sputter.

How astonished she was to find herself dripping wet, and her father still throwing more water over her!

"Dear father!" cried she, "See how you have wet my nice frock, which I put on only this morning!" (Marygold did not know that she had been a little golden statue.)

When King Midas grew to be an old man, he used tell Marygold's children this marvellous story.

"And to tell you the truth, my precious little folks," said King Midas, "ever since that morning, I have hated the very sight of all other gold, except my family!"

— The End —

23. The Seven Ravens

After the Brothers Grimm

READER TIP: Many of the Grimms' fairy tales are very grim. In this story, the young girl loses the chicken bone key and must cut her finger off to open the lock to the glass mountain. If you're worried about this image, feel free to cut that portion of the story.

*O*nce upon a time, there was a man who had seven sons, but no daughters, although he fiercely wished for one. At last, his wife had a baby girl.

The whole family was happy. The father sent his sons down to the river to fetch water to baptize the wee baby girl. One son took the pitcher, and all the rest followed. The boys hurried so much that the pitcher fell into the water and sank out of sight. The boys searched and splashed about but the pitcher was gone. They didn't know what to do because they didn't dare go home empty-handed.

Waiting and waiting, the father became very impatient. In his anger he cried, "I wish those boys were all turned into ravens."

Hardly were the words spoken before he heard the flapping of wings over his head and saw seven coal-black ravens fly past in the sky.

The father was horrified that his careless curse had come true, but there was nothing to do. The parents were sad that their boys were gone and did their best to raise their daughter.

The girl grew up happy and strong and beautiful. She thought she was an only child, because her parents didn't tell her that because of her they had lost their seven boys. They didn't want her to feel sad.

But one day, the girl accidentally heard a woman say, "Oh, yes, she's a strong and beautiful girl, but it was because of her that her seven brothers were lost."

She rushed to her father and mother and asked what had happened. Her parents knew that they had to tell her the truth.

"It wasn't your fault, my dear," her father said. And he told her everything that had happened.

Still, the young girl took it to heart and grew very sad that her brothers were lost because of her. She worried all day and all night about the fate of her missing brothers.

Finally, she decided to set out on a secret journey. She took nothing with her but an old ring that her mother had given her and a loaf of bread to eat. She walked and walked until she came to the end of the world. Then she walked toward the sun, but it was too hot and threatened to burn her. So she ran toward the moon, but it was too cold and threatened to freeze her. At last she went to the stars, and they were very kind and fed her dinner.

The morning star gave her a small chicken bone and said, "You'll need a bone to open the glass mountain where your brothers are." The little girl wrapped the bone carefully in a napkin and put it in her pocket.

And off she went in search of the glass mountain.

Finally, she came to the glass mountain. Its gates were locked tightly shut. She took out her napkin and untied it, but it was empty; the bone was lost.

What could she do? How could she open the gates. She knew her brothers were inside, and she wanted to rescue them, but she had no key.

The girl was brave, as well as beautiful and strong. She cut off her little finger, and put it in the door. The new bone opened the gates to the glass mountain, and she went in.

Inside, she met a little dwarf who said, "Little girl, what are you looking for?"

"I am looking for my seven brothers," said the girl, "the seven ravens."

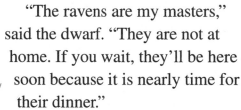

"The ravens are my masters," said the dwarf. "They are not at home. If you wait, they'll be here soon because it is nearly time for their dinner."

The dwarf led her into a dining room where there were seven gold plates and seven crystal glasses. The girl drank a sip from each glass, and took a bite from each place. Then into the last glass she dropped her mother's ring.

Suddenly there was a flapping of wings and a rushing of air, and a cawing of ravens.

"My masters are coming," said the little dwarf.

The seven ravens flew into the room and looked at their plates and glasses.

"Someone has been drinking from my glass," they said, one after another. "Someone has been eating from my plate. It was a human being."

Still, the ravens were hungry, so they ate and drank.

At last the seventh raven came to the bottom of his glass, and he nearly choked on the ring.

He took it from his beak, and at once recognized his mother's ring.

"Is our sister here?" said the ravens. "It is so far from home. Perhaps she has broken the spell. Perhaps we can become people again."

"It would be so good to see her," said the seventh raven.

Just then the girl, who had been hiding behind a door, stepped forward.

The moment her brothers saw her, the spell was broken. They all became humans again. They all hugged their little sister and kissed each other.

Then, with smiles and songs and many tales to tell, they went joyfully home.

— *The End* —

24. The Headless Horseman of Sleepy Hollow

Washington Irving

*O*nce, long ago, a schoolmaster
named Ichabod Crane came to
Sleepy Hollow. He was tall and lank,
with narrow shoulders, long arms and legs,
hands that dangled a mile out of his sleeves,
feet that might have served for shovels, and
his whole frame most loosely hung together.
If you saw him walking along the top of a hill on
a windy day, with his clothes flapping around, you might
have mistaken him for a scarecrow running away from a cornfield.

He was a strict teacher and a fair singing instructor, who spent his
evenings gathered around fires, listening to tales of ghosts and goblins,
including the story the Headless Horseman of Sleepy Hollow. The
Headless Horseman was reputed to be a Hessian soldier who had carelessly stepped in front of a cannon!

The schoolmaster also fancied a lady named Katrina Van Tassel, the
daughter and only child of a rich Dutch farmer.

Since Katrina was so beautiful (and wealthy) she had many other
suitors. The most formidable of these was a burly, roaring, roystering
blade named Brom Van Brunt. He was broad-shouldered, fun, and arrogant. A horseman, a racer, and a fighter, he was nicknamed Brom Bones.

Whenever there were brawls or pranks, the old dames would shake their heads and say, "Ay, there go Brom Bones and his gang!"

Ichabod Crane could not hope to win Katrina's hand in open rivalry, but as the town's singing-master, he made frequent visits to the farmhouse to woo her in private.

When Brom Bones heard of the rivalry, he wanted to duel and threatened to "double the schoolmaster up, and lay him on a shelf of his own schoolhouse."

Ichabod Crane stayed well away.

Did I mention Ichabod Crane's horse? It was as broken-down a mean old plow-horse as you have ever seen, gaunt and shagged. Still he must have been strong once, because he was named Gunpowder. They made quite a sight, Ichabod on Gunpowder; the floppy scarecrow sitting up straight on the sway-backed nag, trodding up and down the country lanes.

One festival night, Ichabod Crane danced for hours with Katrina. All the while, Brom Bones, sat brooding by himself in one corner.

At the end of the dance, talk turned to ghosts, as it frequently did in Sleepy Hollow. And, of course, someone mentioned that they had heard rumors of the Headless Horseman, patrolling the country, and tethering his horse nightly among the graves in the churchyard.

At last, Brom Bones told how one night he had met the horseman, and made him a bet. Whoever reached the town first would win a bowl of punch. Brom Bones would have won, too, but just as they came to the church bridge, the Horseman vanished in a flash of fire.

It was late when Ichabod Crane gave his lady's hand a kiss and headed for home. The night was dark, and the wind blew cold. All the ghost stories grew in his imagination. He heard noises in the underbrush and saw shadows following along beside him.

Then, as he was crossing the haunted stream, just past the hangman's tree, he saw emerging from the trees a large black horse carrying a gigantic rider.

Ichabod nudged Gunpowder to jog a little faster, and at the rise of the next hill, saw with horror that his riding companion, instead of carrying his head on his shoulders, held it bouncing in his lap, with a wicked grin carved on its face.

Ichabod kicked into Gunpowder and snapped his reins. The old nag remembered some long-forgotten fury and took off like a light-

ening bolt. Away they dashed through thick and thin; stones flying and sparks flashing at every bound. Ichabod's flimsy garments fluttered in the air, as he stretched his long, lank body away over his horse's head.

When he saw the church bridge in the distance, Ichabod Crane was ahead of the Horseman, but not by much.

"If I can but reach that bridge," thought Ichabod, "I am safe."

Just then he heard the black steed panting and blowing close behind him; he even fancied that he felt its hot breath.

Just before the bridge, Ichabod looked over his shoulders and saw the goblin rising in his stirrups in the very act of hurling his head at him. Ichabod tried to dodge, but too late.

He tumbled headlong into the dust, and Gunpowder, the black steed, and the goblin rider, rode off.

The next morning, Gunpowder was found, soberly cropping the grass at his master's gate.

But of Ichabod Crane there was no sign. The tracks of the furious race were plainly trampled in the dirt along the road. And just by the edge of the church bridge was found the hat of the unfortunate schoolmaster, and close beside it a shattered pumpkin.

Some folks say that Ichabod Crane made his way out of town, afraid and ashamed, but others still tell the story around a fire of his abduction by the Headless Horseman.

Brom Bones, who shortly after Ichabod's disappearance married Katrina, always laughed at the mention of the pumpkin; which led some to suspect that he knew more about the matter than he chose to tell.

— *The End* —

25. *The Wise Little Girl*

A Russian Tale

Many of the same stories are told by different cultures. Shortly after finding several Russian versions of this story, I also came across a Yiddish version, in which Rachel marries the king.

*O*nce upon a time, in the immense Russian steppe two brothers traveled to market. Dimitri, the rich brother, rode a stallion, and Ivan, the poor brother, rode a young mare. At dusk, they stopped beside an empty hut and tethered their horses outside. Great was their surprise when the next morning they saw three horses outside, instead of two.

During the night, the mare had given birth! After drinking its mother's milk, the foal struggled to its feet, but when the two brothers saw it, the foal was standing beside the stallion.

"It belongs to me!" exclaimed Dimitri. "It's my stallion's foal."

Ivan laughed. "Whoever heard of a stallion having a foal? It was born to my mare!"

"It was standing close to the stallion," shouted Dimitri, "so it's the stallion's foal. Therefore it's mine!"

The brothers decided to bring their quarrel before the judges, and they were still arguing when they reached the town.

They didn't know it was a special day when, once a year, the Emperor himself administered the law. The brothers were ushered into the Emperor's presence and explained their problem.

The Emperor immediately knew who owned the foal. He was just about to decide in favor of the poor brother, when suddenly Ivan developed an unfortunate twitch in his eye.

Annoyed by this disrespectful familiarity from a humble peasant, the Emperor decided to punish Ivan. Since he loved posing riddles and solving them as well, he exclaimed: "I can't decide, so it will be awarded to whichever of you solves the following four riddles: What is the fastest thing in the world? What is the fattest? What's the softest, and what is the most precious? Return in a week's time with your answers!"

Dimitri decided to seek help as soon as he left the courtroom. He remembered a wise woman, who owed him money. He asked her advice, in exchange for canceling part of her debt.

The clever woman demanded that the whole debt be wiped out in exchange for the answers. When Dimitri agreed, she told him: "The fastest thing in the world is my husband's race horse. The fattest is our huge pig! The softest is the bed quilt I made with goose feathers. The most precious is my three-month old nephew. I wouldn't exchange him for all the gold on earth, and that makes him the most precious thing on earth!"

Dimitri wasn't sure the old woman was correct, but he had to take an answer back to the Emperor, or else he might be punished.

In the meantime, Ivan, who was a widower, had gone back to the humble cottage where he lived with his small daughter, Rachel. Only seven years old, the little girl was thoughtful and very clever for her age. When he told her the riddle, the child said: "Tell the Emperor that the fastest thing in the world is the cold north wind in winter. The fattest is the soil in our fields whose crops give life to men and animals alike. The softest is a child's caress, and the most precious is honesty."

A week later, the two brothers returned to the palace. The Emperor was curious to hear what they had to say.

He roared with laughter at Dimitri's foolish answers.

When it was Ivan's turn to speak, the poor brother's wise replies made the Emperor squirm—especially the last one, about honesty, the most precious thing of all.

The Emperor knew that he had been dishonest with the poor brother, but he could not bear to admit it in front of his own counselors, so he angrily demanded:

"Who gave you these answers?"

Ivan told the Emperor that it was his small daughter, Rachel. Still annoyed, the great man said: "For having such a wise and clever daughter, you shall be awarded the foal that your brother claimed, together with a hundred silver ducats. But . . . but . . . in seven days bring me your clever daughter. She must appear before me neither naked nor dressed, neither on foot nor on horseback, neither bearing gifts nor empty-handed. If she does this, you will have your reward. If not, you'll have your head chopped off for your impudence!"

It was clearly impossible! Ivan went home, his eyes brimming with tears, and told his daughter what happened.

The little girl calmly said, "Tomorrow, go and catch a hare and a partridge. Both must be alive. You'll have the foal and the hundred silver ducats. Leave it to me!"

Ivan had no idea what the two creatures were for, but he trusted in his daughter's wisdom and did as she asked.

A week later, the palace was thronged with bystanders, waiting for Ivan and his small daughter.

At last, Rachel, the wise little girl, appeared, draped in a fishing net, riding the hare and holding the partridge in her hand. She was neither naked nor dressed, on foot or on horseback. Scowling, the Emperor told her: "I said neither bearing gifts nor empty-handed!"

The little girl held out the partridge. The Emperor stretched out his hand to grasp it, but the bird fluttered into the air. The third condition had been fulfilled.

The Emperor smiled at the little girl who had so cleverly passed his tests: "Is your father terribly poor, and does he desperately need the foal?"

"Oh, yes!" replied the little girl. "We live on the hares he catches in the rivers and the fish he picks from the trees!"

"Aha!" cried the Emperor triumphantly. "You're not so clever. Whoever heard of hares in the river and fish in the trees!"

To which the little girl swiftly replied: "And whoever heard of a stallion having a foal?"

The Emperor burst out laughing. Ivan was immediately given his hundred silver ducats and the foal, and the Emperor proclaimed: "Only in my kingdom could such a wise little girl be born!"

— The End —

26. The Princess and the Mouse

An Arabian Tale

*F*ar away across the desert lived a princess named Safia. One day, a wicked magician disguised as an old woman approached Safia.

"Princess," he said, "let me be your laundress and wash your sheets."

"Good poor woman," said Princess Safia, "Come to my private quarters and I shall give you my linen to wash."

So the disguised magician followed the princess, and before the girl could see what was happening he bundled her into a laundry bag and ran away as fast as his legs would carry him. Muttering a magic spell, he made her as small as a doll, and put her in a cupboard.

The next day, the magician found the palace in an uproar.

"Princess Safia has vanished, and His Majesty is nearly out of his mind," said the Grand Vizier. "All the fortune tellers have failed to find her."

The wicked magician smiled, for his spell would defy the fortune tellers until the day of his death.

The next day, the Queen was weeping in her garden when the magician entered, disguised as a washer-woman. He put her into a laundry bag and turned her into a doll no bigger than his thumb.

"Ha!" laughed the magician, "Tomorrow I will capture the King and rule the country myself."

Sure enough, the next day, disguised in his usual way, he captured the King, turned him into a doll no bigger than the Queen, and shut him up in the cupboard, too.

"Oh, wise one," the Grand Vizier came to the magician and begged, "please tell us what to do!"

"Until your King and Queen and Princess come again, let me be your ruler," said the magician, and the people agreed. So for a long time the wicked magician ruled the people and gathered much wealth. Sometimes he would send out troops to search for the missing royal family. But, of course, there was no sign of them.

Now, one day a mouse nibbled its way into the cupboard where Princess Safia was hidden.

"Mouse, mouse," said the Princess, "eat a hole in this cupboard and let me out. My father is the King, and he shall reward you."

"But the King and Queen have disappeared," said the mouse. "The magician is on the throne."

"Oh no," wept the Princess. "Can the wicked magician have captured them too?"

They searched the cabinet and found the King and Queen on the cupboard's top shelf. But they were as stiff as wood, because the magician had cast a different spell upon them.

"Princess," said the mouse, "tonight when the moon rises, come with me to the Wise Woman who lives in a hollow tree. She will surely help you."

The mouse nibbled the wood away, and when the moon rose, they hurried to the tree hollow and climbed in.

"To save your family," said the Wise Woman, giving the princess a magic grass seed, "you must find an orange-colored horse by the crossroads. Give him this magic grass-seed to eat, and whisper into his ear 'Take me, Orange Horse, to where the sacred pear tree grows, so that I may pick the pear from its topmost branch.'"

"And then shall I regain my proper size?" asked the Princess.

"When the wicked magician is dead and not before shall you turn back into your normal size," said the Wise Woman. "Ride the horse to the Well of the Green Ogre. Drop the pear into the well. The wicked magician's soul is hidden in that pear, and if it is devoured by the ogre, the magician will die."

"What will happen then?" the Princess asked.

"All the creatures turned into other shapes by the magician will return to their own forms."

So the tiny Princess thanked the Wise Woman, said good-bye to the mouse, and ran on in the moonlight until she reached the cross-roads where stood an Orange Horse.

"Take me, Orange Horse," whispered Safia, "to the tree where the sacred pears grow, so that I may pick the topmost pear from its branches."

The horse put down his head. Safia fed it the magic grass seed and then climbed on. The horse neighed twice and galloped away like the wind.

Soon, Safia found herself in a beautiful orchard with a single pear tree. She climbed into the branches, and picked the pear from the topmost branch.

"Take me to the Well of the Green Ogre," she whispered in the horse's right ear. The horse rode off like the wind, and soon they reached the well.

Inside the well, Safia saw an ogre's head as big as a pumpkin. She took the pear containing the soul of the magician and dropped it right into the Green Ogre's mouth. Instantly he chewed the pear up into tiny pieces.

Safia suddenly found herself growing back to her own size. The wicked magician was dead!

The horse took her back to the crossroads, and just as she was about to thank him, he disappeared before her eyes.

At the palace, she hurried to the magician's room where she found the King and Queen were their normal size again, but very puzzled indeed to find themselves locked in a cupboard. Safia quickly explained.

The King sent soldiers to the royal bedchamber to arrest the magician, but he was dead, as the Wise Woman had predicted.

Safia then went to thank the Wise Woman who lived in the hollow tree. But the tree was gone! Instead, she saw a tall handsome young man dressed in fine clothes.

"Blessings upon you, dear Princess," said he, "The wise woman is gone."

"How do you know this?" demanded the Princess.

"I was the mouse, another victim of the magician's enchantment."

"Come with me to my father so that he can thank you," cried Safia.

Together they went, and the young man knelt before the King.

"You shall stay here and marry my daughter," promised the King, "together you shall rule the kingdom after me."

The wedding feast was celebrated for seven days and seven nights, and Safia and her husband lived happily ever after.

— *The End* —

27. The Little Boy Who Cried "Wolf!"

*O*nce upon a time, in a village not far from here, lived a little shepherd-boy. Every morning he would take his flock into the hills to feed them grass and lead them to water.

Being a shepherd is rather ordinary work, and the boy often found himself bored. He would lie on his back and stare at the clouds, listening idly to the baa-ing of his sheep.

One day he got an idea. He would play a trick on the villagers. He thought the idea over in his mind once, twice, and then, yes, decided that it would be fun.

So, leaving his flock alone in the hills, he ran, ran, ran down from the hills into the village crying out at the top of his lungs: "Wolf! Wolf! Woooolf! There is a wolf in the hills, it is eating my lambs!"

All the villagers who heard his calling immediately stopped working. They dropped their plows and tools, grabbed up sticks and stones, and ran as fast as they could out into the hills to help the poor boy.

But when they got there the wolf was nowhere to be seen.

"Where is the wolf?" the villagers asked.

The little boy could not answer, because he was laughing too hard.

Disgusted at this, the villagers turned on their heels and marched back to their work.

That was fun, the little boy thought. I must remember that.

A few days later, the little boy was again out in the hills, lying on his back, thinking about mischief.

The last time I tried that trick I had so much fun, he thought. Perhaps I should try it again. He thought the idea over once, twice, and then, yes, decided that it would be fun.

So, leaving his flock alone in the hills, he ran, ran, ran down from the hills into the village crying out at the top of his lungs: "Wolf! Wolf! Wooooolf! There is a wolf in the hills, it is eating my lambs!"

Once again, all the villagers who heard his calling immediately stopped working. They dropped their plows and tools, grabbed up sticks and stones, and ran as fast as they could out into the hills to help the poor boy.

"And where is the wolf this time?" the villagers asked.

But the little boy could not answer, because once again he was laughing too hard.

That was fun, the little boy thought. I must remember that trick.

A few days later, though, disaster struck. A wolf, a real live and very hungry wolf came loping over the top of the hill and began killing the lambs.

In great fright, the boy ran for help. He ran, ran, ran down from the hills into the village crying out at the top of his lungs: "Wolf! Wolf! Woooolf! There is a wolf in the hills, it is eating my lambs!"

The villagers heard him, but this time they didn't leave their work or pick up sticks or chase after him into the hills. They all thought it was another horrible trick. No one paid the least attention to his shouts, and when he came up and tugged at their sleeves, they turned away sadly.

When the shepherd boy finally returned to his sheep he found that they were gone, every single one.

It was a hard way to learn the lesson: if you lie to people, no one will believe you, even if you are telling them the truth.

— *The End* —

28. The Country Mouse and the City Mouse

Once upon a time, a country mouse invited her cousin from the city to visit. When the City Mouse arrived, he was shocked to find that the Country mouse had nothing for dinner but an old husk of corn.

"This is it?" said the City Mouse. "In the city we have food of all kinds! Come, let's go to the city and I will show you."

So off they went.

First they stopped at the kitchen cupboard, where they nibbled their way into a huge bag of flour!

The Country Mouse tasted the flour, and thought, "Well, this is living indeed!" She was just thinking how lucky the City Mouse was when the kitchen door opened with a slam, and in came the cook to get some flour.

"Run!" squeaked the City Mouse. "It's the cook!"

Off they ran, scamper-skitter, into the mouse hole. The little Country Mouse was shaking and shivering with relief that they had escaped.

"That's nothing," said the City Mouse. "She'll go away soon, and we can get some more."

Sure enough, when the cook had gone and shut the door, the City Mouse took his cousin to the top shelf of the cupboard. There they found a huge box of raisins.

They quickly gnawed their way into the box, and began pulling out raisins and eating them up.

This was incredible, thought the Country Mouse! Truly delicious.

But just then, there was a scratching at the door and a sharp, loud, meeow!

"What's that?" said the Country Mouse.

"Run!" squeaked the City Mouse. "It's the old Tom cat

Off they ran, scamper-skitter, into the mouse hole. The little Country Mouse was shaking and shivering with relief that they had escaped.

"That," panted the City Mouse, "was the old Tom cat. If he gets a hold of you, you are lost."

"I'm never going to go into that cupboard again," said the Country Mouse.

"I know a better place," said the City Mouse. "Let's go down into the cellar. That's where they keep the really good stuff!"

Down they went into the cellar. It was truly an amazing place. On the walls were shelves lined with chunks of cheese. From the ceiling hung ropes of sausages, and on one table was an entire ham, smoked and waiting to be eaten!

It all smelled so wonderful that the Country Mouse had to try everything. She ran up and down the shelf, nibbling at cheese.

In one corner, she saw an extra rich and very delicious-smelling piece of cheese on a strange looking table. She was just about to sink her teeth into it when her cousin saw her.

"Stop! No!" shouted the City Mouse. "That's a trap!"

"What is a trap?" asked the Country Mouse, skeptically.

"The minute you touch that cheese with your teeth, something from that table comes crashing down on your head, and you're dead."

"My goodness!" squeaked the Country Mouse. She looked at the cheese, and she looked at her cousin. "Please excuse me," she said, "I think I'll go home now. I'd rather have an old husk of corn to eat in peace and comfort than have flour and raisins and cheese, but be frightened to death all the time!"

So, the little Country Mouse went back to her home in the fields, and there she stayed for the rest of her life.

— The End —

29. George Washington and the Cherry Tree

Nearly every historian agrees that this tale is pure fiction. Enjoy!

When George Washington, the first president of the United States of America, was just a boy, he was given a hatchet for his sixth birthday. Now that's not the kind of a gift a six-year-old is likely to receive these days. But in Virginia back then, if you wanted a fire to cook breakfast you needed wood, and they liked to train their young 'uns early.

Well, George, like most little boys, loved his hatchet. He used it constantly. From morning until night, he would chop at just about anything he met. He chopped at tree stumps and fallen logs, at little branches and at big branches.

One day he was tired of chopping away at dead wood. It was a beautiful day, and he found himself standing out on the edge of his father's orchard.

There he found a beautiful young English cherry tree with its flowers all ablossom. One thing led to another, and George took his little hatchet and started a-whacking.

Chopping down even a small cherry tree is hard work, especially for a six-year-old boy with just a little hatchet. He spent the entire day there in the orchard, chop, chop, chopping away. That evening, he could barely keep his eyes open during dinner. His mother was quite surprised when young George went up to bed and without even the littlest fuss fell fast asleep.

The next morning, his father happened to be strolling around the orchard when he found the poor cherry tree (which happened to be one of his favorites) lying sideways across the path.

He asked in the servants and slave quarters who might have done the horrific deed and even offered five guineas for information leading to the arrest of the guilty party. No one spoke a word, and Mr. Washington had a suspicion why.

So, he hid himself behind an apple tree and waited to see if the culprit might show himself.

Not long after, who should arrive but little George carrying his little hatchet.

George was very surprised to see his father looking so stern.

"Tell me, George," his father asked. "Do you know who killed the most beautiful cherry tree in my orchard?"

George stopped in his tracks and hesitated. He knew the truth and was afraid of the penalty.

Then he stood up straight and tall and said, "I cannot tell a lie. Father, it was I. I cut down your cherry tree with my little hatchet."

George's father looked stern, and raised his hand to strike the boy, but then he thought better of it.

"George, my son, I am not pleased that you chopped down my cherry tree. But by telling me the truth, you have shown bravery and heroism worth a thousand cherry trees."

The father hugged his son close, and little George Washington felt very proud.

Two lessons can be learned from this tale. First, always tell the truth.

Second, there are consequences to every action—to atone for his deed, young George went to bed tired every day that week, because his father made him chop enough wood to fill the woodpile for the entire winter.

— *The End* —

30. The Bat and the Weasels

*O*nce there lived a bat, who squeaked and flew about every night with a great flutter and cry. The bat loved to eat flies and to buzz low over the fields of farmers, feeling the silk of tall-growing corn whisper up against his belly.

As the night grew late and dawn approached, the bat was very careful to fly back to his home. He lived in a cave with many other bats. From daybreak until sunset hung he upside down from the ceiling, sleeping soundly.

Then, as night fell, the bat and all his brothers and sisters would fly out from their cave with a great whooshing of wings. So huge was the swarm that it looked like a storm cloud flying into the night air. Then, with sharp squeaks the bats would spin and turn about, each flying in separate directions to search for a night's meal.

One night, the bat was especially hungry, and he flew quickly over the cornfield in search of mosquitoes or gnats. He especially liked gnats, which he ate like popcorn.

Now, bats are not blind as some might think, but their vision is not as strong as that of the falcon or owl. Instead, they rely on a form of radar, seeing in the dark by squeaking out sounds, and listening to the returning echo with their large furry ears.

This evening the bat was so hungry, and in such a great hurry, that he forgot to squeak quite as frequently as usual.

And SMACK! He flew right into the big old scarecrow.

So stunned and surprised was the bat that he fell to the ground with a great thump. In that very instant, a weasel, who had been wandering through the corn looking for baby birds, pounced on the bat.

"Let me go! Let me go!" the bat pleaded.

"And why should I?" said the weasel, its bright eyes shining red in the moonlight. "I am a weasel, the natural enemy of all birds. I think I'm going to eat you for my dinner."

"Wait, wait," said the bat. "I am not a bird!"

"Not a bird?" frowned the weasel. "But you have wings."

"These?" said the bat, trying to hide his leathery wings, "They are nothing. Have you ever seen a bird like me?"

The weasel admitted that he hadn't. "What are you then?" he asked.

"I am a rat," said the bat.

"A rat?" the weasel shuddered. "I could never eat a rat. I tried one once, and it tasted awful. Ah well, you may go."

"Thank you, kind weasel," said the bat, and away he flew.

By now, the bat was very hungry, and more than a little shaken up. He flew away from the corn field and headed toward the cherry orchard where he hoped to find a grasshopper or a beetle.

Once again, he flew fast and low, and once again he forgot to squeak quite as frequently as usual.

SMACK! He flew right into the low branch of a cherry tree and fell to the ground with a great thump.

The next moment, another weasel, who had been wandering through the orchard looking for rats for dinner, pounced on the bat.

"Let me go! Let me go!" the bat pleaded.

"And why should I?" said the weasel, its bright eyes shining red in the moonlight. "I am a weasel, the natural enemy of all rats. I think I'm going to eat you for my dinner."

"Rats?" said the bat. "Wait, wait. I am not a rat"

"Not a rat?" frowned the weasel. "But you have fur and a nose like a rat."

"These?" said the bat, "They are nothing. Have you ever seen a rat with wings?"

The weasel admitted that he hadn't. "What are you then?" he asked.

"I am a bird," said the bat.

"A bird?" the weasel shuddered. "I could never eat a bird. I tried one once, and it tasted awful. Ah well, you may go."

"Thank you, kind weasel," said the bat, and away he flew safe once again.

The moral of the story? Take advantage of your situation, and listen before you speak.

— *The End* —

31. The Lion and the Mouse

The Lion, king of all the land, was fast asleep on a hilltop. It had been a long day. The hunting had been good, and he had eaten a bit too much. Now he was very tired, and he was enjoying his dreams.

Just then, a mouse ran over his face, and woke the Lion up.

"ROAR!" shouted the Lion.

The Mouse was so startled that he fell off the tip of the Lion's nose and was easily caught in the great cat's paw.

"Why did you wake me?" growled the Lion.

"Pardon me, Sire," squeaked the Mouse. "I thought that you were a pile of leaves. I am growing old and my eyesight isn't as sharp as it was."

"SILENCE!"

The Mouse grew very quiet. The Lion began to lick his lips. He wasn't hungry, but the Mouse might make a nice bit of dessert.

"Sire, please don't eat me," begged the Mouse. "I have a wife and sixteen children. If you spare my life, I will surely repay your kindness."

"You'll what?" said the Lion with a wicked grin.

"I'll save your life one day," answered the Mouse, bravely.

It seemed such a good joke, a mouse saving a lion's life, that the Lion burst out laughing. "Very well," said the Lion. "Run along, but in the future be careful about running through piles of leaves."

Now, it so happened that several days later, the Lion was caught by hunters and tied to the ground with a net of ropes. No matter how much he struggled, pulled, or roared, he could not escape.

The Mouse, who lived not far away, recognized the lion's roar and came running.

"Sire," said the Mouse, "why do you roar so?"

"Can't you see?" howled the Lion. "I have been tied to the ground by hunter's ropes."

"Ah," said the Mouse, and he immediately began gnawing away at the many ropes with his sharp teeth.

In a matter of minutes, the Lion was set free.

"You thought it was funny," said the Mouse, "that I thought I would ever be able to save your life. Now you know that even a mouse can help a lion."

"Thank you," said the Lion humbly.

And from that day until this, the Lion and the Mouse were best friends.

— *The End* —

32. The Father and His Seven Sons

*O*nce in a land not far from here, there was a father who had seven sons who constantly argued among themselves.

The seven boys fought like cats and dogs from morning until night, and sometimes later! They argued about who got the most food, who had the best clothes, who could run the fastest, and who could jump the highest. They fought over toys, they fought over girls.

The father, who was a wood chopper by trade, would rush from his house every morning and stay out in the forest quite late just to avoid the sound of seven boys arguing.

The poor mother, who had given up her career as a novelist to take care of her children was a quivering wreck. Every time the boys shouted, she sobbed. Every time they squabbled, she moaned. Years had gone by, and she kept hoping that they would become friends, but now she was coming to wish that she had never stopped writing.

One day the father came home from the forest completely exhausted and discovered that his wife hadn't prepared any dinner.

"I couldn't," she cried. "The boys wouldn't let me. They kept arguing about what we should eat, and who would help me, and then they broke all the eggs in a great fight. Now they've all run off."

Furious, the father went to bed, hungry.

It was late at night when the seven boys finally came home. They had intended to sneak back into the house, but one stepped on another's toes and in an instant they were fighting loudly enough to wake the exhausted father.

"Stop!" shouted the father. He decided that it was time to teach them a lesson. "Each of you bring me a stick."

The seven boys quivered, afraid that their father was going to beat them.

"GO!" their father roared.

Soon the seven boys were back, and each of them held a stick.

One by one the father took the seven sticks from their hands, and he tied them together in a bundle.

"Now," he ordered his boys, "I want you each to try and break this bundle of sticks."

One after another the seven boys tried to break the bundle of sticks, but they could not.

Next, their father untied the bundle, and gave each boy a single stick. "Now try and break the sticks."

The seven sticks snapped easily.

"My sons," said the father, "if you work together and help each other, you will be as strong as the bundle of sticks. Your enemies will not be able to harm you. But if you remain divided among yourselves, your enemies will break you as easily as these sticks."

The seven brothers smiled and hugged each other and hugged their parents. Today they are, one and all, great friends.

— *The End* —

33. The Wolf and the Crane

The wolf was mean and wicked and hungry. He licked his sharp teeth and went out prowling for sheep. When he found a stray, he immediately pounced, and that was the end of the poor lamb.

The wolf was so hungry that he devoured the sheep nearly whole!

It wasn't until every bit of lamb was gone that he noticed an unpleasant feeling in his throat. Because of his haste, one of the lamb's bones had become lodged sideways across the wolf's throat. It hurt terribly.

Moaning, the wolf headed down to the river, where he hoped to wash the bone away with a long drink of water.

He stuck his nose into the river and drank deeply, but if anything the bone became even more deeply lodged.

Just then, a crane happened to notice the wolf's coughing and sputtering.

"What's wrong?" the crane asked.

"There is a bone caught in my throat," the wolf hacked.

"Ah," nodded the crane. "Too bad."

The wolf looked at the long-necked crane, and a plan came into his mind.

"Crane," said the wolf, "if you put your head into my mouth and pull the bone out, I'll give you a dozen fish."

Now, the crane was no fool. He knew that the wolf was in deep trouble. "I'll do it for two dozen," he bargained.

"Agreed!" said the wolf. And he opened his mouth wide.

Holding her breath, the crane stuck her head deep into the wolf's mouth. She poked around as gently as possible until she found the bone lodged deep inside. Then, carefully, but quickly, she pulled out the bone and withdrew her head.

"I've plucked out the bone," said the crane. "Now, how about those fish?"

The wolf grinned and licked his lips, "Why, crane, certainly you have already been fully paid."

"How do you figure that?" asked the crane.

"You put your head into the mouth and jaws of a wolf," the wolf laughed. "And you're still standing there alive and well. That's payment enough, don't you think."

The wolf licked his lips and snapped his jaws, and the crane quickly flew away.

The moral of this story? Expect no reward for serving the wicked, and consider yourself lucky if you escape without injury.

— *The End* —

34. The Traveler and His Dog

*T*he Traveler was getting ready to set on his journey. First he ate his breakfast and fed his dog. The Dog ate every bit.

Then the Traveler washed the dishes, dried them, and put them back in the cupboard. The Dog watched, hoping for another scrap of food.

Upstairs the Traveler went, and upstairs again into the attic. There he found his suitcase, which he brought downstairs into the bedroom.

In the bedroom, he began packing his bag. The Dog followed up the stairs, and lay on the foot of the bed, his tongue lolling about lazily.

The Traveler opened his suitcase and began searching through his dresser drawers. He pulled out shirts and socks and pants and underwear.

He went into his bathroom and packed up his toothbrush and toothpaste, his soap and shampoo, and the special brush that he used to wash his back.

Back in the bedroom, he packed his alarm clock, and the book he was reading before bed. He packed his shoes and his walking stick, and a hat in case it was sunny.

He carried the suitcase downstairs and set it by the door.

The Dog followed him downstairs and lay down in the door step, enjoying the warm sun.

Then the Traveler went from room to room, making sure that all the windows were shut and the lights were off. He checked the faucet in the kitchen sink to make sure it wasn't dripping, and then he ran back upstairs to check the bathroom sink and the shower.

Downstairs again, the Traveler made certain that the stove was turned off and that the milk had been poured out from the refrigerator. (There is nothing worse than coming home from a long trip to find spoiled milk in the fridge.)

He put together an assortment of snacks for the trip, including a peach, a pear, an orange, a plum, and a biscuit for the dog.

Then he remembered that he had forgotten to pack a towel, and hurried back upstairs to get one. He put the towel in his suitcase and managed to close it only by sitting on top.

The Traveler put his wallet in one pocket, and his keys in the other pocket. He picked up the suitcase in one hand and the sack of snacks in the other.

The Dog yawned, slowly stood up and stretched.

"Why are you yawning like that?" said the Traveler. "Everything is ready except you. So, come on, let's go!"

The Dog, wagging his tail happily answered, "Oh, master, I've been ready for quite some time now. I was just waiting for you."

— *The End* —

35. The Dog and His Shadow

One day the Dog was nosing about the farm. He liked to poke his nose into everything, sniffing around here and there. He sniffed in the barn, he sniffed in the shed, he sniffed in the bedroom, and he sniffed in the kitchen.

"Are you under foot again?" asked the Cook. "Get out of here!"

But the Dog just sat on the floor and panted happily.

"Can't you see I can't make dinner while you're around?" said the Cook.

The Dog just barked.

Finally, the Cook gave the dog a piece of bone and pushed him out of the kitchen.

There was a hill not far from the house that would be the perfect place to bury the bone. So, off the Dog trotted down the road.

He came to the bridge and happened to look down into the stream.

What did he see, but another dog staring back at him?

Now, you and I know it was just his shadow, but the Dog thought it was another Dog.

And this dog has a bone even bigger than his own bone!

"Give me that bone!" the dog barked, jumping into the stream. He attacked the other dog fiercely to get the second bone.

But as soon as he barked and bit at the other dog, his own bone fell from his mouth and dropped into the stream, where it was quickly washed away.

It took some time for the Dog to notice that his treasure was gone, because he was so busy attacking the other dog. Eventually, however, it began to dawn on him that he was fighting up a storm, but not coming any closer to winning.

So he climbed back up on shore and shook himself off.

When he realized his bone was gone, he climbed back on the bridge and looked down at the other dog. The other dog's bone was gone too.

He trotted back to the farm house, but the Cook had locked the door and ignored his howls.

Sometimes, the dog thought, it is better to be satisfied with what you have and not to chase after shadows.

— *The End* —

36. Stone Soup

There are dozens of variations on this story. By all accounts, it originated in Germany. I've set this one during the American Revolution.

The winter of 1777 was bitterly cold, especially for the troops of the Continental Army. They had been camped in Valley Forge by the Schuylkill River for months, waiting for General Washington's orders to attack the British, who were no doubt warm and well fed.

Food supplies had grown scarce, and the bitter wind kept every soldier wrapped tightly in as many blankets as he owned.

"What's for dinner, Sergeant?" the Captain asked his cook.

"Nothing, sir," the Cook answered promptly. "The larder is bare."

"Are we going to starve then?" asked the Captain.

"Looks that way, sir."

Not exactly the kind of cheerful optimism that the Captain had wanted to hear. It was too late to go into town, and besides the army's credit was all but exhausted with the tradespeople.

"Pardon me, sir," said Private Black, "but my Grandma taught me a recipe that I think might serve."

The Captain looked at Private Black. The man was a freed slave and frequently found himself excluded from the camaraderie of the company of soldiers.

"Very well," the Captain said. "Proceed."

"Boil up some water," Private Black told the Cook. "We're going to have Stone Soup."

"Stone Soup?" muttered the Cook. "Never heard of it."

When the water was boiling, Private Black opened up his pack and took out three round flat stones. "My Grandma gave me these stones and said that with them, I'll never be hungry."

Then he dropped the stones into the black cauldron. Plop, plop, plop.

"That's it?" asked the Cook.

"It makes a fine broth," said Private Black.

"Hmm, a bit sparse," said the Captain. He brought out a bit of salt pork he'd been saving, and tossed that into the pot.

"Could use some vegetables," said the Gunnery Sergeant. He found an old cabbage at the bottom of his sleeping bag and tossed that in.

"Needs body," said the Quartermaster. He took two potatoes from a pair of old boots.

"I've got these old beans," said the Rifleman from Boston. He poured them in.

Private Black didn't say a word, he just stirred the pot.

The Cook insisted that he take a taste, so he dipped his spoon in. "Needs some

flavoring," he mumbled. He added a handful of salt and a toss of pepper.

"I've got this onion," said the Powder Boy.

"This here turnip would make a nice addition," nodded the Surgeon.

Splash splash, into the pot.

"Smells good," said the Captain.

"Smells ready," said the Cook.

"Dinner is served," said Private Black.

Everyone in the company crawled out of their tents, and with them came a dozen crusts of black bread and a dozen boxes of hardtack for softening, which were broken up and passed all around.

"Who would have thought," said the Captain, "that Stone Soup would taste so good."

"Three cheers for Private Black," said the Cook.

"Hip Hip Hooray!" shouted the entire company of soldiers.

Private Black didn't say much. He just nodded his head in thanks.

And when the soup was all eaten and the pot was cool, he reached down into the bottom, and collected the three stones, which he stored in his back pack for another day.

— The End —

37. The Miser

Once in a poor land lived an old and wealthy miser. He had never earned his money, but was the last of a wealthy family. He lived in a large palace and owned many things.

He spent as little money as possible, keeping only a butler, a maid, a cook, and a stable boy to care for his horses.

When he walked through the halls of his palace, he always felt afraid that the servants were stealing from him. Were there only three paintings on the wall where once there had been four? How many silver forks and knives had the cook taken? What about the furniture? Who could possibly count all that furniture? And the Miser was no expert on horses. Perhaps the young stable boy had exchanged his fine Arabian steeds for old and worn-down nags.

Finally, after many years of fretful worry, the Miser sold everything that he owned. He sold the horses, he sold the paintings, he sold the silver forks and knives, and he even sold the great palace that he lived in. He fired all his servants, and now lived in a small cottage not far from his old palace.

In exchange for all these things, he was given many many gold pieces. These were too cumbersome. It would be too easy for a stranger to sneak in and steal a gold piece or even ten.

So, in a great big cauldron, he melted down the gold pieces into one large lump of gold.

Still, one can't leave a large lump of gold lying around the hut. Any robber could come in and walk off with it.

So, the Miser sneaked out one morning and buried the gold in the ground next to the wall of his old palace.

Every day he went out to the wall and stared at the spot in the dirt until a warm glow came over his face. Then he trotted back to his hut and ate his dinner of gruel and water.

Now, his butler, maid, cook and stable boy were very upset at being fired without warning. They saw that every day, and almost every night, the Miser made trips to the site near the palace wall.

Late one night, when the Miser was fast asleep, they dug into the spot in the dirt and found the large lump of gold. They broke it in four pieces, and each went in a different direction.

In the morning, the Miser rose with the dawn and walked out to the wall where his treasure was buried. There he found only an empty hole!

"Oh woe!" he shouted "Stolen! Stolen! My treasure is stolen!"

He moaned and groaned and tore at his hair.

A neighbor, who was out that morning watering her garden, saw the Miser sobbing and in tears, and asked him whatever was the matter.

He told her that he had buried his entire treasure in the ground and that now it was gone, stolen by thieves.

The neighbor thought for a moment. Then she bent down and picked up a large rock from her garden.

"What is that for?" cried the Miser.

"Take this rock and bury it in the ground where your treasure was buried," the wise woman said. "Pretend that it is your golden treasure. It will do you just as much good, because when the gold was buried there in the ground, you had it not, and you did not make the slightest use of it."

The Miser sobbed uncontrollably, and the wise woman went back to her garden.

Perhaps eventually he learned his lesson. Or perhaps he is there still, standing beside the wall crying after his lost gold

— The End —

38. The Bragging Traveler

One day, the Traveler returned to his small town after many years away. He had traveled far and wide and seen many wondrous things.

"Tell us," said his friends. "Tell us what you have seen in your travels."

"I'm tired," said the Traveler. "My feet are sore, my clothes are dirty. I need a bath and a nap and then some dinner. Let's talk later."

In the evening, after the Traveler had bathed, napped, and eaten his dinner, he went to the social hall, where all his friends had gathered.

The fire was built high, and it crackled warmly.

"Tell us," said his friends, "Tell us now about the wonders you have seen in your travels!"

"I am thirsty," said the traveler, "may I have something to drink?"

His friends filled his mug, and he drained it in one great gulp. They refilled it, and he drank deeply again.

"Tell us!" cried his friends impatiently. "Where have you been? What have you seen?"

"All right," agreed the Traveler. "Now is as good a time as any."

He leaned back in his chair, and closed his eyes for a good long while. Some of his friends were worried that he had fallen asleep, while others leaned forward in their chairs in glowing expectation.

"I climbed mountains," he said. "The tallest mountains in the world. I swam across rivers, and dove into a tidal wave!"

"Impossible!" said one friend.

"Unlikely," said another.

"All true," said the Traveler, placing his palm over his heart. "I spoke with kings and queens, and I even played croquet with a Bishop! I won and lost a fortune gambling and was engaged (for a brief time) to a princess."

"A princess?" said one friend, skeptically.

"Slay any witches?" said another friend, frowning.

"Three!" boasted the traveler. "And I killed two dragons, and bested two knights in a joust. When I was in Rhodes, I jumped so far that no one else in the city could match my incredible leap!"

"Impossible," said one friend.

"Unlikely," said another.

"The Mayor of Rhodes himself, as well as the entire city council, were witnesses!" said the Traveler.

"Well, we don't need to speak to the Mayor of Rhodes to learn whether or not you can jump that far," said the first friend, who had known the Traveler since he was a boy. "Why don't you pretend that this is Rhodes and jump for us?"

The Traveler's face turned scarlet, and he spoke no more that evening.

Next morning, no one in the small town was surprised to find that his bed was empty and his suitcase gone. Since then, many years have gone by, and he has not yet been seen in that town again.

— *The End* —

39. The Tortoise and the Hare

*O*ver the hill and by the stream lived a Tortoise and a Hare. They were neighbors for a long long time, and every day the Hare rose with a laugh on his lips.

"Still asleep?" he called to the Tortoise. "You move so slowly, my friend."

When they were working in their gardens, the Hare would race around and have his planting finished before the Tortoise had even plucked his weeds.

"Still working?" the Hare called. "You move so slowly, my friend."

For many months, the Tortoise listened patiently to the Hare's taunts. Then, one day he decided enough was enough.

"Even though you're as quick as a politician's tongue," the Tortoise said, "I will beat you in a race."

"Impossible!" laughed the Hare. "I will bet you all my carrots that I'll win."

"Agreed," said the Tortoise.

They asked their friend the Fox to lay out the race course and act as referee. It was a long run, from the stream, over the hill, around the great old oak tree, back over the hill, and then at last across the stream to the other side.

On the morning of the race, everyone in the forest rushed out to line the way and watch.

"On your mark," said the Fox. "Get set. Go!"

Away went the Hare, quick as lightning, and in a moment he was up over the hill and well on his way to the old oak tree.

The tortoise for his part had barely left the edge of the stream.

"Go! Go! Go!" shouted all the animals.

By now the Hare had reached the Oak Tree. Underneath the tree was a nice soft patch of moss. He looked back over his shoulder and saw that the Tortoise still hadn't even climbed the edge of the hill.

"It's time for a nap," said the Hare to himself. He lay down and was soon asleep.

The Tortoise for his part never stopped and never paused. He went on slowly to be sure, up the hill, and around the great old oak tree, and was just at the top of the hill when the Hare suddenly awoke with a start.

"Where is that pesky Tortoise?" the Hare muttered.

And then he saw the Tortoise's tail just vanishing down the side of the hill.

The Hare ran and ran and ran as fast as he could, but before he reached the bottom of the hill, the Tortoise was already across the stream, munching on one of the Hare's yummy carrots.

Slow but steady wins the race.

— *The End* —

40. The Brave Tin Soldier

Hans Christian Andersen

As fondly as we remember the stories of Hans Christian Anderson, today they may seem heartless and cruel. Still, the images remain, of the steadfast tin soldier, standing straight and true through all his unkind adventures. At last he returns to his love, and for just an instant they are almost close enough to touch.

The poor little boy's father was very clever, and one day he made twenty-five tin soldiers out of an old tin spoon. They all stood straight and wore splendid uniforms of red and blue. They were all exactly alike, except for one, who had only one leg. He had been the last made, and there was not enough tin to finish him.

The little boy, of course, loved his one-legged Tin Soldier best of all.

On the table where the boy played with his Tin Soldiers was a small black puzzle box, and a beautiful white paper Ballerina who held in her hands a red rose made of tinsel. The father had made the Ballerina for his daughter, and dressed her in a fine silk handkerchief.

"There's the wife for me," thought the Tin Soldier. "She stands as straight and true as a soldier. I would give anything in the world to be with her."

Just then, a little Goblin, who lived in the black puzzle box popped out, and said, "Tin Soldier, you shouldn't wish for things you can't have."

The Tin Soldier stood straight and ignored the Goblin. He was fascinated by the Ballerina, who stood high on one tiptoe with her other leg stretched out. They both stood on one leg, and in that were so similar.

The Goblin was so upset at being ignored that he pushed the Tin Soldier off the table and out the window!

He fell to the ground, and was found by two little boys.

"Look there's a tin soldier!" said one boy.

"Let's put him in a boat," said the other boy.

So they built a small boat, and set the Tin Soldier afloat. Down the tiny stream he floated, standing straight and still.

At the entrance to the sewer stood a rat.

"Give me your passport," demanded the rat.

The Tin Soldier said not a word and floated past the screaming rat into the dark sewer where he swirled around in the darkness and floated out into the great river.

A fish in the river saw the glint from the Soldier's red coat and snapped him up in one bite. A moment later, the fish found itself caught in a net and hauled ashore.

"This is all the goblin's fault," thought the Tin Soldier. "If only the Ballerina were here with me, I wouldn't mind being caught in this fish's belly."

Just then, there was a poke of a knife, and the fish's belly was slit open wide.

"Why look!" said the boy's mother, "here is the lost tin soldier! What a wonderful thing!" The fish had been caught and taken to market, and sold to the family of the very boy whose father had created him.

The mother rinsed the soldier off, dried him, and set him back on the table where all of his brothers welcomed him home with salutes.

The Tin Soldier was very quiet, happy to be back at last in full sight of the Ballerina whom he loved.

Perhaps it was the Goblin's curse, or perhaps it was just a mistake, but at that moment the boy ran into the room in a rage.

He picked up the Tin Soldier, which was the first thing he saw, and threw him into the fireplace.

The Tin Soldier felt the heat of the flames melting first his hat and then his gun. His legs were turning as red as his coat, and soon he knew he would be melted and gone.

Suddenly, though, the door to the room flew open, and a gust of wind caught the Little Ballerina. She blew into the air, and landed in the fire right next to the Tin Soldier.

For a moment they stood beside each other, engulfed in the bright flames.

In the next instant the Ballerina caught on fire, and was gone. The Tin soldier melted down into a little lump.

The next morning, when the mother was cleaning the ashes from the fire, she found nothing left of him but a little tin heart. And of the little dancer, nothing was left but her tinsel rose, which was burned as black as a cinder.

— *The End* —

41. Ten Little Monkeys

This is a favorite for kids. In one version the monkeys didn't "bump" their heads, but "broke" their heads. (And obviously they weren't sent back to bed.) That version teaches a firmer lesson, but also seems a little harsh in the way of punishment.

Ten little monkeys jumping on the bed
One fell off and bumped his head
Mama called the doctor and the doctor said,
"No more little monkeys jumping on the bed!"

Nine little monkeys jumping on the bed
One fell off and bumped his head
Mama called the doctor and the doctor said,
"No more little monkeys jumping on the bed!"

Eight little monkeys jumping on the bed
One fell off and bumped his head
Mama called the doctor and the doctor said,
"No more little monkeys jumping on the bed!"

Seven little monkeys jumping on the bed
One fell off and bumped his head
Mama called the doctor and the doctor said,
"No more little monkeys jumping on the bed!"

Six little monkeys jumping on the bed
One fell off and bumped his head
Mama called the doctor and the doctor said,
"No more little monkeys jumping on the bed!"

Five little monkeys jumping on the bed
One fell off and bumped his head
Mama called the doctor and the doctor said,
  "No more little monkeys jumping on the bed!"

Four little monkeys jumping on the bed
One fell off and bumped his head
  Mama called the doctor and the doctor said,
  "No more little monkeys jumping on the bed!"

Three little monkeys jumping on the bed
One fell off and bumped his head
Mama called the doctor and the doctor said,
"No more little monkeys jumping on the bed!"

Two little monkeys jumping on the bed
One fell off and bumped his head
Mama called the doctor and the doctor said,
"No more little monkeys jumping on the bed!"

One little monkey jumping on the bed
He fell off and bumped his head
Mama called the doctor and the doctor said,
"No more little monkeys jumping on the bed!"

No little monkeys jumping on the bed
None fell off and bumped their heads
Mama called the doctor and the doctor said,
"Put those little monkeys back in bed!"

— The End —

42. Little Bunny Foo Foo

Little Bunny Foo Foo
Hoppin' through the forest,
Scoopin' up the field mice
And boppin' em on the head.

Down came the Good Fairy, and she
*   said:*
Little Bunny Foo Foo
I don't want to see you
Scoopin' up the field mice
And boppin' em on the head.
I'll give you three chances, and then
*   poof!,*
I'll turn you into a goon.

The next day . . . .
Little Bunny Foo Foo
Hoppin' through the forest,
Scoopin' up the field mice
And boppin' em on the head.

Down came the Good Fairy, and she
*   said:*
Little Bunny Foo Foo
I don't want to see you
Scoopin' up the field mice
And boppin' em on the head.
I'll give you two more chances, and
*   then poof!,*
I'll turn you into a goon.

The next day . . . .
Little Bunny Foo Foo
Hoppin' through the forest,
Scoopin' up the field mice
And boppin' em on the head.

Down came the Good Fairy, and she
    said:
Little Bunny Foo Foo
I don't want to see you
Scoopin' up the field mice
And boppin' em on the head.
I'll give you one more chance, and
    then poof!,
I'll turn you into a goon.

The next day . . . .
Little Bunny Foo Foo
Hoppin' through the forest,
Scoopin' up the field mice
And boppin' em on the head.

Down came the Good Fairy, and she
    said:
Little Bunny Foo Foo
I didn't want to see you
Scoopin' up the field mice
And boppin' em on the head.
I gave you three chances
So now I'm gonna turn you into a
    GOON!
POOF!

And the Moral of the story is:
Hare today, Goon tomorrow.

— *The End* —

43. The Ants Go Marching

These are not the official "Ants Go Marching In . . ." lyrics. There are so many variations that listing them all would take a fair-size book. If your family already has an Ants tradition, please change the words!

The ants go marching one by one.
    Hurrah! Hurrah!
The ants go marching one by one.
    Hurrah! Hurrah!
The ants go marching one by one;
The little one stops to suck his thumb,
And they all go marching
Down into the ground
To get out of the rain.
Boom, Boom, Boom!

The ants go marching two by two.
    Hurrah! Hurrah!
The ants go marching two by two.
    Hurrah! Hurrah!
The ants go marching two by two;
The little one stops to tie his shoe,
And they all go marching
Down into the ground
To get out of the rain.
Boom, Boom,
    Boom!

The ants go marching three by three.
    Hurrah! Hurrah!
The ants go marching three by three.
    Hurrah! Hurrah!
The ants go marching three by three;
The little one stops to climb a tree,
And they all go marching
Down into the ground
To get out of the rain.
Boom, Boom, Boom!

The ants go marching four by four.
    Hurrah! Hurrah!
The ants go marching four by four.
    Hurrah! Hurrah!
The ants go marching four by four;
The little one stops to shut the door,
And they all go marching
Down into the ground
To get out of the rain.
Boom, Boom, Boom!

The ants go marching five by five.
    Hurrah! Hurrah!
The ants go marching five by five.
    Hurrah! Hurrah!
The ants go marching five by five;
The little one stops to give a high five,
And they all go marching
Down into the ground
To get out of the rain.
Boom, Boom, Boom!

The ants go marching six by six.
    Hurrah! Hurrah!
The ants go marching six by six.
    Hurrah! Hurrah!
The ants go marching six by six;
The little one stops to pick up sticks,
And they all go marching
down into the ground
To get out of the rain.
Boom, Boom, Boom!

The ants go marching seven by seven.
    Hurrah! Hurrah!
The ants go marching seven by seven.
    Hurrah! Hurrah!
The ants go marching seven by seven;
The little one stops to look up at heaven,
And they all go marching
Down into the ground
To get out of the rain.
Boom, Boom, Boom!

The ants go marching eight by eight.
    Hurrah! Hurrah!
The ants go marching eight by eight.
Hurrah! Hurrah!
The ants go marching eight by eight;
The little one stops to shut the gate,
And they all go marching
Down into the ground
To get out of the rain.
Boom, Boom, Boom!

The ants go marching nine by nine.
    Hurrah! Hurrah!
The ants go marching nine by nine.
    Hurrah! Hurrah!
The ants go marching nine by nine;
The little one stops to straighten the line,
And they all go marching
Down into the ground
To get out of the rain.
Boom, Boom, Boom!

The ants go marching ten by ten.
    Hurrah! Hurrah!
The ants go marching ten by ten.
    Hurrah! Hurrah!
The ants go marching ten by ten;
The little one stops to shout
The End!

— The End —

114

44. Ten Little Indians

It's short and sweet, probably not politically correct, but great for a boy or a girl with the giggles.

One little, two little, three little Indians
Four little, five little, six little Indians
Seven little, eight little, nine little Indians
Ten little Indian boys.

Ten little, nine little, eight little Indians
Seven little, six little, five little Indians
Four little, three little, two little Indians
One little Indian boy and girl

— *The End* —

45. Diddle, Diddle, Dumpling

READER TIP: Change the name "John" to your child's name.
If she's a girl, say, "Diddle, diddle, dumpling, my girl Sue . . . ."
If the name's too many syllables, either abbreviate, or cram
them all in as quickly as possible.

Diddle, diddle, dumpling,
my son, John,
Went to bed
with his trousers on,
One shoe off
and one shoe on!
Diddle, diddle, dumpling,
my son, John!

— *The End* —

46. Wee Willie Winkie

The original spoilsport

Wee Willie Winkie
Runs through the town,
Upstairs and downstairs
In his nightgown.
Rapping at the windows,
Crying through the lock,
"Are the children all in bed?
For it's now eight o'clock."

— *The End* —

47. Winken, Blinken, and Nod

Eugene Field

Winken, Blinken, and Nod one night
Sailed off in a wooden shoe,
Sailed off on a river of crystal light,
Into a sea of dew.

"Where are you going, and what do
    you wish?"
The old moon asked the three.
"We have come to fish for the herring
    fish
That live in the beautiful sea;
Nets of silver and gold have we!"
Said Winken,
Blinken,
And Nod.

The old moon laughed and sang a
    song,
As they rocked in the wooden shoe,
And the wind that sped them all night
    long
Ruffled the waves of dew.

The little stars were the herring fish
That lived in the beautiful sea.
"Now cast your nets wherever you
 wish—
Never afeard are we";
So cried the stars to the fisherman
 three:
Winken,
Blinken,
And Nod.

All night long their nets they threw
To the stars in the twinkling foam—
Then down from the skies came the
 wooden shoe
Bringing the fisherman home;

'Twas all so pretty a sail it seemed
As if it could not be,
And some folks thought 'twas a dream
 they'd dreamed
Of sailing that beautiful sea—

But I shall name you the fishermen
 three:
Winken,
Blinken,
And Nod.

Winken and Blinken are two little
 eyes,
And Nod is a little head,
And the wooden shoes that sailed the
 skies
Is the wee one's trundle-bed.

So shut your eyes while mother sings
Of wonderful sights that be,
And you shall see the beautiful things
As you rock in the misty sea,
Where the old shoe rocked the fish-
 erman three:
Winken,
Blinken,
And Nod.

— *The End* —

48. I Know an Old Lady Who Swallowed a Fly

I know an old lady who swallowed a fly.
I don't know why she swallowed the fly.
Perhaps she'll die.

I know an old lady who swallowed a spider
That wiggled and jiggled and tickled inside her.
She swallowed the spider to catch the fly.
I don't know why she swallowed the fly.
Perhaps she'll die.

I know an old lady who swallowed a bird.
How absurd to swallow a bird.
She swallowed the bird to catch the spider
That wiggled and jiggled and tickled inside her.
She swallowed the spider to catch the fly.
I don't know why she swallowed the fly.
Perhaps she'll die.

I know an old lady who swallowed a cat.
Think of that to swallow a cat!
She swallowed the cat to catch the bird,
She swallowed the bird to catch the spider
That wiggled and jiggled and tickled inside her.
She swallowed the spider to catch the fly.
I don't know why she swallowed the fly.
Perhaps she'll die.

I know an old lady who swallowed a dog.
Oh what a hog, to swallow a dog!

She swallowed the dog to catch the cat,
She swallowed the cat to catch the bird,
She swallowed the bird to catch the spider
That wiggled and jiggled and tickled inside her.
She swallowed the spider to catch the fly.
I don't know why she swallowed the fly.
Perhaps she'll die.

I know an old lady who swallowed a goat.
She open her throat, and swallowed a goat!
She swallowed the goat to catch the dog,
She swallowed the dog to catch the cat,
She swallowed the cat to catch the bird,
She swallowed the bird to catch the spider
That wiggled and jiggled and tickled inside her.
She swallowed the spider to catch the fly.
I don't know why she swallowed the fly.
Perhaps she'll die.

I know an old lady who swallowed a cow.
I don't know how she swallowed a cow!
She swallowed the cow to catch the goat,
She swallowed the goat to catch the dog,
She swallowed the dog to catch the cat,
She swallowed the cat to catch the bird,
She swallowed the bird to catch the spider
That wiggled and jiggled and tickled inside her.
She swallowed the spider to catch the fly.
I don't know why she swallowed the fly.
Perhaps she'll die.

I know an old lady who swallowed a horse.
She's dead, of course!

— The End —

49. This Old Man

This old man, he played one,
He played knick knack on his thumb,
With a
Knick, knack, paddy whack,
Give the dog a bone;
This old man came rolling home.

This old man, he played two,
He played knick knack on my shoe,
With a
Knick, knack, paddy whack,
Give the dog a bone;
This old man came rolling home.

This old man, he played three,
He played knick knack on my knee,
With a
Knick, knack, paddy whack,
Give the dog a bone;
This old man came rolling home.

This old man, he played four,
He played knick knack on my door,
With a

Knick, knack, paddy whack,
Give the dog a bone;
This old man came rolling home.

This old man, he played five,
He played knick knack on my hive,
With a
Knick, knack, paddy whack,
Give the dog a bone;
This old man came rolling home.

This old man, he played six,
He played knick knack on my sticks
With a
Knick, knack, paddy whack,
Give the dog a bone;
This old man came rolling home.

This old man, he played seven,
He played knick knack on my hen,
With a
Knick, knack, paddy whack,
Give the dog a bone;
This old man came rolling home.

This old man, he played eight,
He played knick knack on my gate,
With a
Knick, knack, paddy whack,
Give the dog a bone;
This old man came rolling home.

This old man, he played nine,
He played knick knack on my spine,
With a
Knick, knack, paddy whack,
Give the dog a bone;
This old man came rolling home.

This old man, he played ten,
He played knick knack on my shin,
With a
Knick, knack, paddy whack,
Give the dog a bone;
This old man came rolling home.

— *The End* —

50. The Tale of Scheherazade

By all rights, the tale of Scheherazade should begin any collection of stories. It is what is commonly called a "Frame Tale," that is a story that has within it many, many more stories. In the original versions, the stories were quite long and frequently bawdy. Each day at dawn, Scheherazade would interrupt her story, and her sister would beg her to continue. "If the King wills me to live another day," the brave girl replied. Think of it a bit like a cliff-hanger in a television show. Except instead of trying to keep an audience in suspense until the next season, the world's greatest storyteller paused to save her life for yet another day.

It is related that there was once in a land far away a king who had been so foully betrayed by his wife that he made a vow. Each night King Shahryar required his Grand Wazir to bring him a new bride. Each night he was married. But the next morning, he ordered the bride's head cut off.

This horror continued for many years, and the people of the land moaned under its weight.

One day, the Wazir's eldest daughter Scheherazade came to her father.

"Oh, father," she cried, "how long will you allow this slaughter of women to continue? Shall I tell you my idea to save this land from destruction?"

"Please, my daughter," said the Wazir. "Tell me."

"I have a favor to ask," said Scheherazade. "Will you grant it to me?"

"Please, my daughter," said her father. "I can deny you nothing that is fair and reasonable."

Now, Scheherazade was not an ordinary woman. Her father had her well educated, and she had read every book in the royal library. She knew stories of kings, works of the poets and had studied philosophy, the sciences, and the arts. Not only was she well read, but also she was pleasant and polite, wise and witty, and well bred.

And, of course, she was beautiful beyond words. In fact, for many years the Wazir had kept his two daughters (the youngest was named Dunyazad) far from the sight of the king, whose vow he both feared and hated.

"I would like you," Scheherazade paused, considering for a moment, "to give me in marriage to King Shahryar. I have contrived a plan to live and to free the daughters of our fair country from his miserable curse."

"By Allah!" cried the Wazir. "Have you gone mad? I have contrived for years to keep you away from him, and now you wish me to bring him my eldest and most beautiful daughter?"

"You must," Scheherazade said. "Make me his wife."

The Wazir ranted and raved, shouted and screamed, he argued and begged, but in the end it was all useless. His daughter never relented, and he at last agreed to her wish.

He went to his King, and told him who his bride was to be.

The King roared with amazement. "Oh, my most faithful Counselor, why? You know what I have sworn. You know that tomorrow morning I shall say to you, 'Slay her!' And if you do not, I will slay you in her place without fail."

"She is," her father said his head bowed low with sadness, "determined."

"Bring her tonight," said King Shahryar. "So it shall be."

That evening, as they prepared for her wedding, Scheherazade spoke in confidence to her sister, Dunyazad.

"Duny," she said, "pay attention to what I am going to tell you. After the wedding, I will ask the king to send for you so that we may spend my last few hours together. You must not be sleepy. Ask me to tell you a story. I will tell you a story that will save our kingdom."

Dunyazad bowed her head and said, "I will, my sister."

That very evening King Shahryar was married to Scheherazade. When the ceremonies were complete and they were in the royal bed chambers, Scheherazade dropped to her knees and began to weep.

"What's the matter?" asked the King.

"Oh, great and powerful King," Scheherazade replied. "I have a younger sister, and I would like to say good-bye to her before I leave this world."

The king sent at once for Dunyazad, and the young girl sat on the foot of the bed.

"Oh, sister," Dunyazad said, "before the sun rises, tell me a delightful story to while away the last few hours of our waking life."

"That would please me," Scheherazade said. "If our wise and auspicious king will permit me, then I will begin."

"Tell on," said the King, who was for once having trouble sleeping. "Proceed with the story."

So, Scheherazade rejoiced, and on this, the first night of the Thousand and One Nights, she began to spin her tale.

— *The End* —

51. The Tale of the Merchant and the Genie

*I*t is related, O auspicious King, Scheherazade began her story, that there was a wealthy merchant who traveled frequently from city to city. One day, he was traveling on his horse, and the day was particularly hot. He sat beneath a tree and took from his pack some broken bread, a handful of dry dates, and began to eat.

When he had finished eating the dates, he threw away the stones, as was his custom. (For in a desert, who knows what seeds may some day take root and provide shelter and shade for another?)

He rose to remount his horse, but found his way blocked by an Ifrit!

Now, an Ifrit is a genie of the largest and most terrible height. This genie had drawn a sword, and said, "Stand still, so that I can kill you, even as you have killed my son!"

"How did I slay your son," the Merchant asked.

"When you ate your dates and threw away the stones," replied the genie. "One of the stones struck my son through his heart as he was walking by, and he died immediately."

"Pardon me!" cried the Merchant falling through his knees. "I would never have killed your son if I knew he was there.

"That is no excuse!" roared the genie. "Prepare to die!"

"Wait, oh great one!" begged the Merchant. "Please allow me to travel back to my home and say good-bye to my children and wife."

The Genie relented. He would give the Merchant one week to conclude his affairs, and then he would come and take his life.

In another instant the Genie was gone, and the Merchant stood alone under the unfortunate copse of trees. True to his word, he traveled back to his home and bid his wife and children good-bye. On the last day of his life, he went to the great mosque and prayed. Afterward, he sat outside the mosque and began to weep.

Presently, two sheiks came across the tearful merchant. One sheik traveled with a gazelle and the other with two large dogs. "What has happened?" the sheiks asked. "Why do you weep?"

The merchant told his tale, and the two sheiks asked if they might wait with him, so he should not face his death alone. The merchant nodded, and the two sheiks sat down with the gazelle and two dogs beside them.

An instant later, the genie appeared, his sword drawn and revenge in his eyes.

"Wait, wait!" shouted the first sheik. "If I tell you the story of myself and this gazelle, and you consider it wonderful, will you give me half of this merchant's blood?"

"Why not?" said the Genie. "If the story is good, then I will give you half of the merchant's blood."

— *The End* —

52. The First Sheik's Story

*K*now, oh Genie, that this gazelle was my wife who was a magician herself. We had been married for nearly thirty years, but had no child. As was the custom of our time, I took a damsel to be my wife and soon had a newborn son.

My first wife was most jealous of the young boy and his mother.

When the boy was fifteen years old, tall and fair, business called me to travel far away. While I was gone, my wicked wife used her magic to change my son into a calf and his mother into a cow.

When I returned, she told me, "Your damsel is dead, and your son has ran away. I don't know where he went."

For a year I grieved and ate nothing but cheese and dates. Then, at the Great Festival of Allah, I ordered my herdsman to bring me a fat cow for our feast.

He brought me the one who had been my damsel. I rolled up my sleeves and took the knife to slay the calf, but the cow lowed and began to weep.

I had never seen a cow cry, and I said to my herdsman, "Bring me another."

He said to me, "This is the best there is. I will slay her for you."

He killed the poor cow, but instead of finding meat, inside her skin there was nothing but bones.

"Bring me a calf then," I ordered. The herdsman brought to me the calf that was my son.

The calf also began to cry. It broke loose from its tether and ran to me, rubbing its head against my legs most piteously.

"Do I need to kill this one too?" said the herdsman.

"No," I cried, resolve swelling in me. "I will slay it myself." I took the knife in my hand and held it to the throat of the calf. . . .

And Scheherazade noticed the light of dawn creeping in through the window, and stopped talking.

"What a wonderful story!" Dunyazad said. "Can you tell me the end?"

"If the King wills me to live another day," the brave girl replied, "I will finish the tale."

The King, who was utterly entranced by the story, agreed. "I will not slay you until I have heard the rest of your story."

That morning, the Wazir came to the bed chambers, prepared to kill his first and most beloved daughter. He was most surprised when the King did not give him the order, but went about the business of the day.

When the second night finally fell, Dunyazad said to her sister Scheherazade, "Please, good sister, finish the story of the Merchant and the Genie."

130

"Gladly," said Scheherazade, "if the good and auspicious King will permit me."

"Tell thy tale," said the King.

Just as the merchant was about to kill the calf (Scheherazade continued), he saw it weeping, and his heart relented.

"Keep this calf among my cattle," he told his herdsman.

All this, the sheik told the Genie, who listened in wonder to the story.

"Oh, lord Genie," the sheik said, "While all this occurred, my wicked wife watched. She turned to me and ordered me to kill the calf, but I would not. Instead I sent it away with my herdsman."

The next day the herdsman returned. "Oh my master," he said. "I have good news for you. My daughter learned magic in her childhood from an old woman. Yesterday, when I brought that calf home, she took one look at it and began to first laugh and then cry. I asked her what the matter was, and she said, "This calf is the son of our master, who has been bewitched by his wicked step mother. I laugh because at long last he is found. I cry because the first fat cow that you slew was the boy's poor mother.""

"Is this true what your daughter says? Bring her to me now! Bring the calf as well."

The herdsman hurried to fetch his daughter and the calf, and all stood before me.

"Oh maiden," I begged, "will you release my son? I shall give you all my cattle and property."

The good girl smiled and answered, "Master, I am not greedy. I have only two conditions. First I would like to marry your son. Second I would like to bewitch the witch who bewitched him, otherwise none of us will ever be safe."

Hearing these words, Oh Genie, I immediately agreed. "You may have that, and all the cattle that are in your father's charge."

The herdsman's daughter took a cup and filled it with water. Then she spoke the counterspell.

"If Almighty Allah created you a calf," whispered the girl, "then remain a calf. If you are enchanted, return to your proper form!"

The calf trembled and shook and became a man!

I fell on my knees and begged his pardon. He told me what his life had been like as a calf and the sorrow he felt at the death of his mother.

Then, Oh Genie, I married the girl to my son. She ordered my wicked wife brought before us.

"She is not ugly to look at," said the herdsman's daughter, "but her tongue is most wicked." And then she transformed my wife into this gazelle, who travels with me even unto this day.

And so my tale comes to an end.

The Genie turned to the first sheik and said, "Your tale is strange and well told. I gladly give you half of this merchant's blood!"

The Genie stood and held his sword high.

"Wait, Oh Genie," said the second sheik. "If I tell you a tale even more wonderful, about these two dogs, about what happened to me because of my brothers, will you grant me the half of this man's blood?"

"Gladly," replied the Genie. "If your story is even more marvelous and wonderful."

— *The End* —

53. The Second Sheik's Story

*K*now, oh king of the Genies, that these two dogs are my brothers! When our father died, he left us each a thousand gold pieces. I opened a shop with my share and sold wonderful silks and fine linens. Both of my brothers took their gold pieces and became traveling merchants. They went their own separate ways, exploring the world, buying and selling spices.

Once, after my brothers were gone for a year, a beggar came to my shop. I reached into my pocket to give him a copper, when he spoke.

"Have I changed so much that you don't even recognize me?"

I looked closer and to my surprise, saw that it was my oldest brother. Quickly, I hurried him into my shop and began asking him questions.

"Don't ask," he said. "I have wasted my money and have nothing left."

I brought him home, bathed him, and gave him new clothes. From the profits of my shop, I gave him a thousand gold pieces.

"Pretend that you didn't ever leave our city," I told him. "Use this money to banish any bad luck."

He took the gold happily and opened a shop for himself.

A year later, my second brother returned from his travels in the same pitiful beggarly state as my eldest brother.

"Oh, brother," I wept, "did not the example of our older brother show you the danger of traveling?"

He shed tears, and I took him to bathe and gave him fresh clothes. As with my older brother, I gave him a thousand gold pieces from the profits of my shop.

He too opened a shop, and for a time all was well.

Then, one day, both of my brothers came to my shop and asked that I travel with them to seek fortune.

I refused, saying, "What's so great about traveling? You both came back empty-handed. Why should I want to leave my home?"

They persisted, but I refused, and eventually both went back to their shops.

Every year for six years, my brothers urged me to sell all and to travel. At last, I agreed, but first I wanted to see what they had earned from their shops.

I learned that they had saved not a single gold piece! They had spent it all on fine food and drink. I did not criticize them, but since my own fortune had grown by six thousand gold pieces, I gladly divided it in half with them.

"These three thousand gold pieces are for us to trade with," I said. "Let us bury the rest underground, in case something should happen to us on our travels. That way we'll at least have a thousand to reopen our shops."

With one thousand gold pieces each we purchased goods and hired a ship, and away we went. We traveled and bought and sold. For every gold piece we had invested, we soon earned ten!

Then, as we came back to our ship we found at the shore of the sea a maiden clad in worn and ragged gear.

She kissed my hand and said, "Oh, sir, are you kind? Are you charitable? I will repay you."

"Yes, I am kind, and I believe in good works," I said. "You don't have to repay me."

"Marry me then," she said, "and take me to your city. I will be a wonderful wife for you."

My heart melted at these words, and I agreed. I gave her new clothes and found that she was beautiful as well. We found a place for her in our ship, and away we sailed. As we traveled, I spent more and more time with my new wife and less with my brothers.

They became jealous, both of my wife and of the money and merchandise I had accumulated.

"Let us slay our brother," they said, "and seize all his money."

While my wife and I were asleep, they took us from our cabins and threw us into the sea!

And Scheherazade noticed the light of dawn creeping in through the window and stopped talking.

"Such a marvelous tale!" Dunyazad said. "Can you tell me the end?"

"If the King wills me to live another day," Scheherazade said, "I will finish the tale."

King Shahryar agreed. "I will not slay you until I have heard the rest of your story."

When the second night finally fell, Dunyazad said to her sister Scheherazade, "Please, good sister, finish the story of the Merchant and the Genie."

"Of course," said Scheherazade, "if the good and auspicious King will permit me."

"Tell thy tale," said the King.

As soon as my brothers had thrown us from the boat, the second Sheik continued, my wife awoke, startled from her sleep. She turned into an Ifritah, a wonderfully powerful spirit. She picked me up from the sea and carried me to an island.

"Now you know that I am a she-Genie," she said, "but you did not know that when we were married. You were kind to me, and so I have saved your life. However, your wicked brothers have made me angry, and now I must go and kill them."

I thanked her for saving my life, but begged her not to kill my brothers.

"Nevertheless, I must," she said.

I begged and pleaded for my brothers' lives, but she would not relent. At last she picked me up and flew me back to the roof of my own house. I dug up the hidden gold and reopened my shop.

Onc evening, I came home and found these two dogs tied up at the door to my house. When they saw me, they stood up and whined and howled, nuzzling their noses against my legs.

Before I knew what had happened, my wife told me. "These two dogs are your brothers. I would have killed them, but my sister said that I should be wise and forgiving. Instead, my sister has turned them into dogs, and so they will remain for ten years."

That, said the sheik, is why I am here. I am searching for my wife's sister, so that she may remove the curse on these two dogs, who are my brothers. As I was passing by the mosque, I saw this young man and stayed to see what would became of him. That is my tale!

The Genie turned to the second sheik and said, "Your tale is even stranger than the first. I gladly give you half of this merchant's blood!"

The Genie shook with pleasure, and cried, "I have given you the remainder of the merchant's punishment, and for your sake I have released him!"

The merchant embraced the two old men, and thanked them with cheers and tears and laughter.

— *The End* —

54. Scheherazade's Story Concludes

"Yet that, good King," said Scheherazade "is not even half so wonderful as the Fisherman's Story. . . ."

"What," asked the king, "is the Fisherman's Story?"

The evening was young, and Scheherazade was wise. So she spun her tales night after night, story after story for a thousand and one nights.

The years passed, and during that long time, Scheherazade had borne the king three sons. At last, she came to the king and said, "I have been your wife for a thousand and one nights. I have told you stories of the world, of men and of Genies. May I ask one small favor of your Highness?"

"Ask, Oh Scheherazade," said the King, "and it shall be granted to you."

She ordered the servants to bring forth their three children, and with the babes held tightly in her arms, she said, "Oh, King of the Age, these are your children. I beg you to release me from the doom of death for their sake. If you kill me, they will become motherless."

The King wept and hugged his boys to him.

"By Allah, Oh Scheherazade," he said. "I pardoned you long ago, long before these boys came. You are wise and pious and pure."

The next morning, the King had his wazir brought before him. "Thank you, for giving me your noble daughter as my wife. She has helped me to see the evil of my ways, and I do truly repent."

Then King Shahryar spoke and withdrew the evil curse that he had ordered on his land. He gave Scheherazade's sister, Dunyazad to his brother, and the two began to rule in kindness and wisdom. Word of this miracle spread far and wide, and from that day until this, the kingdom was filled with wonder and happiness.

— *The End* —

55. The Frog Prince

*O*nce upon a time, there was a princess who loved to play with her golden ball. She loved to throw the ball high in the air and catch it. Every day she would play in the garden with her ball.

One day, she decided to see how high she could throw the ball. She threw it up high and caught it easily. Then she threw it even higher and still it was easy to catch. At last, she threw the ball as high as she possibly could. It flew so high that she lost sight of it in the sun, and when it came down, she didn't catch it.

Instead, the ball rolled away and landed with a plop in the pond.

The Princess stood at the edge of the pond and peered in, but she could not see her golden ball anywhere.

"Excuse me, Princess," said a voice, "I can get your ball for you. Croak. Ribbit. Nee-deep!"

The Princess looked around and could not see anyone near by, except for a small green ugly slimy frog.

"Did you say something to me?" the Princess asked the frog.

"Yes," answered the frog. "I said that I could get your ball for you. Croak. Ribbit. Nee-deep!"

"I'm not accustomed to talking with frogs," said the Princess haughtily. "Especially not the gross green slimy ugly kind."

"Well, then," burped the frog, "you shall never see your ball again." He turned to hop away.

"Wait, wait!" cried the Princess. "I'm sorry. Will you please get my ball for me?"

"Pretty please?" said the frog. "Croak. Ribbit. Nee-deep!"

"Pretty please," begged the Princess. "I am a princess. I'll give you anything. All the flies you want, your very own lily pad."

"I already have all the flies I want and my own lily pad," said the Frog, "But I will ask you one small favor."

"Of course," said the Princess. "Only, please get my ball."

So the frog swam down into the pond, and in a few minutes came back with the ball.

"Ptui!" he said, dropping the ball at the Princess's feet. "Here is your ball. Croak. Ribbit. Nee-deep!"

She picked the ball up, and rubbed it in the grass, because it was kind of gross and slimy from the frog's mouth.

"Thank you, good frog," she said, and she turned to go back to her play.

"Wait," said the frog. "Aren't you forgetting your promise?"

"Oh, sure," said the Princess. "What do you want?"

"Nothing much," said the frog. "Only a single kiss from you. Croak. Ribbit. Nee-deep!"

"Kiss a frog?" said the Princess. "Eww, gross! You're green and ugly and slimy and gooey!" She shuddered and ran away.

That evening at dinner, the Princess sat with her golden ball at the table next to her father, the King.

"Your ball looks a little green today," said the King.

"Oh, that," said the Princess frowning. "It fell into the pond. I got it out, though."

The King nodded suspiciously. He knew how little his daughter liked to get her feet wet.

Just then, the butler came into the dining room.

"A frog to see you, your Majesty."

"A what?" said the King.

"A what?" said the Princess.

"A frog," sniffed the butler. "He says he has business with the Princess."

"Send him away," said the Princess.

"Bring him in," ordered the King.

A few minutes later, in hopped the Frog.

"Oh, it's you," said the Princess. "I thought it was another frog."

"Do you know this frog?" said the King.

"I rescued your daughter's golden ball," said the frog. "But she has broken her promise to me."

"Is that true?" asked the King.

"He wanted me to kiss him," said the Princess. "Ick!"

"No daughter of mine will break her promise," said the King. "Do as you must."

"No, sire," said the Frog. "I will not have her ordered to kiss me. She must do it willingly."

"Never!" shouted the Princess.

The frog sniffed and turned to go.

"Wait," said the King. "You seem like a nice enough frog. My child has need of a playmate. Would you like to stay with her and share her meals and keep her company?"

"Daddy!" said the Princess, but the King silenced her protests with a look.

"I would be happy to share her company," said the frog politely, although he was a little dubious about it.

So for many many weeks, the frog and the Princess were together every waking hour of the day. They ate together, played together, and even rode horses together. (Well, the Princess rode the horse, and the frog sat on her shoulder.)

At the end of six months, as they were going up to bed, the Princess turned to the frog and without really thinking said, "Good night, Frog," and gave him a little kiss on the top of his head.

There was a thunderclap and a lightening bolt, and the frog vanished in a puff of smoke.

Instead, standing before the Princess was a handsome man with gorgeous brown hair and beautiful blue eyes.

"Who are you?" said the Princess, stepping back. "What have you done with my frog?"

"I am your frog," said the man. "I am also a Prince. I was enchanted by a wicked fairy and turned into a frog. Only the kiss of a beautiful Princess could restore me."

"Well, why didn't you say so months ago," said the Princess. "I would have kissed you gladly."

"Because," said the Prince, "you had to do it of your own free will, without knowing the truth."

"I don't believe that you're really my frog," said the Princess. "Prove it."

"Hmm," thought the Prince. "Croak. Ribbit. Nee-deep!"

"Froggy!" exclaimed the Princess.

With that, the two embraced. They played together for many years and became good friends. Eventually they got married, and of course they lived happily ever after.

— *The End* —

56. The Baker's Dozen

In the city of Albany, New York, in the days before the British ruled the land, Volckert Jan Pietersen Van Amsterdam owned a bakery. The snow was high on the ground, but inside the bakery was warm and smelled heavenly. Baas (which is Dutch for Boss) Van Amsterdam was famous throughout the city for inventing New Year's cakes, and for the wonderfully round gingerbread babies, which it is said he modeled after his own plump children. ("These cakes," he always said, "are soft and sweet, but not quite as sweet as my own precious boys and girls.")

One winter, the snows were higher than ever, and the holidays were particularly busy. The Baas was in his bake shop from well before dawn until well after dusk. He had to shovel the snow from his door, light the fire in the stove for heat, and then set the fire in his ovens. Then he had to prepare the dough and the batter for cakes and cookies and every kind of treat imaginable. Everyone wanted their cakes and breads just so for Christmas and New Year's. He hardly had time to sit down and think, let alone spend time with his family. When he finally returned home at night, he was always exhausted. He barely spoke to his wife and precious boys and girls, eating a hearty dinner, and falling into fast, but short, sleep before rising again for the next day's business.

At last, it was the evening of December 31, the final day of the year, and time to close his shop! January 1, New Years day was a holiday and Baas Van Amsterdam was looking forward to the day of rest. He shut the shop's door, closed the oven, and began to put out the lights.

Just then, there was a knock at the door. Rap, rap, rap.

"Go away," snapped Baas Van Amsterdam. "We're closed."

He didn't mean to sound harsh, but it had been a long and trying week. Whenever people are in a hurry, they grow angry and mean spirited, and he had picked up some of the habit from his customers.

He listened for a moment and heard nothing. He began loading up a bag full of cakes to take home to his children when again there was a knock at the door. Rap, rap, rap.

"I said we're closed!"

Rap, rap, rap.

Finally, in utter exasperation, he went to the door and threw it wide open. "What do you want?"

There stood an old woman, ugly and shriveled. Her shoulders were stooped and her eyesight so poor that she had to squint just to see Baas Van Amsterdam's face in the fading day light.

Still, old or not, he told her again, "We're closed!"

"I want a dozen of your New Year's Cookies!" the old woman shouted.

Baas Van Amsterdam clapped his hands over his ears. "I'm not deaf!"

"A dozen cookies! Give to me a dozen cookies!"

Now, New Year's eve is a haunted time, perched as it is on the cusp of the years. Perhaps, Baas Van Amsterdam worried, this was an

evil witch knocking at his door. If he refused to give her cookies, then she might cast a curse upon him and his entire family. He couldn't have that.

So, with a great shrug, he escorted her inside, and again lit the lamps.

"A dozen cookies!" the old dame shouted. "Give to me a dozen!"

"Fine, fine," Baas Van Amsterdam shouted back. He took her bag from her and found twelve of his best New Year's cookies. "Here you are good woman. Have a happy New Year."

The old woman frowned and peered into her bag. She held it right up to her face and stared into the bottom.

"This isn't a dozen. I said, give to me a dozen cookies!"

"I did," said the bewildered baker.

"No," said the old woman. "This is only twelve! I want a dozen!"

"But twelve is a dozen."

"Give to me a dozen!"

"Look," said the impatient man, "if you want another one, go get it from the devil!"

With that, he pushed her out of his door and locked it tight.

All of a sudden, he felt a rapping inside his head, and then all up and down his arms. He felt as if someone was beating him with a stick. He watched in horror as two of his best wedding cakes slid from their places on shelves and landed with a splat on the floor. The old woman, he realized, really was a witch!

In utter despair, Baas Van Amsterdam ran round his shop, trying to protect his baked goods, all the while feeling as if he was being beaten and tripped by invisible fiends. Cookies smashed, pies flung themselves across the room, and cakes exploded like cannon shot, splattering batter and frosting everywhere.

Finally, the poor man called on St. Nicholas for help and advice. For a moment, the spirits stopped their torment. "Perhaps," said a voice, "you should be more generous. Find it in your heart to spread some of your good fortune to others."

"But I gave her a dozen," said the Baas Van Amsterdam.

And then, the torment began anew.

"I will, I will," shouted the bewildered baker. "I will be more generous!"

He threw open the door, fully intending to shout after the old woman to come back, but she was standing right there.

"I want a dozen New Year's Cookies," said the old hag.

"Here," said Baas Van Amsterdam. "Have another cookie! Please. Anything to stop this."

The old woman watched as the baker put the extra cookie into her bag. Then she nodded solemnly. She picked up one of the gingerbread babies, and made him put his hand on its belly. "Swear to me," she yelled, "that from now on, you will be more generous and that all of your dozens shall be thirteen!"

"I swear! I swear!"

"The curse is broken," she hollered.

And in a clap, she was gone. All his cakes were back up on their shelves, the pies on theirs, and the cookies that had been broken were intact. The shop was clean, and the light of the day was fading fast. The only sign of her presence were the missing thirteen cookies and the slight ringing in the poor baker's ears.

Without any more hesitation, Baas Van Amsterdam hurried home from his shop and hugged his wife and babies into his arms.

But from that day until this, a Baker's dozen has been thirteen, and now you know why.

— The End —

57. The Emperor's New Clothes

*O*nce upon a time, in land far far from here lived an Emperor. He was the most powerful Emperor in the entire world! He ruled every country from ocean to ocean and a dozen islands as well. He was wealthy beyond belief. His counting rooms held millions upon millions of gold pieces. His stables held thousands upon thousands of horses. He had hundreds of houses and a dozen palaces, each one more splendid than the next.

You would think that with all this money and wealth and power, the Emperor would be happy, but he was not. Every day he looked at himself in the mirror and frowned.

"There is something wrong," he thought. "Something's not quite right here."

He would brood for days and weeks at a time, and when he began to brood, his ministers and advisors and generals would shake and quiver. They all knew that when the Emperor was in bad spirits, something big was brewing. He would pace up and down the halls of one or another of his great palace, frowning the whole time.

And then, just when everything seemed darkest and full of despair, he would hit upon a new plan. "I'll go out and conquer another country!" he'd say. An instant later he would summon his ministers and advisors and generals, and they would begin planning a war. During the war, the Emperor would be very busy, and very happy. Then, when the war was over and the battles all won, he would parade through the newly conquered country and wave triumphantly at all the people.

Then he would go back to the palace, peer into the mirror, and instantly the old feeling would come back. "Something is wrong. Something's not quite right here."

This had gone on for decades, and at last, the Emperor had conquered every country in the world! He had paraded triumphantly through every city, and was both adored and feared by good people everywhere.

So, when he called his ministers and advisors and generals together to plan the next war, they were forced to give him the bad news.

"There are no other countries to conquer," said the Prime Minister.

"You are the Emperor of the entire world," said the Chief Advisor.

"You rule the whole planet!" said the Head General.

"Posh!" sniffed the Emperor, and then he threw them all out of his chambers.

The doors to the Emperor's bedrooms stayed shut, and none but the servants bearing his meals dared to sneak in. Even they were afraid, because the Emperor ate nothing and drank even less.

"Perhaps there will be a rebellion," suggested the Prime Minister. "That would cheer him up."

"We could start one," said the Head General.

"Hush!" ordered the Chief Minister. "He'll cut off your head if he hears you say something like that."

The Head General nodded, because he knew it was true. The Emperor had a very bad temper, and no one dared to disobey or criticize him.

Now, it just happened that around that time, a pair of strangers entered the capital city. They stayed at a local inn and did their best to find out what was going on in the great city. Almost immediately, they heard rumors that the Emperor was in another of his funks.

"Is he now?" said Ingot, the skinny stranger.

"Perhaps we can help," said Rempar, the fat stranger.

"Oh, I don't think so," said the Innkeeper. "The Emperor has the finest advisors and ministers and generals, and they haven't been able to help him."

"Ah," said Ingot, "but does he have the world's best tailors?"

"The world's best tailors?" said the innkeeper.

"The world's best tailors," echoed Rempar. "Yes, indeed."

"Well," the Innkeeper scratched his beard. "I don't think he does."

(In fact, for all his wonderful conquests, the Emperor was not known as a fine dresser. He did all right at formal functions, but never quite managed the kind of noble bearing that everyone expected of the ruler of the entire planet.)

"We'll go to see him," said Ingot.

"Tomorrow," said Rempar.

"Good luck," said the innkeeper. "Whenever the Emperor's unsatisfied, he has a bad habit of cutting off the offender's heads."

Ingot looked at Rempar, and they both shrugged.

The next morning, bright and early there was a knock on the palace door.

"Who goes there?" shouted the palace guard.

"Tailors," came the shout back.

"Tailors?" said the palace guard.

"Tailors to see the Emperor."

"Go away," shouted the guard. "The Emperor sees nobody."

"He'll be very angry if you send us away!"

Just then, the Captain of the Guard approached. "What's going on here so early in the morning?"

"Tailors," said the guard. "To see the Emperor. They say he'll be angry if we send them away."

"We don't want to make the Emperor angry," said the Captain of the Guard. He hurried off to see the Commander of the Watch. The Commander of the Watch rushed to the Garrison Colonel. The Garrison Colonel knocked on the Head General's door.

"Tailors to see the Emperor," the Garrison Colonel said.

"Well, show them in," said the Head General. "Why not?"

So, word was passed back down the line, and at last the two tailors were let into the palace and brought before the Emperor.

"Who are you?" the Emperor snarled.

"We are Ingot and Rempar, the world's finest tailors," the two bowed very low. "We have sewn and tailed for all the best Sultans and Kings and Queens and Princesses in the world. We have dressed Dukes and Barons and Marquises and Earls. Our work is the finest in the world, and by far the most flattering."

The Emperor's eyes narrowed. "Why haven't I heard of you."

"We've been away," said Ingot.

"Learning how to make thread from diamonds," said Rempar, "and cloth from rubies, emeralds, and sapphires."

"You can do that?" asked the Emperor.

The two bowed low. "Indeed we can. And it would be our pleasure to make the finest suit of clothing in the world for your highness."

"How much will it cost me?" asked the Emperor. Even though he was the ruler of the planet, he was no fool to be taken advantage of.

"Absolutely nothing," said Rempar.

"We work only to serve your majesty," said Ingot.

The Emperor scratched his chin. "Sounds like a good deal. I will be leading the New Year's parade through the Capital in four months. I would like to wear a suit made out of diamond and rubies and emeralds."

"And sapphires," added Rempar.

"You shall need shoes, too," said Ingot. "Perhaps pearl slippers."

"And since New Year's is quite cold, you'll need a coat," suggested Rempar. "Perhaps fine spun gold and platinum."

"Excellent!" shouted the Emperor. "Get to work."

"Well," said Rempar, "we'll need a few things. . . ."

"Whatever you need," said the Emperor. He turned to his ministers. "See to it that these tailors have whatever they need."

The tailors handed the Prime Minister a list, and a very long list it was. They needed work rooms in the palace and tools and tables and needles and looms. And they needed mules and pack horses to bring their secret supplies, from their cave in the mountains.

Then, of course, they needed the raw materials. They needed piles of diamonds, heaps of emeralds, stacks of gold coins, barrels of sapphires, and scads of rubies.

Soon, such a ruckus was heard from the workshop. Banging and whirring. Screeching and whizzing.

The Emperor was more cheerful already. He began to stroll around the palace most happily. For once, it looked that another war had been averted. (A fact that only his generals were unhappy about.)

He had not, you see, been looking forward to the New Year's parade. As the ruler of everywhere on the planet, he would have walked through the streets of the great capital knowing that he had accomplished everything. There was nothing left for him to conquer. It had all seemed quite depressing.

But now that he had the two world's greatest tailors working for him, well, he would be able to walk through the city triumphantly!

After two months of banging and clatter from the tailors' workshop, the Emperor was beginning to get a little anxious. At last, he knocked on the door.

"How's it going in there?" he asked.

"Quite well," said Rempar, opening the door. "Come in."

So, the Emperor and his ministers and advisors and generals strode into the room.

It was filled from top to bottom with machinery. The looms were rattling and clanking. Sewing machines were whirring and whizzing. In one corner, a button machine was stamping loudly.

But nowhere did anyone see a single stitch of clothes.

"Ahem," said the Emperor. "I'd like to see my suit."

"Oh, it's not done yet," said Ingot. "But look, here is the emerald and diamond shirt cloth."

He held his arms up as if holding the finest sheet of linen.

"Notice the stitching," said Rempar. "The fine embroidery."

The Emperor stared closely at the space between Ingot's arms. He didn't see anything.

"I have worked for weeks just to get the texture so smooth," said Ingot. "Feel this."

The Emperor held out his fingers and rubbed them where Ingot had pointed to. He didn't feel anything.

"Isn't that the smoothest shirt you have ever felt?" asked Rempar.

"I don't. . . ." the Emperor began, but Ingot cut him off.

"Your Majesty, if you'll pardon my saying, but even as the ruler of the entire world, you are unaccustomed to such finery. These are very ancient and secret techniques. It requires time and understanding to appreciate them."

"Ah," said the Emperor, nodding as if he understood.

"What's going on over there?" asked the Prime Minister, pointing to an empty loom that seemed to be shuttling back and forth but not making anything at all.

"That's the gold and platinum robe," answered Rempar. "We've only got a few feet of it made so far. The thread work is so fine that it takes quite a long time."

"And that?" the Head General pointed to the sewing machine.

"The sapphire trousers, of course!" said Ingot.

"Of course," said the Emperor. "Wonderful work."

"Wonderful work," nodded the Chief Advisor.

"Fabulous," agreed the Prime Minister.

"Swell," said the Head General, shaking his head in wonder.

"I have never seen finer," said the Emperor enthusiastically. "Are you sure it will be done by New Year's."

"Guaranteed," said Rempar.

"One hundred percent," nodded Ingot.

Then the two tailors paused in their work and took the Emperor's measurements.

"Oh, my," frowned Rempar, "I believe we've miscalculated."

"Is something wrong?" the Emperor asked.

"Well," said Ingot, "It seems that your Highness is a bit taller than we had estimated."

"Is that a problem?" asked the Emperor.

"We will need more materials," said Ingot. "But we can still meet the deadline."

"It will be done!" shouted the Emperor happily.

He ordered more diamonds and jewels, gold and platinum and pearls to be sent to the tailor's workshops. Every day the tailors sent their mules and pack horses off to the mountains for supplies, and still the banging and noise from the workshop continued.

At last it was New Year's. Time for the Emperor to dress for his parade.

The Emperor came alone to the Tailor's workshop. All his ministers and advisors and generals waited outside. The two men bowed and escorted him in. They stripped him down to his underwear, and stood him in front of the mirror.

"Here is your shirt, your majesty," said Ingot, helping the Emperor into the emerald and diamond shirt. "Is it not smooth and light."

"It's not very warm," frowned the Emperor. He still couldn't see the shirt, couldn't see even the buttons.

"Ah, but you must wait for the robe," said Rempar, helping the Emperor into the Sapphire trousers.

"Very light," said the Emperor. "I can't even feel them."

"Don't forget the pearl slippers," Ingot said.

"And the ruby gloves."

"Here at last is the gold and platinum robe."

"Splendid!" said Rempar.

"Wonderful," agreed Ingot.

The Emperor looked at himself in the mirror, and began to feel a little nervous. He seemed as naked as the day he was born. "Bring in my ministers. Let us see what they have to say."

One by one the ministers came in. Each had nothing but wonderful things to say about the Emperor's new clothes. The Advisors filled the room with compliments. Even the Generals got into the spirit of things, praising the wonderful stitching and the fine handiwork of the two tailors.

At last, the Emperor felt quite cheered by all this enthusiasm. "To the parade!" he cried.

Off they went, the Emperor leading his ministers and advisors and generals and the entire army through the city.

There was a hush as the Emperor passed. No one said a word.

"They are all marveling in my splendor," whispered the Emperor to his Prime Minister. "They have never seen anything finer!"

Just then, a little boy standing in the front row began to laugh.

"Why is he laughing?" asked the Emperor.

"Perhaps his sister is tickling him," suggested the Chief Advisor.

"Bring him here," said the Emperor.

The Head General grabbed the boy and brought him directly in front of the Emperor.

"What's so funny youngster?" the Emperor asked.

"You're not wearing any clothes!" said the boy giggling. "Nothing at all!"

And then the entire crowd burst into laughter.

The Emperor stared down at his finery and realized that he had been tricked!

The Prime Minister took off his warm coat and threw it on the shivering Emperor. Then, everyone raced back to the palace, but Rempar and Ingot were long gone.

"Oh, what will I do?" moaned the Emperor. "The people will think I am a fool."

Just then, the little boy coughed. In the hurry, the Head General had forgotten to leave him behind.

"What is it youngster?" asked the Emperor.

"Your Majesty doesn't need fine clothing or to conquer new lands. I like you fine just the way you are."

The young boy gave the Emperor a hug and was immediately made a prince. All the advisors and ministers and generals were fired.

The new advisors and ministers and generals searched the land far and wide for the two tailors who had stolen the Emperor's diamonds and emeralds and sapphires, rubies and platinum and gold, but they were never ever found.

Still, from that day until the day of his death, the Emperor was happy, because he knew that he was fine just the way he was.

— *The End* —

58. The World's Greatest Fisherman

*O*nce, near the ocean, in the time of my grandfather's grandfather lived the world's greatest fisherman. Now, he was very old and his bones creaked. He didn't go to sea anymore, but still everyone in the small fishing village knew that he was the world's greatest fisherman.

One day, a young fisherman came into the village and boasted that he was the world's greatest fisherman.

"Not true," said the tackle shop owner. "Why we have the world's greatest fisherman right here in this village."

"I should challenge him to a fishing contest," said the young fisherman.

"Well, young feller," said the tackle shop owner, "p'rhaps ye should."

Well, the youngster went down to the fisherman's cabin, and told the old man that he wanted to have a competition.

"Whoever catches the biggest fish will be declared the greatest fisherman in the world," said the younster.

"Aye," said the old man, squinting. "Why not?"

The next day was a fine sunny day, and the two men met at the pier. The young fisherman carried the newest and best equipment money could buy. He had a fancy rod and reel and a box filled with all kinds of lures and hooks. The old fisherman had nothing but an old pole with a length of twine and a rusty hook at one end.

"Ha!" laughed the young fisherman, "this'll be a piece of cake. What're you using for bait?"

The old fisherman pulled out a can of worms and hooked one on. Then they sat down, and the contest began.

Within minutes, the youngster had a hook. It was a large fish, at least two feet long. "I win already!" said the youngster.

The old man shrugged. "Not done yet, fellah. Keep fishing."

The youngster put the fish in his creel, and tossed his line back in.

Half an hour later, he hooked another one. Three feet long this one was, and it put up quite a fight. Finally, the youngster managed to bring it to shore and haul it onto the dock. "Got another one!" he said. "Do you conceed?"

"Nope," said the old man. He hadn't even gotten a nibble. All he did was sit there, calmly puffing on his pipe.

For the next three hours, the youngster pulled up one fish bigger than the next! His creel was filled with fish. The last one had been nearly five feet long, and still the old man would not conceed.

At last the young fisherman found that he had hooked the biggest fish he'd ever seen. Off in the distance it looked to be seven feet long. He struggled and pulled, tugged and let it run. After three hours of heaving and fighting, he finally

brought almost all the way in to shore when the line snapped with a TWANG!

"Whew," said the youngster. "Now that was the biggest fish I've ever seen."

"Not bad," said the old fisherman, puffing on his pipe. "Seen bigger, but not bad."

"Not bad?" the young man was outraged. "Why since we've started this morning, I've caught more than a dozen fish, and you haven't landed a single one. How can you possibly say that you're a better fisherman than I am?"

The old man shrugged. "I've just caught bigger fish. That's all."

"Well, I don't believe it!" said the youngster. With that, he picked up his equipment, gathered up his fish, and marched off the dock, and right out of the village.

The old fisherman shrugged, and puffed on his pipe.

A few hours later, just before sunset, the old man brought in a fish nearly nine feet long. He needed the help of three men to bring it into shore.

The entire village stood up and cheered. They prepared a great feast that evening, and celebrated because they all knew that they had the world's greatest fisherman.

"Too bad that young feller didn't stick around," said the the tackle store owner. "I doubt if ever he hears the tale that he'll believe it. Mighty tasty fish, though."

"Too impatient," said the old fisherman. "Maybe someday he'll learn. Maybe not."

And they ate and drank and danced late into the night.

— The End —

59. The Two Monks and the Gross Slimy Monster

One day, two monks were walking along the road. These monks were holy men, who wore long orange robes and shaved their heads. Their monastery had very strict rules. They were not allowed to eat meat, could not marry, owned no possessions (except their clothes—and even this was a point of argument at times), and were not allowed to carry any money. There were rules about when they should sleep, when they should eat, and even rules about who they could touch and talk with. For example, they were not supposed to talk with young unmarried women, nor were they supposed to touch anything unclean.

The weather was fine, and the monks were enjoying their walk. The older monk had been in the monastery for twenty years, but the younger one had only been there for just two years. They did not talk as they walked, but meditated on the beauty of the world.

All of a sudden, at the edge of a rushing stream, they saw a gross slimy monster. It was hideous. It had bulging eyes that popped out of its head on long tentacles. Its mouth was filled with fangs that dripped poisonous venom. Its skin was green and slimy, covered with bumps, lumps, scales, and warts. It had seven fingers on each of its three hands and no legs, just a long wiggly tail, like an enormous snail or a slug!

As soon as they saw the gross slimy monster, the younger monk shrieked loudly and turned around to run.

The older monk put a hand on the younger one's shoulder. "Master," said the young monk, "We must get out of here, or else the gross slimy monster will surely eat us."

"You have missed something," said the older monk. "Look closer, Grasshopper." (Grasshopper was the younger monk's nickname.)

The young monk stayed where he was and shivered. He managed to turn his head to look at the monster, and everything he saw repulsed him. Its skin was the color of moldy stale bread in some parts, and the color of the gross slimy stuff that grows underneath the bathtub in other parts. And the smell! Phew. A stable full of cows smelled better.

"I can't see anything," he said at last.

"It is crying," said the older monk. The old man stepped forward. The young man tried to hold him back, but the old man shrugged him away.

"What is the matter?" the older monk asked.

"I can't cross the stream," croaked the monster. It was a truly disgusting voice, the voice of an old lady who has eaten far too many children and has an upset stomach. "I have to visit my fiancee's sister, and the stream is going too fast. There used to be a bridge, but it has been washed away."

"That's too bad," said the younger monk. He took the older monk's robe by the sleeve. "Let's get out of here."

"May I help you?" asked the older monk.

"How could you possibly help me?" said the gross slimy monster. Her voice sounded positively filled with despair.

"We could carry you across," said the older monk. "You don't look too heavy, and I have this young fellow here to help me."

The gross slimy monster turned all of her seventeen eyes toward the older monk. "Oh, would you?" she slurped. "That would be so kind!"

"Yes, yes, far too kind," said the younger monk. "We really. . . ."

"Silence!" ordered the older monk.

"But she might eat us!" said the youngster.

"She won't, though," the old monk said. "Will you?"

"Oh, no. I would never eat a monk. They're far too stringy, and besides, the Lord Buddha would be very angry with me."

"You see," said the older one. "Come."

The young monk saw that further protest was useless. With a great effort, they lifted the gross slimy monster. Grunting and moaning the whole way, the young monk led, and the old monk took the rear. It was hard going in the stream. The water rushed quickly by and was very cold. The rocks were wet and slippery sometimes, and sharp at others.

"She's going to kill us," thought the young monk. "She'll eat us in the middle of the stream and then we'll all die. Or she'll wait until we drop her on the other side, and we're exhausted, and then she'll bite us and chew us into tiny little pieces to carry with her to her fiancee's sister. . . ."

At last the two monks and their gross slimy load reached the far side of the stream. The monks gently lowered the monster down, and she opened her mouth.

"Ah!" shouted the young monk. He jumped back.

"Thank you," wheezed the monster. "You are kind souls."

And off she slithered.

The two monks recrossed the stream, taking care to wash themselves thoroughly—getting all the gross green slime off took a while. At last they were back on the road, walking along in the warm sun, and drying off.

The younger monk was furious. He tried to meditate, tried to pay attention to the birds in the trees, but he no longer saw them. Instead he just got madder and madder.

At last, they stopped under a coconut tree for a break. The older monk sat down calmly and began to meditate. The younger one threw himself down with a thump. At last he spoke.

"How can you just sit there? I can't believe you even talked with her. She could have eaten us! You made me carry her all the way across that stream. We're not supposed to touch unmarried women, let alone unmarried female gross slimy monsters. What would have happened if she had eaten you but left me alive? How would I have explained that to everyone at the monastery?"

"Yes, I carried her across the stream," the older monk said, smiling at the younger monk. "But I left her on the other shore. You have carried her all this way as if she is still with us."

The younger monk scratched his head.

"Would you like a coconut?" asked the older monk.

"Yes, master," said the younger one.

And that is the end of the story.

The moral: Some monks live wonderful and peaceful lives, filled with valuable lessons, but they still don't know how to end a story.

— *The End* —

60. The Ballad of East and West

Rudyard Kipling

You may never have thought of "The Ballad of East and West" as a proper bedtime story. Try reading it aloud, though, and see how much fun it is.

Oh, East is East, and West is West, and never the twain shall meet,
Till Earth and Sky stand presently at God's great Judgment Seat;
But there is neither East nor West, Border, nor Breed, nor Birth,
When two strong men stand face to face, tho' they come from the ends of the earth!

Kamal is out with twenty men to raise the Border-side,
And he has lifted the Colonel's mare that is the Colonel's pride·
He has lifted her out of the stable-door between the dawn and the day,
And turned the calkins upon her feet, and ridden her far away.

Then up and spoke the Colonel's son that led a troop of the Guides:
"Is there never a man of all my men can say where Kamal hides?"
Then up and spoke Mahommed Khan, the son of the Ressaldar:
"If ye know the track of the morning-mist, ye know where his pickets are.
"At dusk he harries the Abazai—at dawn he is into Bonair,
"But he must go by Fort Bukloh to his own place to fare,
"So if ye gallop to Fort Bukloh as fast as a bird can fly,
"By the favour of God ye may cut him off ere he win to the Tongue of Jagai.
"But if he be past the Tongue of Jagai, right swiftly turn ye then,
"For the length and the breadth of that grisly plain is sown with Kamal's men.
"There is rock to the left, and rock to the right, and low lean thorn between,
"And ye may hear a breech-bolt snick where never a man is seen."

The Colonel's son has taken a horse, and a raw rough dun was he,
With the mouth of a bell and the heart of Hell
and the head of the gallows-tree.
The Colonel's son to the Fort has won, they bid him stay to eat—
Who rides at the tail of a Border thief, he sits not long at his meat.
He's up and away from Fort Bukloh as fast as he can fly,
Till he was aware of his father's mare in the gut of the Tongue of Jagai,
Till he was aware of his father's mare with Kamal upon her back,
And when he could spy the white of her eye, he made the pistol crack.

He has fired once, he has fired twice, but the whistling ball went wide.
"Ye shoot like a soldier," Kamal said. "Show now if ye can ride."
It's up and over the Tongue of Jagai, as blown dustdevils go,
The dun he fled like a stag of ten, but the mare like a barren doe.
The dun he leaned against the bit and slugged his head above,
But the red mare played with the snaffle-bars, as a maiden plays with a glove.
There was rock to the left and rock to the right, and low lean thorn between,
And thrice he heard a breech-bolt snick tho' never a man was seen.

They have ridden the low moon out of the sky, their hoofs drum up the dawn,
The dun he went like a wounded bull, but the mare like a new-roused fawn.
The dun he fell at a water-course—in a woful heap fell he,
And Kamal has turned the red mare back, and pulled the rider free.

He has knocked the pistol out of his hand—small room was there to strive,
"'Twas only by favour of mine," quoth he, "ye rode so long alive:
"There was not a rock for twenty mile, there was not a clump of tree,
"But covered a man of my own men with his rifle cocked on his knee.
"If I had raised my bridle-hand, as I have held it low,
"The little jackals that flee so fast were feasting all in a row:
"If I had bowed my head on my breast, as I have held it high,
"The kite that whistles above us now were gorged till she could not fly."

Lightly answered the Colonel's son: "Do good to bird and beast,
"But count who come for the broken meats before thou makest a feast.
"If there should follow a thousand swords to carry my bones away,
"Belike the price of a jackal's meal were more than a thief could pay.
"They will feed their horse on the standing crop, their men on the garnered grain,
"The thatch of the byres will serve their fires when all the cattle are slain.
"But if thou thinkest the price be fair,—thy brethren wait to sup,
"The hound is kin to the jackal-spawn,—howl, dog, and call them up!
"And if thou thinkest the price be high, in steer and gear and stack,
"Give me my father's mare again, and I'll fight my own way back!"

Kamal has gripped him by the hand and set him upon his feet.
"No talk shall be of dogs," said he, "when wolf and gray wolf meet.
"May I eat dirt if thou hast hurt of me in deed or breath;
"What dam of lances brought thee forth to jest at the dawn with Death?"
Lightly answered the Colonel's son: "I hold by the blood of my clan:
"Take up the mare for my father's gift— by God, she has carried a man!"

The red mare ran to the Colonel's son, and nuzzled against his breast;
"We be two strong men," said Kamal then, "but she loveth the
    younger best.
"So she shall go with a lifter's dower, my turquoise-studded rein,
"My broidered saddle and saddle-cloth, and silver stirrups twain."
The Colonel's son a pistol drew and held it muzzle-end,
"Ye have taken the one from a foe," said he; "will ye take the mate
    from a friend?"

"A gift for a gift," said Kamal straight; "a limb for the risk of a limb.
"Thy father has sent his son to me, I'll send my son to him!"
With that he whistled his only son, that dropped from a mountain-crest—
He trod the ling like a buck in spring, and he looked like a lance in rest.
"Now here is thy master," Kamal said, "who leads a troop of the Guides,
"And thou must ride at his left side as shield on shoulder rides.

"Till Death or I cut loose the tie, at camp and board and bed,
"Thy life is his—thy fate it is to guard him with thy head.
"So, thou must eat the White Queen's meat, and all her foes are thine,
"And thou must harry thy father's hold for the peace of the Borderline,
"And thou must make a trooper tough and hack thy way to power—
"Belike they will raise thee to Ressaldar when I am hanged in Peshawur."

They have looked each other between the eyes, and there they found no fault,
They have taken the Oath of the Brother-in-Blood on leavened bread and salt:
They have taken the Oath of the Brother-in-Blood on fire and fresh-cut sod,
On the hilt and the haft of the Khyber knife, and the Wondrous Names of God.
The Colonel's son he rides the mare and Kamal's boy the dun,
And two have come back to Fort Bukloh where there went forth but one.
And when they drew to the Quarter-Guard, full twenty swords flew clear—
There was not a man but carried his feud with the blood of the mountaineer.
"Ha' done! ha' done!" said the Colonel's son. "Put up the steel at your sides!
"Last night ye had struck at a Border thief—to-night 'tis a man of the Guides!"

Oh, East is East, and West is West, and never the twain shall meet,
Till Earth and Sky stand presently at God's great Judgment Seat;
But there is neither East nor West, Border, nor Breed, nor Birth,
When two strong men stand face to face, tho' they come from the ends of the earth

— The End —

168

61. Paul Bunyan Meets Babe the Blue Ox

Paul Bunyan is one of those mythical fellows who populate the edges of American History. Along with Johnny Appleseed, Mike Fink (of riverboat fame), and Pecos Bill, he lived on the wild frontiers in the days before civilization got too close. His stories were told around campfires and in bunk houses all across the United States and may still be told today in logging camps. Now, not every word of these stories can be taken as the gospel truth. Late at night, men have been known to stretch the truth just a shade.

To say that Paul Bunyan was a giant would be an understatement. Giants are much too small. Paul Bunyan was so big that when he was born, his Mammy had to put his cradle in the ocean just to rock him asleep. One evening, when Paul was teething, he tossed and turned so much that he created a tidal wave that threatened to wipe out the city of New York. When he got a little bigger, he pulled up giant trees and chewed on them for a pacifier.

Well, you can surely see that the crowded East Coast was no place for a fellow of Paul's size. He could eat an entire pig for breakfast, a cow for lunch, and still have room for an apple orchard's worth of pies for dessert. He had a hard time walking down the street, too. After all, each of his feet were as big as a train engine, so he had to be very careful where he set them down. Once, on a trip in upstate New York, Paul Bunyan tripped and sprawled out so long and hard that he made a ditch five miles long. The governor of New York saw a possible profit in it, so he convinced Paul to take another few falls, and in no time at all, the Erie Canal was dug.

Still, the neighbors complained about Paul. When he set out his washing to dry, it blocked out the sun, and when he snored at night it sounded like a thunderstorm. Nobody for miles could sleep, and they all went around wearing wet clothes.

Finally, Paul decided to set out West to make his fortune.

Now, that happened to be the winter of the blue snow. Everybody knows that snow is usually white, or maybe a bit grey around the edges in the city. This snow, though, was blue through and through. It was the color of robin's eggs, the ocean, or the sky on a clear day. The snow was high, but that didn't bother Paul any. He was walking West (since there wasn't a horse alive that could carry him without getting a hernia) when all of a sudden he heard the most pitiful wail.

"Mlooooooooooo!" came the sound. "Mlooooo!"

At first Paul thought it was the wind. So he licked his finger and stuck it in the air, but there wasn't a wind blowing. The sound just continued.

"Mlooooo!"

Well, Paul was nothing if not curious, so he began to poke around the snow drifts, and pretty soon he saw two blue triangles peeking up out of a snow drift. He reached down into the snow, felt around, and was surprised when he found something alive and kicking down there. He closed his hand around it and picked it up.

It was a little baby ox, small and thin and shivering from the cold. So cold was the ox that its skin had turned completely blue! The poor thing's parents must have been frightened by the strange blue snow and ran off.

Well, Paul lifted the ox up and looked it in the eye.

"Mlooo!" said the ox, nearly deafening Paul.

"You sure do have some strong lungs," said Paul. "I think I'll call you Babe."

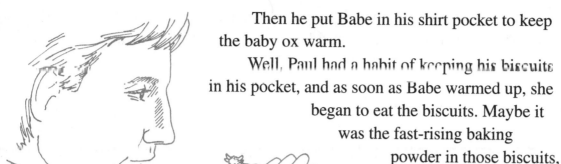

Then he put Babe in his shirt pocket to keep the baby ox warm.

Well, Paul had a habit of keeping his biscuits in his pocket, and as soon as Babe warmed up, she began to eat the biscuits. Maybe it was the fast-rising baking powder in those biscuits, or maybe it was just being so close to Paul, but pretty soon Babe began to grow.

She grew and she grew and she grew. In a matter of days she was bigger than Paul's pocket, so he had to carry her in the palm of his hand. Then she got even bigger. Inside of a month, she was the biggest ox the world has ever seen. Her horns were the size of telegraph poles, and her hooves were so big it took a ton of iron just to make shoes for her.

Even though Babe was as big as a small building, that wasn't the strangest thing about her. No, sir, the strangest thing about Babe was that she stayed blue. You'd have thought that once she warmed up her skin would turn a normal ox color of brown or maybe a little red, but nope, she was blue. She had blue fur the color of a blue jay's feathers and blue eyes the color of gigantic sapphires. Even her telegraph pole-sized horns were blue.

They made quite a pair, Paul Bunyan and Babe the Blue Ox wending their way West to find their fortune.

About this time Paul finally figured out what he could do as a career. This happened almost by accident. Paul was traveling through the Westernmost parts of Ohio and he needed a place to sleep. He came across a farm, and asked if he might bunk down for the night.

"Surely," the Farmer said. "Only I haven't cleared a field big enough for you."

Paul looked around and saw that the Farmer was right. The cabin was much too small for Paul, and all around the cabin were woods.

"Tell you what," Paul said. "If I can make myself a place to sleep, can I stay the night?"

"Sure," shrugged the Farmer, who figured he had nothing to lose in the deal.

Paul took the Farmer's spare tin roof and attached it to a long pine tree, and made the world's first double-bladed ax. When he swung that ax it was like watching a whirlwind come to life. In twenty minutes, Paul had cleared the woods for three miles in all directions.

Then he was so tired, he just fell right asleep. Babe lay down next to him, and the two made a rather cute pair of snoring hills.

The next morning, the Farmer came out and whistled in surprise.

"My goodness!" he said. "That was twenty years' work for me. You'll make a terrific lumberjack!"

"A lumberjack?" Paul said. "Why what's that?"

"Why, a lumberjack's somebody who cuts down trees. The trees here are nothing compared to those out in the great North Woods. I hear they're looking for lumberjacks that way."

"Well," said Paul, "that's where we'll go."

And off they went to the great North Woods.

— *The End* —

62. Paul Bunyan Finds His Camp

$\mathcal{N}$ow, it took Paul Bunyan and Babe the Blue Ox a while to get to the Great North Woods, and they had a lot of adventures along the way, enough to fill a book this size fifteen times over. So, we're going to skip all that nonsense and just tell you about Paul Bunyan's lumberjack camp, which was known as the Big Onion.

Now, why you may wonder would you name a logging camp the Big Onion? Well, after Paul and his fellow loggers (by now he was famous and had more than a hundred loggers working for him) cleared the Great Plains of Kansas, they were looking for a new challenge and a new home.

"We need a base of operations," said Sven Olaffson, Paul's foreman. "Why every time we send loggers out into the woods, half of them don't come back home, because they don't know where home is!"

Paul Bunyan agreed, but it wasn't so easy even in those days to find prime real estate for a bunch of rowdy working men to call home. Paul went to real estate agents and asked around various towns.

At last, the settlers in this particular stretch of the Great North Woods told them that there was a valley not too far off that the Indians called "The Place of Great Tears."

"Nobody'll go there," said the Mayor of a nearby town. "As soon as you get too close, everybody breaks down crying."

"Well," Paul said, smelling an opportunity, "We'll just see about that."

Off he and Babe went to investigate this valley.

Sure enough, as soon as they got within range, they began to sniff, and their eyes started to water. Pretty soon both Paul Bunyan and Babe the Blue Ox were crying.

Now, when you and I cry, it's nothing special. A few tears and we feel better. But once Paul and Babe started crying, they couldn't stop.

They cried and they cried, and pretty soon the entire valley was filled with their tears.

"This will never do," sobbed Paul. "We can't build our bunk houses under water."

So, even though he kept crying, Paul got out a shovel and began to dig a drainage ditch. Babe, through tears of her own, helped to move the earth around. Pretty soon they'd managed to cut a drain for the water, and away it rushed!

So powerful was the flow of those tears that it couldn't drain anywhere on the Great Plains, so it kept on going all the way down to New Orleans. Today, they call that drainage ditch the Mississippi River, and it's a mile wide in some places.

Now, while Paul and Babe were digging, they found that their crying actually got worse.

"I'm not sad," Paul told Babe, "But I sure do want to cry."

"Mooo-hooo!" Babe agreed.

Well, the two of them sat down and cried so much that it eroded the dirt around the edges of the valley. What do you think they saw there? Yep, it was the biggest onion the world has ever seen. Some folks say that it was the size of the state of Rhode Island, but I think they're exaggerating just a little.

Still bawling like a baby, Paul dug up the onion and threw it into a nearby hot spring. Almost immediately their crying stopped. He and Babe danced a jig for joy.

And that, my friends is how the Big Onion Logging Camp got its name.

— *The End* —

63. Paul Bunyan and Sourdough Slim

The Big Onion was some camp, too. As soon as word got out that Paul Bunyan was looking for loggers, every man and boy for hundreds of miles grabbed his ax and headed for the camp.

Pretty soon the bunk house that Paul had built was too small. They couldn't expand flatwise over the land, so Paul just built another floor. A week later he built another floor. And then another. Inside of a year the bunk house was so high that they had to build a hinge in the top to let the moon pass through. Some of the hands that lived at the top never actually made it to work. By the time they heard the breakfast bell and got downstairs to eat, it was already dinner time.

Now, feeding this many men was a chore that would have boggled the minds of Europe's finest politicians. Fortunately, Paul hired Sourdough Slim, the best camp cook in the United States.

Sourdough Slim was a gawky man with a rawhide face who never ever smiled. He was always too busy.

You see, every morning he had to make flapjacks. When you and I make flapjacks it's a bit of a chore, because there's never enough stove space for all the flapjacks to get cooked at once. Sourdough Slim fixed that problem by building a griddle the size of an ice skating rink. Every morning he had fifteen of his assistants strap slabs of bacon to their feet and go skating around on the hot griddle to grease it up. He invented the cement mixer to stir up all the batter, and he used to pour it out with a catapult that sent balls of wet batter flying way up into the sky, landing on the griddle with a great hissing splat.

Flipping those flapjacks was some task, too. All the fifteen assistants would skate around with snow shovels, flipping flapjacks and loading them into wheelbarrows to feed the hands. But, mmmm, were they good. Of course there still were never enough to go around, but nobody ever complained. Do you know why? Because Sourdough Slim had a rule. Anybody who complained had to clean the dishes, and let me tell you that with that many lumberjacks there were alot of plates. Nobody wanted to do that, so after breakfast every lumberjack had to load his plates in a special cart that Babe dragged down to the river. They pushed the cart through the rapids, and in no time the dishes were cleaned.

One day, a couple of careless teamsters dumped a ton of dried peas right in the middle of the camp. Paul Bunyan was just about to order them to do the laundry. (If there's one thing worse than doing dishes for a logging camp, it's doing the laundry. Imagine all those pairs of dirty underwear and smelly shirts. Whoo-eee!)

Just then, Sourdough Slim had an idea. "Take those peas and shovel them into the hot spring," Slim ordered.

The teamsters hopped to it.

"What're you doing?" Paul asked Slim.

"Making lunch," Slim answered, scowling. "That's the spring with the big onion, right?"

"Ah-yuh," Paul nodded.

"Right," Slim said. "Throw in a couple of hams, forty pounds of salt and ten bushels of carrots."

Then Sourdough Slim went off to the flour mill with fifty pounds of pepper to grind.

Paul scratched his head, thinking that perhaps his cook had finally gone around the bend.

That afternoon, though, a smell began to waft through the North Woods. It was a fine rich smell, earthy and sweet. Paul's stomach began to grumble, and everybody for thirty miles thought that there was an earthquake.

Just then, Sourdough Slim rang the dinner bell. Now, when I say dinner bell, most of you will think of those little fancy bells that people ring in fine society houses. Or perhaps you'll think of a little triangle that cowboys have in their bunk houses. Well, the dinner bell at the Big Onion was something else completely. It was a triangle, to be sure, made from a half mile of welded railroad ties. To ring it, Slim and all fifteen of his assistants had to take rail pounding hammers and strike all at the same time. If any one of the sixteen men was off by even a fraction of a second, the bell would only sound a muffled thud.

This afternoon, though, they did it right. It sounded like this.

"Ready?" Slim began. "One . . . Two . . . Three. . . ."

"DONGGGGGGGGGG!"

Why some people say you could hear that dinner bell all the way to San Francisco, and there are folks in that city who to this day blame Paul Bunyan for their earthquakes.

When the loggers heard the dinner bell, they came a-running. The noise of their coming was so loud it scared every animal in earshot. A great heard of buffaloes tore out of the woods into the Great Plains, and the Indians there for a short time thought that the great old days had finally returned.

When the loggers got to the camp they sat round the huge tables and stared in surprise at the empty bowl set before them.

"Where's the food?" Paul demanded. His bowl, which was the size of a riverboat barge was empty, too.

"Over in the hot spring," Sourdough Slim yelled back. "Go get it yerself!"

Paul was skeptical, but he trundled over to the hot spring and dipped the huge ladle in.

When he pulled it out, he was surprised to see that the spring water wasn't thin and clear anymore. No, sir, it was thick and gooey, and completely green.

"What do you call this gunk?" Paul asked Slim.

"That's pea soup, you big galoot," Sourdough Slim answered back.

"Looks disgusting," Paul said.

"That's it!" Slim shouted. "I've cooked for you for five years now without a single word of thanks. Now I make something wondrous and new and you disparage it without even giving it a single taste. That's it! I quit!"

"Wait a minute, Slim," Paul said. "Before you quit, let me taste this stuff."

Paul screwed up his face and closed his eyes. He picked up a big spoonful and thought about holding his nose.

Slim's frown got even angrier. There's nothing a cook hates more than to see folks eat food like it's medicine.

Well, at last Paul managed to put the spoon into his mouth, and close his great cave of jaws around it. He chewed slowly, and then broke into a wide smile.

"Hey, Slim," Paul said. "This is good stuff."

"Yer darn tootin!" Slim answered back. And some folk say that he even cracked a bit of a smile himself. I don't know if that's true, but he certainly didn't quit the day he invented pea soup.

— *The End* —

64. Min Tzu Chien

*Not only is "Min Tzu Chien" a Cinderella-style story,
but also it has a boy hero, and it is told from a completely
different cultural perspective.*

Thousands of years ago in China
there lived a little boy named Min Tzu
Chien. He was a disciple of Confusius and known
to be a loyal and dutiful son. It was not always easy
for little Min Tzu Chien to be nice to his family.
His mother had died when he was very little, and
his father had remarried. His father and stepmother
had two more sons. Together they all lived, the father, stepmother, two
sons, and Min Tzu Chien, in a tiny hut not far from the palace.

Even though Min Tzu Chien was the oldest son, his Stepmother
loved her own sons best. She fed her sons more rice and gave them finer
clothes to wear. While Min Tzu Chien's clothing grew old and ragged,
his two brothers always had fresh new and clean silks. When dinner was
over, it was the sons' duty to clean the table and wash the dishes, but the
Stepmother allowed her two sons to play in the yard, while Min Tzu
Chien worked in the kitchen. Soon she began putting him to work in the
fields as well. He was in charge of planting the rice and harvesting all the
vegetables. When crows came to the fields, he rose at dawn to sit alone
in the rice paddy to scare them away, while his two brothers slept late
into the day and grew fat.

Where was Min Tzu Chien's father during all this? Well, he worked
at the palace as an assistant to the emperor. He left the house very early

in the morning (long before dawn) and came home long after dark. He barely had enough strength to eat dinner, and his faithful son did not want to bother his father with his inconsequential tales of woe.

One winter, the emperor was feeling generous and gave the father a large sack of goose feathers for coats. In those days, most coats were made out of cotton, so the goose feathers were a truly special gift. The father brought the sack home and gave it to the stepmother.

"Make three warm coats for our sons," he said. "Then they will be the handsomest and warmest boys in the city."

The second wife bowed very low and thanked her husband for the feathers. She immediately set to her task cutting the cloth for the coats.

Soon the coats were nearly ready. The stepmother waited until the father was at the palace, and then she stuffed her two sons' coat linings full of all the goose feathers. In Min Tzu Chien's coat lining she put only grass and weeds.

Winter grew cold that year. There was snow and great gusts of wind. Min Tzu Chien could not understand why he was never able to stay warm. It did not matter that he wore his brand-new coat, he shivered and shook, and his fingers and lips turned bright blue. All the while, his fat brothers played in the snow and felt as cozy as tea in a pot.

One day, Min Tzu Chien and his father were out for a walk. There was only a little snow on the ground, but still Min Tzu Chien wobbled as he walked. His face was grey and his feet weak and wobbly. The father could not understand why his son was walking so slowly and erratically.

The boy seemed to be drunk, and the father felt very ashamed. At last Min Tzu Chien stumbled and fell.

"So, this is what it has come to!" his father roared. "I leave you alone to take care of my house and you become a drunkard!" He picked up a stick and was about to beat the poor boy, but then he saw something and stopped.

When Min Tzu Chien fell, his coat had torn open on a rock. The grass and weeds inside the coat's lining were exposed.

At the sight of the poor torn coat, Min Tzu Chien's father realized that he had been blind. He dropped his stick and hugged his first-born son.

"I have made a poor choice in a wife," he told Min Tzu Chien. "I will ask the emperor to behead her."

But Min Tzu Chien stopped his father. "If you kill our mother, my stepmother's sons who are still my brothers will continue to live with us," he said. "After a time, you will probably get married again. It is most difficult for a woman not to love her own children best. So, if by your new wife you have more children, instead of one poor son there would be three."

His father nodded at Min Tzu Chien's wise words and decided not to have his wife beheaded.

Later, when the stepmother heard what Min Tzu Chien had said, her heart melted. She realized that she had been needlessly cruel to the good boy and vowed to change her ways. Soon, she was treating him just as well (if not better) than her own sons.

At last, the emperor heard of Min Tzu Chien's wisdom, and he appointed the young boy his chancellor. They lived happily for many years.

— The End —

65. The Shaggy Dog's Tail, a Shaggy Dog Tale

READER'S TIP: As you will see, this story can go on forever—or until the little one drifts off to sleep. It is designed for days when your brain is off-line. After the first few times, you can tell it without any thought whatsoever. If the child says, "No, tell me a different story!" then you can change it to a shaggy sheep or goat or squirrel, or whatever suits your fancy. This can be quite a fun game as long as you don't get annoyed. Hopefully, this *won't* become your child's favorite story.

Once upon a time, there was a baby shaggy dog who didn't want to go to bed.

The baby shaggy dog pulled on the daddy shaggy dog's tail.

"Tell me a story," said the baby shaggy dog.

"Ok," said the daddy shaggy dog. "Let me think. Oh, I remember one. . . ."

Once upon a time there was a baby shaggy dog who didn't want to go to bed.

The baby shaggy dog pulled on the daddy shaggy dog's tail.

"Tell me a story," said the baby shaggy dog.

"Ok," said the daddy shaggy dog. "Let me think. Oh, I remember one. . . ."

Once upon a time there was a baby shaggy dog who didn't want to go to bed.

The baby shaggy dog pulled on the daddy shaggy dog's tail.

"Tell me a story," said the baby shaggy dog.

"Ok," said the daddy shaggy dog. "Let me think. Oh, I remember one. . . ."

Once upon a time there was a baby shaggy dog who didn't want to go to bed.

The baby shaggy dog pulled on the daddy shaggy dog's tail.

"Tell me a story," said the baby shaggy dog.

"Ok," said the daddy shaggy dog. "Let me think. Oh, I remember one. . . ."

Once upon a time there was a baby shaggy dog who didn't want to go to bed.

The baby shaggy dog pulled on the daddy shaggy dog's tail.

"Tell me a story," said the baby shaggy dog.

"Ok," said the daddy shaggy dog. "Let me think. Oh, I remember one. . . ."

Once upon a time there was a baby shaggy dog who didn't want to go to bed.

The baby shaggy dog pulled on the daddy shaggy dog's tail.

"Tell me a story," said the baby shaggy dog.

"Ok," said the daddy shaggy dog. "Let me think. Oh, I remember one. . . ."

— *The End* —

66. Noah and the Great Flood

This version of the story of Noah is largely taken from the King James Bible. It may be a little difficult for younger children to understand the language, but you can use it as an opportunity to teach them.

*T*here were giants in the earth in those days, and wicked days they were. The earth was corrupt and filled with violence. God looked down upon humanity, and saw that wickedness and sin were great. The LORD repented that he had made man on the earth, and it grieved him at his heart.

And the LORD said, "I will destroy man whom I have created from the face of the earth; both man, and beast, and the creeping thing, and the fowls of the air."

But Noah found grace in the eyes of the LORD.

God said unto Noah, "Behold, I shall bring a flood of waters to destroy all life. Every thing that is on the earth shall die.

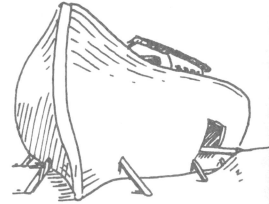

"But with thee will I establish my covenant; and thou shalt come into the ark, thou, and thy sons, and thy wife, and thy sons' wives with thee.

"Make an ark of gopher wood with many rooms. The ark shall be three stories high.

"And of every living thing of all flesh, two of every sort shalt thou bring into the ark, to keep them alive with thee. They shall be male and female. Birds and cattle, creeping things and flying things.

"And you shall take food for thee and for them.

"I will cause it to rain upon the earth forty days and forty nights; and every living substance that I have made will I destroy from off the face of the earth."

Noah did all that the LORD commanded him.

Of clean beasts, and of beasts that are not clean, and of fowls, and of every thing that creepeth upon the earth, there went in two and two unto Noah into the ark, the male and the female, as God had commanded.

They, and every beast, and all the cattle, and every thing that creepeth upon the earth, and every fowl, every bird of every sort went in unto Noah into the ark, two and two of all flesh, wherein is the breath of life. They went in male and female, as God had commanded.

And it came to pass that the waters of the flood were upon the earth. The fountains of the great deep broke up, and the windows of heaven were opened

Noah went in, and his sons, and his wife, and his sons' wives with him, into the ark, because of the waters of the flood. And Noah was six hundred years old when the flood of waters was upon the earth.

It rained upon the earth forty
days and forty nights. The waters
increased, and the ark was lifted up
above the earth.

And the waters rose, covering the earth;
and all the high hills, and the mountains were covered.
All flesh died that moved upon the earth, both of fowl, and of
cattle, and of beast, and of every creeping thing that creepeth upon the
earth, and every man: all in whose nostrils was the breath of life, of all
that was in the dry land, died.

And every living substance was destroyed which was upon the
face of the ground, both man, and cattle, and the creeping things, and
the fowl of the heaven; and they were destroyed from the earth: and
Noah only remained alive, and they that were with him in the ark.

And the waters stayed upon the earth a hundred and fifty days.

God remembered Noah, and every living thing, and all the cattle
that was with him in the ark: and God made a wind to pass over the
earth, and the waters receded.

And the ark rested upon the mountains of Ararat. The waters decreased continually until the tops of the mountains were seen. At the end of forty days, that Noah opened the window of the ark which he had made.

He sent forth a dove to see if the waters were abated from off the face of the ground.

But the dove found no rest for the sole of her foot, and she returned unto him into the ark, for the waters were on the face of the whole earth: then he put forth his hand, and took her, and pulled her in unto him into the ark.

Noah stayed yet other seven days; and again he sent forth the dove out of the ark.

The dove returned to him in the evening; and, lo, in her mouth was an olive leaf, so Noah knew that the waters were abated from off the earth.

He stayed yet other seven days; and again sent forth the dove; but it returned not again unto him any more.

The waters were dried up from off the earth: and Noah removed the covering of the ark, and looked, and, behold, the face of the ground was dry.

And God spake unto Noah, saying, "Go forth from the ark, thou, and thy wife, and thy sons, and thy sons' wives with thee. Bring forth with thee every living thing that is with thee, of all flesh, both of fowl, and of cattle, and of every creeping thing that creepeth upon the earth; that they may breed abundantly in the earth, and be fruitful, and multiply upon the earth."

And Noah went forth, and his sons, and his wife, and his sons' wives with him. Every beast, every creeping thing, and every fowl, and whatsoever creepeth upon the earth, after their kinds, went forth out of the ark.

Noah built an altar unto the LORD offered burnt offerings on the altar.

The LORD smelled a sweet savour; and the LORD said in his heart, "I will not again curse the ground any more for man's sake; for the imagination of man's heart is evil from his youth; neither will I again smite any more every thing living, as I have done. While the earth remaineth, seedtime and harvest, and cold and heat, and summer and winter, and day and night shall not cease."

And God blessed Noah and his sons, and said unto them, "Be fruitful, and multiply, and replenish the earth.

"I will establish my covenant with you; neither shall all flesh be cut off any more by the waters of a flood; neither shall there any more be a flood to destroy the earth."

And God said, "This is the token of the covenant which I make between me and you and every living creature that is with you, for perpetual generations:

"I do set my bow in the cloud, and it shall be for a token of a covenant between me and the earth. And it shall come to pass, when I bring a cloud over the earth, that the bow shall be seen in the cloud, and I will remember my covenant, which is between me and you and every living creature of all flesh; and the waters shall no more become a flood to destroy all flesh."

— *The End* —

67. The King and His Fool

Way back when kings ruled the world there lived a man named George, who thought that his King was a fool. The King, you see, had made a law that whoever came before him and asked for pardon would receive it. So, George made a habit of knocking the hats off rich men's heads and then going in front of the King and asking for his pardon. He would break windows and steal apples, and then rush into the courtroom and ask for the King's pardon. George wasn't a bad man, just mischievous. He liked to get into trouble, and knew that he would be safe. Since it was the law, the King always said, "All right, you are pardoned."

Eventually, though, the King got tired of pardoning George for silly things. So, he had George brought into the throne room and issued an order.

"The next time you come before me," the King said, "make sure that you are not walking and not riding. Make sure that you're not dressed and not naked."

"Your royal majesty the great and wonderful King," George said. "I can do that."

Right away, George went out and he poached a deer from the King's very own forest. That was against the law back then, and the penalty was death. George didn't mind, though. While the guards were chasing him, he tore his shirt in half. Just as he reached the palace, he grabbed a sheep from the courtyard and threw one leg over its back. Chased by the King's guard's, George and the sheep hop-hobbled into the court room.

"Your majesty," George said, "Oh, supreme ruler of this entire land. I've killed one of your deer. Please pardon me."

"I thought I ordered that the next time you come before me you neither walk nor ride, that you're neither dressed nor naked!"

"Surely your great and wonderful highness, I have done just that," George said. "I'm only wearing half a shirt, so I'm neither dressed nor naked. And I've only got one leg on the back of this sheep, so I'm neither walking nor riding."

The King saw that George had outfoxed him, so he decided to make George the King's fool. It was the fool's job to keep the King amused, and since George was always getting into trouble, the King figured that George already was well on the way.

George wasn't sure he much liked being called a fool. He had to hang around the palace and wear a floppy fool's hat with bells on the ends. But he decided to use the King's decision to his advantage. He figured he could use his position to show the King how foolish so many of his laws were.

For instance, there was one law that said that anybody could burn down their own house without any penalty at all. That, George thought, was a stupid law.

So, George built a house right next to the palace. And he filled it full of dry twigs and branches and logs. He poured oil on the logs and then decided it was time to light it up.

George went into the throne room and plucked a torch from the wall.

"Where are you going, George?" the King asked.

"I'm going to burn my house down," George said.

"But your house is right next to the palace. It will surely set the palace on fire."

"Your most stupendous and grand majesty, the law says that I can burn down my own house without asking anybody's permission."

"Well, we'll just have to change that law, won't we," said the King. And so the law was changed immediately.

All this time, the King kept pardoning George for anything he did, and he was really and truly sick of the whole thing. At last he decided enough was enough.

"George," he said, "You can do whatever you want."

"Really?" George said.

"Yes," said the King. "Whatever you ask for, it shall be yours."

"Ok," George said. "I want to be king, and you can be the fool."

"Darn it!" the King said, stomping his feet. But his word was law, and a minute later, there was George sitting on the throne, and there was the King standing around in a floppy fool's hat with bells on the ends.

George didn't much want to be king, so after a few minutes, he gave the throne back on one condition.

"From now on, you can't give anybody anything without finding out what it is they want first," George said.

"Agreed," said the King.

George handed the King his scepter, and the King handed George his floppy hat back.

"Now, Mister smartypants," said the King, "You are banished. I never want to see you in my country ever again."

George didn't want to leave. He had a wife and a family and a budding career as the King's fool. Then he thought of a plan.

He went to the next country over and filled his boots with dirt. Then he put a whole pile of dirt in his hat and on top of his hat. Then he went back to court.

"What are you doing back here?" cried the King. "I thought I told you I'd cut off your head if I ever saw you on my land!"

"But your fabulous Kingship, I'm not on your land," George said. "Nor am I under your land. I'm standing on the next country's land."

Well, the King saw that George had outfoxed him once again, and he decided to pardon him and keep him around as a fool.

From then on, for as long as they both lived, the King made foolish laws, and George got them all changed.

— *The End* —

68. The Fool and the Rich Man

Once upon a time, there was a rich man who made all his money by taking advantage of poor and foolish folk. He tried to get everyone to work too hard for too long for too little money. Then he'd always try to cheat them out of their money to boot.

He was riding into town one day and he saw a fool standing on a corner drawing with a stick in the dirt.

"Hey, you!" he said. "You want to work for me? I'll give you a dollar a day."

"Is it hard work?" asked the Fool.

"Not hard by half," said the Rich Man, but he had his fingers crossed. He wanted the fool to harvest the crops, chop some wood, and move some boulders.

"Ok," said the fool. "Can I ride on your horse?"

"Of course not," said the Rich Man. "You've got to walk along behind me."

Well, off they went. The Rich Man rode ahead, and the Fool walked behind.

"Come on," said the Rich Man. "Come on!"

"I'm a-coming," said the Fool.

But he walked so slow that by the time he reached the Rich Man's house it was time for supper.

The Rich Man's wife gave him supper, and the Fool went straight to bed.

The next morning, the Rich Man woke the fool up at the crack of dawn.

"Get up lazybones!" the Rich Man shouted. "You've got to go to work."

"First pay me for yesterday," said the Fool.

"You didn't work yesterday," said the Rich Man.

"You said you'd give me a dollar a day," said the Fool. "Yesterday was a day, right?"

The Rich Man had to agree. He paid the Fool his dollar, but he didn't much mind. He decided that he'd have the Fool clean the stables and milk the cows, too.

After the Fool pocketed the dollar he said, "How about some breakfast. A man works much better after he's eaten some breakfast."

So the Rich Man woke his wife, who cooked up a good breakfast of eggs and bacon and ham and coffee and sausages and flapjacks and butter and biscuits and gravy and steak.

The Fool ate so quickly you'd have thought he'd missed all his meals for a month. Before the Rich Man could even sit down at his place all the food was gone.

"Well," said the Rich Man, "get out into the fields and start working on the harvest."

"How about lunch?" said the Fool. "I want to work really hard for you all day. You don't want me coming back in the middle of the day for lunch and then having to walk all the way back out again, do you?"

"I reckon not," said the Rich Man. So he told his wife to make lunch for the Fool.

She got to work and fried up a chicken and sliced up some ham and baked some bread and made a cake.

The Fool ate it all as soon as it reached the table, and the Rich Man didn't even get to eat a single bite.

"Get to work now!" said the Rich Man.

"Well, what about supper?" said the Fool. "You don't really want me breaking off work early to walk all the way back here from the fields for supper."

"No, I guess I don't," said the Rich Man. "Fix him some supper."

The Rich Man's wife was pretty angry by now, but she did as her husband told. She fried up some fish and baked some more bread and roasted some vegetables and even made a pie.

Once again, the Fool ate it all as soon as it reached the table and once again the Rich Man didn't get a single bite.

"Ok," said the Rich Man, "You've had your breakfast, you've had your lunch, and you've had your supper. Now get out into the fields and go to work!"

"I can't do that," said the Fool.

"Why not?" cried the Rich Man.

"I don't know about your house, but in my house after supper everybody goes to bed. Good night."

And off he went back to bed.

By the way, the Rich Man's wife was so mad at her husband for making her cook so much that she forced the Rich Man himself out into the fields, and he had to harvest the crops, chop the wood, move the stones, milk the cows, and clean the stables all by himself.

— *The End* —

69. The Monkey's Paw

READER TIP: This story is scary, *very* scary. It is probably not appropriate for most kids. Still, it's the kind of bedtime story that is good for a Halloween night when everybody wants to be scared.

*M*anchester was a dirty town, and Professor Shepherd hated living there. Every one worked in the steel industry or in the coal mines. The air was polluted and the streets were dirty. At night cut-throats lurked in the lanes, and during the day the smell from the refineries stank up the air. But, it was the only place where he'd been able to find a job, and his son had a job in the steel mill, so he had to stay.

One day, Armstrong, a friend of the Professor's from the university wrote that he was coming to visit.

Professor Shepherd was shocked when Armstrong finally arrived. His face was wrinkled, his back was bent, and his hair had gone completely white. Politely, the Professor ushered his friend into the house, and said nothing.

Over dinner, though, the suspense got to be too much. At last, the Professor asked, "Armstrong, when I last saw you you were young and healthy. Now you look old and haggard. What has happened?"

"After dinner," Armstrong said. "I'll tell you everything."

When dinner was finished, Armstrong, the Professor, and the Missus went into the parlor, where a warm fire was burning.

"You know that I've been traveling abroad," said Armstrong. "Well, it was in India that I stumbled across this cursed thing."

Armstrong reached into his pocket and pulled out a small and shriveled thing.

He held onto it tightly, but the Professor and Mrs. Shepherd could see that it was a tiny hand about six inches long, dark and hairy and shriveled.

Mrs. Shepherd shuddered.

"What is it?" the Professor asked.

"Better I should never have set eyes on this cursed thing," Armstrong said. "This is the Monkey's Paw. It is a magical thing that will grant its owner three wishes."

"Nonsense," said the Professor. He was a scientific man who did not believe in such superstition.

"I think three wishes would be rather nice," said Mrs. Shepherd.

"Yes," agreed Armstrong, "but the Monkey's Paw is a curse. Its wishes always come out wrong. It has made me into the wreck that you see standing here."

"Why don't you just wish things back the way they were?" asked Mrs. Shepherd.

"I wish I could," Armstrong said. "But it's too late. I've used my three wishes. I can't even throw the thing away."

"Why not?" Mrs. Shepherd asked.

"Part of the curse. It must be given willingly to someone."

"Well, I'll take it," said Mrs. Shepherd.

"No," said Armstrong. He grew pale. "You don't know what you're saying."

"Don't be a fool," Professor Shepherd said. "It's all in your imagination Armstrong. Give the thing to my wife and maybe you'll sleep well tonight."

Reluctantly, Armstrong handed the thing to Mrs. Shepherd. "Be careful," he warned. "Don't use it. I beg you."

"Oh, pish," said Professor Shepherd.

For once his wife agreed, "Pish indeed."

That night, Armstrong went to bed early. Mrs. Shepherd and the Professor were finishing their glasses in front of the fire.

"What a strange story," said Mrs. Shepherd.

"Poor fellow," said the Professor. "He's gone quite mad."

"I wonder if the thing really works," said the Missus. She held the Monkey's Paw in her hand.

"Why don't you give it a try?" suggested the Professor.

"All right," said the Missus. "Want to be rich?"

"Of course," said her husband.

The wife held the Monkey's Paw in the palm of her right hand and said, "Monkey's Paw, Monkey's Paw, I wish that I was a rich woman."

The Monkey's Paw began to twitch. Mrs. Shepherd dropped it on the ground. Its fingers opened and closed three times, and then it was still.

"Did you see that?" said the wife.

"I'm not sure," said the husband.

Just then, there was a knock on the door.

"I wonder who that could be," said the husband.

It was the foreman from the steel mill where their son worked. He looked very sad.

"What's the matter?" said the wife.

"There's been an accident," said the foreman. "Your son fell into the machinery. Here is a check for a million pounds."

In shock, the husband took the check, and shut the door.

His wife burst into tears. "My son!" she cried. "My son!"

Her husband tried to comfort her, but she would not be still. She broke free from his hugs and ran back into the parlor. She snatched the Monkey's Paw from the floor.

"Monkey's Paw," she cried. "Monkey's Paw. I want my son alive and back at home."

Once again the Paw twitched, and again she dropped it onto the floor. It opened and closed its fingers three times and then was still.

They both looked toward the front door, but heard nothing.

"Cursed thing," said the Professor.

Just then there was a scraping at the door, a horrible sound like wet nails on a demon's chalkboard. There was a gurgling and a pounding and then a sluggish moan.

"My son!" cried the woman.

"No," shouted the Professor.

They both ran to the door. The wife tried to open it. The Professor bolted it tight.

"My son is home!" said the wife.

"Don't let him into the house," said the husband.

"It's cold outside," said the wife. "And dangerous. He wants his mother."

"No!" said the husband.

His wife pushed him away from the door and began to unlock the bolts.

The Professor ran back into the parlor and snatched up the Monkey's Paw.

"Monkey's Paw," he shouted. "Monkey's Paw, I wish my son was dead again."

The Paw twitched. Its fingers opened and closed three times, and then it was still.

At exactly that moment the pounding and groaning and scratching at the door stopped.

Mrs. Shepherd opened the door and found nothing but claw marks red with blood upon the door.

"My son!" she shouted.

Her husband stared at the Monkey's Paw and threw the cursed thing into the fire. It burned brightly for a moment, and then was gone.

When they went upstairs to wake Armstrong they found his bed empty, as if it had never been slept in.

The Professor tried to comfort his wife, but neither she nor he was ever again the same.

— *The End* —

70. The Red Snowman

I wrote this story with my son, Max, and my wife Alicia. We drew a picture of it first, and then made up the story between the three of us.

*O*nce upon a time, on top of a little mountain was a big silver castle. Inside the big silver castle lived a red snowman. He was a very happy snowman, and he loved to tend his garden.

One summer, the sun grew very hot, and the Red Snowman began to melt. He needed to get some more snow, otherwise he would melt away into nothing.

So, he quickly left his castle, climbed down the small mountain, and climbed up a big mountain.

The top of the big mountain was covered with snow. It was cold and deep, and best of all it was red.

But, as the snowman stepped toward the snow, out jumped a gigantic purple lion.

"Roar!" said the Purple Lion, "What do you want?"

"I just want some more snow," said the Red Snowman.

"More snow?" growled the lion. "Why do you need more snow?"

"So I don't melt away into nothing," said the Red Snowman.

"I see," said the Lion. "I will give you all the red snow you want, on one condition."

"What is that?" the snowman asked.

"You must travel into the great green forest," said the Lion. "Bring me whatever you find at the tallest tree in the forest."

The Red Snowman hurried down the mountain. He had never been in the great green forest and didn't know what he would find at the tallest tree.

Finally, he stood at the foot of the tallest tree in the forest.

There he saw a blue mouse.

"Ah ha!" said the Red Snowman. He snatched the Blue Mouse up.

"Eeek!" squeaked the Blue Mouse. "What are you doing?"

"I am taking you to the Purple Lion, so that he will give me more snow."

"More snow?" said the mouse "Why do you need more snow?"

"So that I don't melt away into nothing," said the snowman.

"If you bring me to the Purple Lion, he will eat me up in one bite," said the Blue Mouse.

"I don't know what to do." The snowman felt sad. "All I want is to go back to my castle and work in my garden."

"I have an idea," said the mouse. "At the top of the tallest tree is a golden apple. You could give that to the lion."

"Then he would give me some snow," said the snowman. "But snowmen can't climb trees."

"Mice can!" said the mouse. "I will bring you the golden apple on one condition. Take me back to your castle and let me work in your garden."

The snowman agreed. The mouse raced to the top of the tree and plucked the golden apple.

Then, the two friends hurried out of the great green forest and climbed the tall mountain.

"Roar!" said the Purple Lion when they reached the top. "What do you want?"

"I have traveled to the tallest tree in the great green forest," said the snowman. "I am bringing you what I found."

"The Blue Mouse!" said the lion, his teeth gleaming white. "I will eat him up in one bite."

"No!" squeaked the mouse.

"Not the mouse," said the snowman. "We have brought you a golden apple."

"I have always wanted a golden apple," said the Purple Lion. "You may have all the snow that you want."

"Thank you," said the Red Snowman.

"You're welcome," said the lion, politely.

The Red Snowman rolled and rolled around in the red snow, until he felt completely better.

Then he and the Blue Mouse traveled down the big mountain, and up the little mountain, until they reached the big silver castle.

"What a beautiful garden!" said the Blue Mouse.

"Welcome home," said the Red Snowman.

And together they lived happily ever after.

— *The End*—

71. The Brave Little Tailor

*O*ne morning, the Tailor sat at his bench, mending as usual. Since it was still early, he had his breakfast spread out on the table beside him. Jam and toast, tea and sugar. He sang quietly as he worked.

"Stitch it in. Stitch it out. Never mind. Don't you shout."

It must have been the sugar and the jam, but no sooner had he finished singing than he noticed that the workshop was filled with flies.

"What are you doing eating my breakfast?" shouted the Tailor.

He leaped up and took a great red swatch of cloth and slammed it down hard on the table.

All of the buzzing stopped in an instant. Pleased with himself, the Tailor looked down and saw that he had killed seven flies all in one blow."

206

"All in one blow!" he said to himself. "Seven with one blow! Now that is something special."

So, he took the red cloth and made himself a broad belt, and on the belt he stitched the words, "Seven with one blow!"

"Now, I am tired of tailoring," said the Tailor to himself. "Someone such as I, who can kill seven with one blow is surely destined for greater things. It's time I set off to see the world."

He knew he would be hungry, so he put a piece of soft cheese in one pocket. In his other pocket, he put his pet canary bird, who had always wanted to see the world herself. Then he put his cloth cutting knife in his belt, hung a sign on his door, and headed off down the road.

It wasn't long before the Tailor came across a great huge giant in the road.

"Fee, Fi, Fo, Fum, I smell the blood of an Englishman," said the Giant.

"I'm German," said the Tailor, "and you won't eat me. I have killed seven with one blow!"

The Giant saw the red belt and trembled. "You are clearly a great warrior," the Giant said. "But are you strong?"

"I can squeeze water from this stone," said the Tailor. He took the cheese from his pocket and squeezed it until water dripped through his fingers.

"You are strong," said the Giant, "but can you throw far?"

"I can throw this rock so high it will never come down!" said the Tailor. He took the canary bird from his pocket and threw it high up in the air, and it never came down.

"Yes, but can you lift heavy things?" asked the Giant.

"Why don't we move that tree?" asked the Tailor, pointing to the tallest tree in the forest."

The Giant tore the tree from the ground.

"I'll take the big part," the Tailor said, pointing toward the leaves, "and you take that skinny bit."

So, the Giant grabbed a hold of the trunk, and the tailor jumped into the branches of the tree. The Giant carried the tree for miles before dropping from exhaustion. Just before the tree hit the ground, the Tailor jumped out.

"What, tired already?" he said. "I'm hungry. Those cherries look good."

The Giant looked up and saw a tall cherry tree. He pulled down the top of the tree and asked the Tailor to hold it while he picked the cherries.

Of course as soon as the giant let go, the Tailor flew up into the air and landed on the other side of the tree.

"What," cried the Giant, "are you so weak that you can't hold a cherry tree?"

"Nonsense," said the Tailor. "I thought I saw some archers in the woods shooting at us, so I jumped over the tree. Can you do that?"

The Giant tried jumping over the cherry tree, but got stuck in the high branches.

Off the Tailor went down the road.

Not long afterward, he saw a great castle in the distance.

"I should like to live in a place like that," said the Tailor.

He marched right up to the door of the royal castle and knocked loudly.

"I would like to see the king," he shouted.

The guards saw that "Seven with one blow" was written on his sash and let him into the castle.

"Who is there?" said the King.

"He must be a great warrior," whispered the guards, "because he has killed seven with one blow."

"What do you want?" asked the King.

"Do you have a daughter?" asked the Tailor. "I would like to marry her."

The King began to laugh. Even though the tailor had an impressive looking sash, he was still dressed like a poor tailor. He carried only a cloth cutting knife in his belt and was rather short and scrawny.

"I have killed seven with one blow," the tailor said, "and defeated the Giant of the road. I will pass any test that you give me."

"Well," said the King, "since you're so good with giants. . . ."

He told the tailor that there were two wicked giants who were terrorizing the countryside. "If you kill them, then you shall have my daughter's hand in marriage."

The daughter, who was a beautiful princess peeked into the throne room and decided she liked what she saw. All the other suitors her father had brought her were haughty and fine, stuffed shirts, or muscle-bound dolts. This looked like an intelligent and gentle man, and she hoped that he would come home safe from defeating the giants.

"I shall do it, your Majesty," said the Tailor, who had spotted the Princess and decided that he too loved her at first sight.

So, off the Tailor went with a troop of men. Soon they heard the rumbling of the Giants off in the distance.

"I will go on by myself," said the Tailor.

He left his horse behind, and sneaked on ahead through the forest. Finally, he saw the two giants, fast asleep under a large oak tree. The Tailor filled his pockets with rocks, large and small, and climbed up the oak tree.

Then, when he was safely hidden in its leaves, he dropped a rock on one of the giant's heads.

"Ouch!" yelped the Giant. "Why did you hit me?"

"I didn't hit you," mumbled the second Giant. "Go back to sleep."

They both dozed off and a few minutes later, the Tailor dropped a second rock on the other giant.

"Oww!" screeched the second Giant. "Now you hit me!"

"Nonsense," snorted the first Giant. "You're just dreaming."

They settled down again, and as soon as they were asleep, the tailor took a big rock and dropped it right on the first Giant's nose.

"YAARGH!" shouted the first Giant, and he immediately began hitting the second Giant.

The two of them fought and fought, rolling in the dirt and tearing up trees all around. At last they fell, both of them quite dead. Giants, once they get angry have a hard time knowing when to stop.

The Tailor hopped down from his tree, thankful that they hadn't knocked over his tree. He stabbed them each a few times with his cloth cutting knife, and then went back to the soldiers.

"They're dead," said the Tailor. "You can look for yourselves."

When they all returned to the palace, the soldiers told the king that they had heard a terrible fighting, and that the brave hero had emerged from the forest without even a scratch!

The King still did not want this scrawny pip-squeak marrying his daughter, so he said, "Before you can get married, you have to catch the unicorn for a wedding present. It is very fast, and has gored hundreds of brave warriors with its sharp horn."

"No problem," said the Tailor.

Back into the woods he rode until he came near the clearing where the unicorn lived. "Wait here," he told the other soldiers. Taking nothing but a rope and a hatchet, he went on ahead.

In a short while, he saw the unicorn. It was a beautiful creature, a large horse with a long sharp horn sticking out of the front of its head.

As soon as it sniffed the tailor it charged.

Rather than fighting, the Tailor did the only sensible thing someone should do when faced with a charging unicorn.

He ran right up a tree.

The Unicorn was so startled that it didn't stop. It ran right into the tree, smack, and its horn got stuck there.

"There there," said the Tailor, "I won't hurt you. Here, let me help you get free."

First the tailor put the rope around the unicorn's neck, and then very carefully he chopped away at the tree until the Unicorn was free.

Then, of course, he rode the Unicorn back to the palace, where he presented her as a gift to his beautiful bride-to-be.

The King was furious. It's all luck, he thought. Still, he had given his promise.

The Tailor and the Princess were married, and you would think that they would have lived happily ever after, wouldn't you?

Well, they would have, except the King was still angry. He set his spy to keep an eye on the Tailor. One night, the spy heard the Tailor singing in his sleep.

"Stitch it in. Stitch it out," the Tailor sang as he snoozed. "Never mind. Don't you shout."

"He's a tailor," the spy said to the king.

"Then we shall kill him," said the king. He ordered all his men to stand in ambush outside the Tailor's bedroom.

Fortunately, the Tailor was well liked, and the guard who had initially admitted him to the palace told him of the plot.

That evening the Tailor only pretended to be asleep. Then he began to sing,

"Stitch it in. Stitch it out. Never mind. Don't you shout.

"I defeated the big giant in the road

"And killed two more as I was told

"Captured the unicorn don't you know

"And I killed seven with one blow

"Who is next? Come on out!

"Stitch it in. Stitch it out. Never mind. Don't you shout."

When the men laying the ambush for the Tailor heard this song, they ran off in absolute terror!

The King heard about this, and he became so suspicious that the Tailor was going to kill him that he worried himself to death. After that, the Tailor and his wife ruled the country for many years, and they lived happily ever after.

— *The End* —

72. Rapunzel

READER TIP: The story of Rapunzel seems ordinary enough, until the ending where the Prince loses his eyes and wanders blind for twenty years. If this is a bit harsh for your taste, skip the blinding and turn his wandering into a search.

*O*nce upon a time, a man and a woman lived in a small house near a beautiful walled garden. They had lived there for a long time and had never seen their neighbor, but somehow the garden grew and flowered and was tended to for many years.

The man and woman wanted a child more than anything else, and at long last the woman became pregnant. Like many pregnant women, she found herself hungry for strange things. She especially wanted a salad made from the leaves of the rampion from the garden next door.

The rampion, which is also called Rapunzel, looked beautiful. It had red and green leaves, and she knew that even its roots were edible and would taste rather like a beet.

The woman stopped eating altogether and grew sadder and sadder, and her husband came to her.

"What is the matter?" he asked.

"I am not hungry for anything except the rampion in the garden next door," she said.

"Then I will get some for you," the husband said.

The next night, in the bright light of the moon, he climbed over the high brick wall into the beautiful garden and picked a small basket full of the rampion.

He rushed back over the wall and gave the leaves to his wife, who immediately ate them happily.

The next night, however, she wanted more, and he was forced to make two trips over the wall just to satisfy her hunger.

The next night his wife was even hungrier still. It would take at least three trips to satisfy her appetite. The man was very nervous. He made the first two trips without incident.

But then, just as he was about to escape back over the wall, he felt a hand fall on his shoulder.

He spun about and saw an ugly old fairy standing there frowning.

"How dare you," she hissed, "steal into my garden and steal my rampion like a common thief. You shall die for that."

"Have mercy," he said. "Please. I had to. My wife saw your rampion, and she wanted it so much that she stopped eating. Both she and our child-to-be would have died."

"A daughter I think," said the fairy, thinking aloud. "All right, I will let you live on one condition."

"Anything," said the man.

"Your wife shall have as much rampion as she likes, and you shall live," said the fairy, "but when your daughter is twelve years old, you will give her to me. I will take care of her like a mother, but you shall never see her again."

The man, who was afraid for his life, agreed to everything. The wife cried horribly when she heard of the bargain, but she agreed that her husband had no choice.

When the child was born, the fairy appeared and gave her the name of Rapunzel. Then, she vanished and did not reappear until the girl's twelfth birthday.

"I have come for you, Rapunzel," said the fairy.

"I will go with you," said the girl, because she did not want her father to die.

The fairy shut Rapunzel up in the top of a glass tower in the middle of a forest. There was no door to this tower, and no stairs. There was only one window high up at the top, far too high for any ladder to reach.

When the fairy wanted to go up, she stood at the bottom and cried, "Rapunzel, Rapunzel, let down your golden hair."

Rapunzel, who had gloriously long hair, would unfasten her braids, loop them around a hook on the window, and drop the tresses down to the fairy who was standing far below. Then the woman would climb up the hair.

A number of years passed, and one day a prince riding through the forest happened to hear a song. It was faint, but beautiful, a girl's voice. He rode toward it and saw the tall tower. In the window, high up, he saw a beautiful girl, singing loudly and clearly to herself.

The Prince wanted to climb the tower, but he saw right away that it was impossible. There was no door. There were no stairs. He rode home,

saddened, but then every day he came back to the edge of the forest and listened to the girl sing, and waited for a glimpse of her face in the window.

One day while he was waiting, he saw the Fairy arrive and shout, "Rapunzel, Rapunzel, let down your golden hair."

He watched the wicked woman climb the hair and devised a plan.

The next day when it grew dark, he went to the tower and cried, "Rapunzel, Rapunzel, let down your golden hair."

Down came the beautiful golden hair, and up climbed the Prince.

At first, Rapunzel was frightened, because she didn't expect a man to climb in her window. The Prince, however, talked quietly and told her that he had heard her singing for many months and that he had fallen in love with her.

Rapunzel saw that her suitor was quite handsome and eloquent, and she fell in love with him as well.

The Prince asked her to marry him, and she immediately agreed.

"But how will you escape from this prison?" the Prince asked.

"Bring a length of silk with you every time you visit," Rapunzel said. I will weave a ladder, and when it is ready I will come with you."

So, the Prince returned every evening, and every evening they talked while she wove the ladder of silk.

One day, the fairy came to visit and began sniffing. "I smell a man. Who has been visiting you?"

"A handsome Prince," said Rapunzel boldly. "Why, when you climb my hair, do you weigh so much more than he does?"

The Fairy was outraged at this insult. She cut off all of Rapunzel's hair, and threw the poor girl into a desert far away from the forest.

She burned the silk ladder, and then, the Fairy waited in the tower for the Prince to arrive.

That evening, he rode his horse up to the base of the tower and cried, "Rapunzel, Rapunzel, let down your golden hair."

The Fairy tied Rapunzel's hair to the hook by the window and lowered it down. The Prince climbed the golden hair and was surprised. Instead of his beautiful Rapunzel, the he found himself face to face with the evil Fairy.

"You tried to steal my prize," the Fairy cried, "but the golden bird is no longer singing in her nest. She is gone, far far away, and you will never see her again."

All at once, the Prince drew his sword and slew the Fairy. Only afterwards did he realize that he had forgotten to ask her where he could find his Rapunzel.

The Prince, in agony, jumped from the high tower, and while he did not die from the fall, he fell into a bush of thorns, which blinded him.

He wandered, blind through the forest bemoaning his fate, and searching for the loss of his dear wife.

For ten years he roamed the world, until at last he came to the desert where Rapunzel lived with the two twins she had given birth to, a boy and a girl.

From far away, the Prince heard singing, and as he drew closer, he became more and more certain that it was his beloved.

When Rapunzel saw him, she recognized him immediately, hugging him, kissing him, and crying.

Two of her tears fell in his eyes, and immediately he could see again.

The Prince led Rapunzel and his family back to his kingdom and together they lived happily ever after.

— The End —

73. The Boy and the Gold Pieces

$\mathcal{M}$any years ago in a land far away from here lived a boy who was very, very poor. His father had no job, and his mother had no job. Sometimes, when the father got work, they would eat beans. Sometimes when the mother got work, they would eat bread, but it was only rarely that the mother and father found work at the same time. And then, the boy was left in charge of his five brothers and sisters.

One afternoon, the boy decided that he would find a job and make enough money for his entire family to live for many, many years. He had heard that in the big city there were many opportunities for people to make money, so he traveled there. It was a

long and difficult trip. He had to walk the whole way, and by the time he arrived he was very hungry. But he did not have any money. His clothes were old and tattered, and he was very, very dirty.

Everyone in the city walked past him as if he did not exist. They ignored him or, if they did see him, quickly turned away.

At last, a young girl, not much older than the boy, came up and gave him a copper.

"No," the boy said. "I will not take this."

"Why not?" asked the girl.

"I am not a beggar," the boy said. "I have come to the city to make my fortune. My family is very hungry, and I would like to find work to support them."

The girl thought this was wonderful, and she clapped her hands together. "I know just the right person you should meet," she said. "Come with me."

She led him through the streets of the crowded city until they came to a large building. It had stone columns and a pair of heavy brass doors.

"Surely you are not going to arrest me," the boy cried. He thought the building was a jail.

"No no," laughed the girl. "This is the bank where my father works. He will certainly help you get a job."

She led him inside, and all at once the boy was amazed. Never had he seen ceilings so high. And the ceilings were painted with pictures of factories and farms. On the walls were portraits of imposing-looking men. One whole wall had a bank of tellers, people who sat behind tall glass windows, and took deposits and cashed checks.

"Follow me," the girl said.

The boy followed, very conscious of the shabbiness of his clothing, and the dirt that he still wore from his travels.

Finally, the girl led him into a large room with deep red carpeting. Inside was a very imposing man. He looked just like all the other men in the portraits on the walls. He had white hair and big bushy side burns. His mustache drooped, and his mouth seemed to be frozen in a perpetual scowl.

But he smiled when he saw the girl, and he laughed softly when she gave him a kiss on the cheek.

"Father," said the girl, "this boy has traveled a long way because he wants to get a job. I offered him a copper, but he said that he would not beg. He wants to work. He has a large family that is very poor and he would like to support them."

The father's scowl returned. "Do you know who I am?" he asked.

"No, sir," said the boy.

"Well, he's polite at least," thought the father.

Then he said, "I am the president of this bank. I understand that you want a job."

"Oh, yes, sir," said the boy, his face brightening. "Please, I would like a job. I may not look like much, but I can read and I can count, and I can follow directions, and. . . ."

"Slow down," said the father. "First I have a test for you. Come with me."

The man stood up, and the boy followed him into a little back room.

The old man showed him a table that held a beautiful crystal pitcher that was nearly filled with gold pieces. The boy's eyes widened in amazement. He had never seen so many gold pieces in his entire life. One gold piece would feed his family for two months. The pitcher itself might give them food enough for ten or twenty years!

"You may take as many gold pieces as you can hold in your hand," said the old man.

The boy raced to the pitcher and reached his hand in.

He grabbed as many gold pieces as he could possibly hold, but when he tried to pull his hand out, he found it was stuck in the neck of the pitcher.

He immediately burst into tears. A handful of gold coins would feed his family for a long time, and he did not want to let go.

Then he realized something. If he broke the pitcher all the coins would spill out, but he could still hold onto the ones he had.

He lifted the pitcher up high above the table. Perhaps he would cut himself, but any pain would be worth it to help his family.

Then, just as he was about to send the pitcher crashing down on the table he stopped himself. One by one, he let go of the gold pieces. At last, sadly, he removed his hand from the neck of the pitcher, completely empty.

"You know," said the girl's father, "if you had been satisfied with only half a handful, you could have withdrawn your hand easily."

"Yes," said the boy, "but I did not come here to beg or to receive charity."

He picked up the crystal pitcher with one hand, and poured gold pieces into his other hand. "I came here to show you that I was smart and could work for you," he said. He looked at the gold pieces in his hand, and then one by one dropped them back into the crystal pitcher.

The old man looked very pleased. "No, no, don't put them all back."

"I won't take charity, sir," said the boy.

"Then consider that gold piece an advance against your pay," the man said. "I can't have my youngest clerk looking like a ragamuffin."

The boy was overjoyed! He worked hard and sent money back to his family, and his mother and father and all of his brothers and sisters came to live with him in the city. Then, when he was old enough, he married the old man's daughter. In time, he became the manager and eventually the president of the bank.

If you go down to the bank, perhaps you will see his portrait hanging on the wall. He is the one who doesn't frown quite as much as all the others.

— The End —

74. Clever Doris

Once upon a time, there was girl named Clever Doris. She lived on the edge of town with her mother and father. One day, a merchant came to town and said that he was looking for a clever girl to marry. Of course everyone in town said that he should immediately marry Clever Doris.

The merchant (whose name was Stanley) invited Clever Doris and her family back to his house for dinner. When they were finished eating, he asked Doris to go into the basement and fetch the ice cream from the freezer for dessert.

Clever Doris went into the basement, opened up the freezer door, and was just about to take the ice cream out when she saw something that made her very sad.

She looked up over the freezer and saw that the ceiling was loose and rotting. She immediately began to cry.

"If I marry Stanley," she thought, "and we have a child named Hans, and he grows up and I send him into the basement to get ice cream from the freezer, the ceiling will fall down on his head and kill him."

She sat down on the floor in front of the freezer and began to cry.

Now, everyone upstairs was waiting for their dessert.

"I wonder what could have happened to Doris," said her father.

"Maybe she's stubbed her toe," suggested Stanley.

"Why don't I go down and have a look," said her mother.

Her mother went downstairs and saw Clever Doris sitting on the floor in front of the open freezer crying her eyes out.

"What is wrong, Doris?" said her mother. "Why are you crying."

"Because," Doris said, "If I marry Stanley, and we have a child named Hans, and he grows up and I send him into the basement to get ice cream from the freezer, the ceiling will fall down on his head and kill him."

"That's terrible!" said her mother. "What a clever girl you are!" And she too sat down and began to weep.

After a while, since the mother did not come upstairs either, the two men began to worry.

At last, Stanley said, "Perhaps I should see if everything is all right."

"Nonsense," said Doris's father. "I'll do it. I'm sure they're just having a little chat."

Imagine his surprise when he climbed down the steps to the basement and saw his daughter and his wife sitting in front of the open freezer, bawling like two newborn babies!

"What's the matter, Doris?" said her father. "Are you all right? Why are you crying?"

"Because," said Doris, "If I marry Stanley, and we have a child named Hans, and he grows up and I send him into the basement to get ice cream from the freezer, the ceiling will fall down on his head and kill him."

"Oh my goodness!" said her father. "What a clever girl you are!" And he too sat down and began to weep.

At last, Stanley the Merchant grew tired of sitting alone and waiting for his ice cream. He poked his head down through the basement door and said, "Is everything all right?"

Imagine his surprise when all he heard were the bawling of Doris and her mother and her father.

"Perhaps the ceiling has collapsed and they are all dying!" thought Stanley, and he raced downstairs to check on his guests.

He found them all sitting in front of the open freezer, quite well but crying like three newborn babies.

"Why are you all crying?" Stanley asked. "Are you hurt? Is something wrong?"

"If I marry you, Stanley," said Doris, "and we have a child named Hans, and he grows up and I send him into the basement to get ice cream from the freezer, the ceiling will fall down on his head and kill him."

"You're kidding?" said Stanley.

"No," wailed the poor girl.

"No," cried the Doris's mother. "She's far too clever."

"It's such a shame," said her father.

"There, there," Stanley said, patting the girl on the shoulder. "You are very clever indeed. We will have the carpenters come and fix the ceiling. Then when we get married and have a child named Hans, and he grows up, and you send him down into the basement to get ice cream from the freezer the ceiling will NOT fall down on his head and kill him."

"You mean it?" Clever Doris said, jumping to her feet.

"Yes, I will marry you tomorrow," said the Stanley. "You are a very sweet and caring person, and I love you."

They hugged and kissed, and Doris's parents hugged and kissed each other.

They had a big wedding and lived happily until. . . .

— *The End* —

75. How Clever Doris Lost Herself

*S*everal months after Clever Doris married Stanley the Merchant, Stanley had to go away on a business trip. They had had a beautiful wedding, with a lot of cake and ice cream, and then taken a long long honeymoon. This was the first time that the new bride and groom would be apart.

"Don't go," said Clever Doris. "What will happen if you travel to another country, and get lost, and forget where you live? Then you won't be able to come back home, and if we have a child named Hans he will never ever get to know his father."

"Clever Doris," said Stanley the Merchant, "I will never forget where I live, and I will always come back home to where I live. If we have a child named Hans I will always come home and play with him. I promise. Besides, I'm not going to another country, only a town a few miles away. I'll be back tonight."

Doris was very much reassured by Stanley's promise, and she began to smile and hum.

"Tell me, Doris," Stanley said. "What will you do while I am away?"

"I think that I'll go into the garden and pick the tomatoes," Doris said. "That way I can make a nice tomato sauce for dinner."

"Sounds delicious," Stanley said, and he kissed his wife on the nose.

Now, Clever Doris had never been much of a housekeeper. She was studying to become a lawyer and had never really paid attention in Home Economics Class.

"I'll have to pick the tomatoes before I make the sauce," Doris said. "But perhaps I should have some lunch and then go out into the garden. What shall I do? Shall I eat my lunch first or pick the tomatoes first? I think I'll eat my lunch first."

Clever Doris made herself some lunch and ate it all up. Then she washed the dishes and put them all away.

Then she went out into the garden and looked at all the tomato plants.

"There are far too many tomatoes to carry in my arms," she said. "What should I do? Should I pick them first or go back to the house and get a basket? I think I'll go back to the house and get a basket first."

Clever Doris went back to the house and got two baskets to fill with tomatoes.

By the time she got back to the garden, she was feeling very tired.

"Oh my I feel tired," she said. "Should I pick the tomatoes first, or should I go to sleep and take a nap? I think I'll take a nap first."

So, she found a soft spot in between the tomato plants and lay down. The ground was very comfortable and the sun very warm. In a few minutes, Clever Doris fell asleep.

Now, Stanley the Merchant's business went much quicker than he had expected, and he came home from his trip early.

"Doris," he said when he arrived at the house. "Doris, where are you?"

But he heard no answer. He searched the house from top to bottom, taking extra care to check in the basement and make sure that Doris wasn't sitting in front of the freezer. (Even though they'd had the ceiling fixed, he wanted to make certain.)

At last, he went into the kitchen and noticed that there weren't any dirty dishes. "Perhaps," he thought, she's been out in the garden all day. "What a hard-working wife I've found. She did not even come home to eat lunch!"

He went out into the garden to see if she needed his help and was very surprised to find that his wife had not picked a single tomato and had fallen asleep in between the rows.

He hurried to the tool shed and found a pair of tiny bells. Then he sneaked back to the garden. Doris was still asleep. So, Stanley tied the bells to Doris's shoes. She didn't even stir.

Then Stanley ran back home and waited for Doris.

The sun set, and still Doris was not home, so Stanley went up to bed.

Finally, when it was completely dark, Clever Doris woke up.

"Oh, my, I've been asleep a long time," she said. "I wonder if everything is all right."

But when she stood up the bells tied to her shoes jingled, and she became quite worried. "My feet don't jingle," Clever Doris said. She took two steps and heard a jingle with each step. "If my feet don't jingle, but I jingle every time I take a step then I must not be Clever Doris. Oh my!"

Clever Doris immediately ran back to the house, her feet jingling with every step.

Now, Stanley the Merchant heard her jingling steps approaching, and he locked the door.

Clever Doris was surprised to find the door locked, because she knew that she had left her keys inside. So, she knocked on the door.

"Who is it?" Stanley said.

"Clever Doris," Doris said.

"I don't think so," Stanley said. "Clever Doris is already inside. She is upstairs asleep in her bed."

Clever Doris was completely horrified. "Oh no," she said, "Then I'm not me. And if I'm not me, who am I?"

She ran from door to door in the town, but when people heard the bells jingling on her feet they would not let her in.

Then, she ran out of the town, and no one there heard from her until. . . .

— *The End* —

76. Clever Doris Returns

*T*en years went by, and Stanley the Merchant grew very rich. But he was also very lonely. His wife, Clever Doris, had fallen asleep in the garden, and he'd played a mean trick on her and she'd run away. He'd waited a long time for her to return and had searched the countryside for signs of her, but none were found. Eventually, he decided that he wanted to remarry.

Stanley put ads in the local newspapers announcing that he intended to marry the cleverest woman that he could find.

All the neighbors rolled their eyes. "There he goes again," they said. "Won't Stanley ever learn?"

Stanley paid them no attention. Soon, he began receiving applications. Some of the women were brilliant. They had invented wonderful things. Others had written long and interesting books. Stanley invited them over for dinner (one at a time) and asked them to go into the basement to get some ice cream for him. Some of them refused, and some of them were very puzzled when he asked why they were back so soon. None of them fell in love with Stanley, and Stanley didn't fall in love with any of them.

Then, one day there was a knock at the door.

230

Stanley opened the door and saw a young boy.

"What do you want?" the boy said.

Stanley was quite surprised by this. Usually when you open the door, you're the one to ask, "What do you want?" not the stranger standing outside.

Still, Stanley decided to take the boy at face value. "I'm looking for a wife."

"I heard you were already married," said the Boy.

Now, how can he know that, Stanley wondered.

"Yes," Stanley said. "I was married to Clever Doris, but I played a mean trick on her once and she ran away. I searched everywhere for her, but never found her. Now I think enough time has passed, and I would like to get married."

"My mother is very clever," said the Boy. "I'll bet you a million dollars that you will be married to her."

"I'm sure your mother is very clever," Stanley said, humoring the boy, "but a million dollars is all the money that I have. Besides, what would I get if I win the bet?"

"Hmm," thought the boy. "Then I would be your son and do whatever you ask me to."

The merchant, who had always wanted a son, thought this was a fine idea. "All right, boy, it's a deal."

They shook hands.

"Now you must come and meet my mother," said the boy.

"All right," Stanley said. And he followed the boy down the road. "What is your name?"

"My name is Hans," the boy said.

"I have always wanted to have a son named Hans," Stanley said, remembering his wife, Clever Doris.

The boy, Hans, led Stanley through town and back, up and down every street.

"Where are we going?" said Stanley

"To my mother's house," said Hans. "We're almost there."

At last, the boy led Stanley up to a door. "Here is my mother's house."

"But this is my house!" Stanley said.

"Open the door, then," Hans said.

Stanley patted his pockets, but realized that he had forgotten his keys. "This is foolish. If you are a robber, I will have you arrested."

"I am not a robber," said the boy. "I am your son Hans."

Hans knocked on the door. "Mother, mother, let us in. I've brought your husband home."

"No one will answer," Stanley said.

But no sooner had he spoken then he heard a strange jingling sound.

At first he thought it was a ghost, and he became very frightened. Then the door opened and he found himself face to face with his wife, Clever Doris.

"Doris," Stanley said. "You're home!"

"Of course I'm home," Clever Doris said. "I've been home all day. Where have you been?"

"This boy has led me all over the town, up and down every street," Stanley said.

"That boy is your son, Hans," Doris said.

Stanley looked at the boy with a look of surprise. "But where have you been? I looked everywhere for you?"

"I went to law school," Doris said. "And I raised Hans on my own. I decided that you were much too mean to me."

"I'm very sorry," Stanley said, softly. "I wish you had let me apologize a long time ago."

"I came back," Doris said, "only because I heard you wanted to get married again."

"I do," Stanley cried.

"Well," said the boy, "You are already married to my mother! You owe me a million dollars!"

"I do indeed," said Stanley, and he patted the boy on the head.

Doris put her hands on her hips. "Pay the boy, Stanley."

"What?" Stanley said, "You can't be serious."

"A contract is a contract." Clever Doris waited. "I'm not going to let you back inside until you pay him."

At last, Stanley drew out his checkbook and wrote a check to Hans for a million dollars.

As soon as he paid the boy, Hans ran up and hugged his father tightly. Then Doris hugged Stanley as well.

"Will you forgive me?" Stanley asked.

"Of course," both Clever Doris and Clever Hans said.

Clever Hans went into the basement, went to the freezer, and got some ice cream to celebrate.

And then, at long long last, they lived happily (if a bit mixed up) ever after.

— *The End* —

77. Rip Van Winkle

Washington Irving

*M*any years ago, high in the Catskill mountains lived a peaceable sort of fellow named Rip Van Winkle. Now, Rip Van Winkle was not much pestered by an abundance of ambition. Nor did he have the hard habit of working his fingers to the bone, as his wife was frequently wont to complain. In fact, if you gave Dame Van Winkle half a chance, she could itemize a laundry list of her husband's grievances until your ears turned blue.

Around the village, Rip Van Winkle was a very popular fellow. The women took pity on him for his browbeating wife. The children would shout with joy whenever he approached. He played games with them, taught them to fly kites and shoot marbles, and told them long stories of ghosts, witches, and Indians.

If Rip had one failing it was his uncanny ability to find employment and business anywhere but on his own farm. He could sit on a wet rock with a long rod and fish all day without a single nibble. He would carry his musket on his shoulder for hours, trudging with his dog, Wolf, through woods and swamps, and up hill and down dale, to shoot a few squirrels or wild pigeons. He would never refuse to assist a neighbor even in the roughest toil and was a foremost man at all country frolics for husking Indian corn or building stone fences. The women of the village asked him to run their errands and to do such little odd jobs as their less obliging husbands would not do for them.

In a word Rip was ready to attend to anybody's business but his own. Keeping his farm in order, he found it impossible.

In fact, he declared it was of no use to work on his farm; it was the most pestilent little piece of ground in the whole country. Everything about it went wrong and would go wrong, in spite of him. His fences were continually falling to pieces; his cow would either go astray or get among the cabbages. Weeds were sure to grow quicker in his fields than anywhere else. The rain always made a point of setting in just as he had some outdoor work to do. It was the worst conditioned farm in the neighborhood.

Even his children were ragged and wild as if they belonged to nobody. His son Rip, an urchin who looked just like the elder Rip, promised to inherit the habits, with the old clothes of his father.

Still, Rip Van Winkle was happy. If left to himself, he would have whistled life away in perfect contentment. But his wife kept continually shouting in his ears about his idleness, his carelessness, and the ruin he was bringing on his family. Morning, noon, and night, her tongue was incessantly going, and everything he said or did was sure to produce a torrent of household eloquence.

Rip's only friend at home was his dog Wolf. As frequently as possible, both Rip and Wolf would sneak out of the house and sit on the bench outside the town's inn, under the sign with the picture of His Majesty George the Third. There they would to sit in the shade through a long lazy summer's day, talking listlessly over village gossip or telling endless sleepy stories about nothing with other lazy worthies like

Derrick Van Bummel, the schoolmaster, or Nicholas Vedder, the landlord of the inn.

Still, Dame Van Winkle wouldn't let Rip lounge about for long. Soon enough, she chased him from the inn and set him back to work.

Now, one fine autumn day, Rip put his musket on his shoulder, whistled Wolf to his side, and climbed up to one of the highest parts of the Catskill mountains. He was after his favorite sport of squirrel shooting, and the still solitudes had echoed and reechoed with the reports of his gun.

At last, panting and fatigued, he threw himself on a green knoll and snoozed peaceably.

"Rip Van Winkle!" said a voice. And he woke with a start. Was that his wife, calling him all this way? Surely it was only his imagination, still it was time to be on his way. He stood up and was about to head back into the village when he heard the voice hallooing again. "Rip Van Winkle! Rip Van Winkle!"

He looked round, but could see nothing but a crow winging its solitary flight across the mountain. At the same time, though, Wolf bristled up his back, and gave a low growl.

Then Rip saw a strange, short, square-built man lumbering up the trail toward him. He had thick bushy hair and a grizzled beard. His trousers were of the antique Dutch fashion: breeches with buttons down the sides and bunches at the knees. He bore on his shoulder a stout keg that seemed full of liquor and made signs for Rip to approach and assist him with the load.

Rip, quite naturally fell in, and lifted the barrel to his own shoulder. Then, he followed the short fellow up into the mountains, wondering where it was they might be going.

As they ascended, Rip every now and then heard long rolling peals, like distant thunder, that seemed to issue out of a deep ravine, or rather cleft, between lofty rocks, toward which their rugged path conducted. He paused for an instant, but supposing it to be the muttering of one of those transient thunder showers that often take place in mountain heights, he proceeded.

Finally, they came to a small hollow in the mountains, like a small amphitheater, surrounded on all sides by perpendicular precipices. Strangest of all were the fellows he saw in the amphitheater.

On a level spot in the center was a company of odd-looking personages playing at nine-pins. They were all dressed in a quaint, outlandish fashion; some wore short doublets, others jerkins, with long knives in their belts, and most of them had enormous breeches, of a style similar to that of the guide's. Their faces, too, were peculiar: one had a large beard, broad face, and small piggish eyes: the face of another seemed to consist entirely of nose and was surmounted by a white sugar-loaf hat, set off with a little red cock's tail. They all had beards of various shapes and colors. There was one who seemed to be the commander. He was a stout old gentleman, with a weather-beaten countenance; he wore a high crowned hat and feather.

What seemed particularly odd to Rip was that though these folks were evidently amusing themselves, they maintained the gravest faces, the most mysterious silence, and were, withal, the most melancholy party of pleasure seekers he had ever witnessed. Nothing interrupted the stillness of the scene but the noise of the balls, which, whenever they were rolled, echoed along the mountains like rumbling peals of thunder.

As Rip and his companion approached them, the men suddenly stopped their play and stared at him. Rip's knees knocked, and his heart turned cold. The guide poured the contents of the keg into large flagons and asked Rip to help him serve.

All drank deeply, and even Rip raised his glass. One taste provoked another; and he visited the flagon so often his senses were overpowered, his eyes swam in his head, his head gradually declined, and he fell into a deep sleep.

On waking, he found himself on the green knoll whence he had first seen the old man of the glen. He rubbed his eyes—it was a bright sunny morning. The birds were hopping and twittering among the bushes, and the eagle was wheeling aloft, and breasting the pure mountain breeze.

"Surely," thought Rip, "I have not slept here all night." He recalled the occurrences before he fell asleep—the strange man with a keg of liquor, the mountain ravine, the wild retreat among the rocks, the woebegone party at nine-pins, the flagon—"Oh! that flagon! that wicked flagon!" thought Rip, "what excuse shall I make to Dame Van Winkle!"

He looked round for his gun, but in place of the clean, well-oiled musket, he found an old firelock lying by him, the barrel encrusted with rust, the lock falling off, and the stock worm-eaten. Perhaps those fellows had played a trick on him, poisoning his drink and robbing his gun. Wolf, too, had disappeared, but he might have strayed away after a squirrel or partridge. Rip whistled and shouted, but all in vain; the echoes repeated his whistle and shout, but no dog was to be seen.

As he rose to walk, he found himself stiff in the joints and wanting in his usual activity. "These mountain beds do not agree with me," thought Rip.

He again called and whistled after his dog; he was answered only by the cawing of a flock of idle crows. What was to be done? The morning was passing away, and Rip felt famished. He grieved to give up his dog and gun; he dreaded to meet his wife; but it would not do to starve among the mountains. He shook his head, shouldered the rusty firelock, and, with a heart full of trouble and anxiety, turned his steps homeward.

As he approached the village he met a number of people, but none whom he knew, which somewhat surprised him, for he had thought himself acquainted with every one in the country round. Their clothing, too, seemed different. They all stared at him in surprise and stroked their chins. The constant recurrence of this gesture induced Rip, involuntarily, to do the same, when, to his astonishment, he found his beard had grown a foot long!

A troop of strange children ran at his heels, hooting after him, and pointing at his gray beard. The very village was altered; it was larger and more populous. There were rows of houses that he had never seen before. Strange names were over the doors, strange faces at the windows—everything was strange.

It was with some difficulty that he found the way to his own house, which he approached with silent awe, expecting every moment to hear the shrill voice of Dame Van Winkle. He found the house gone to decay—the roof fallen in, the windows shattered, and the doors off the hinges. A half-starved dog that looked like

Wolf was skulking about it. Rip called him by name, but the cur snarled, showed his teeth, and passed on. This was an unkind cut indeed. "My very dog," sighed poor Rip, "has forgotten me!"

The house was empty, forlorn, and apparently abandoned. He called loudly for his wife and children. The lonely chambers rang for a moment with his voice, and then all again was silence.

He now went to his old resort, the village inn, but it too was gone. Instead he found a large hotel, and even its sign was strange. Gone was the ruby face of King George. The red coat was changed for one of blue, and the new fellow's head was decorated with a cocked hat. Underneath was painted in large characters, GENERAL WASHINGTON.

"Are you a Federal or Democrat?" said one fellow who wore a cocked hat.

"What brings you to the election with a gun on your shoulder?" asked another. "Do you mean to breed a riot in the village?"

"Alas! gentlemen," cried Rip, somewhat dismayed, "I am a poor, quiet man, a native of this place, and a loyal subject of the King, God bless him!"

Here a general shout burst from the bystanders—"A Tory! a Tory! a spy! a refugee! hustle him! away with him!"

At last, the crowd was quieted. The first fellow asked, "If you are from this village, then who are your neighbors?"

Rip thought for a moment, and inquired, "Where's Nicholas Vedder?"

"Nicholas Vedder! why, he is dead and gone these eighteen years! There was a wooden tombstone in the churchyard that used to tell all about him, but that's rotten and gone too."

"Where's Brom Dutcher? or Van Bummel, the schoolmaster?"

"They went off to the army at the beginning of the war. Dutcher never came back. Van Brummel is a great militia general and is now in Congress."

Rip's heart died away. At last he cried out in despair, "Does nobody here know Rip Van Winkle?"

"Oh, Rip Van Winkle!" exclaimed two or three, "Oh, to be sure! that's Rip Van Winkle yonder, leaning against the tree."

Rip looked, and beheld a precise counterpart of himself, as he went up the mountain: apparently as lazy, and certainly as ragged. The poor fellow was now completely confounded. He doubted his own identity and whether he was himself or another man.

"Here," said the man with the cocked hat. "Who are you? What's your name?"

"I'm not sure," said the old fellow.

At this critical moment a fresh comely woman pressed through the throng to get a peep at the gray-bearded man. She had a chubby child in her arms, which, frightened at his looks, began to cry. "Hush, Rip," cried she, "hush, you little fool; the old man won't hurt you." The name of the child, the air of the mother, the tone of her voice, all awakened a train of recollections in his mind. "What is your name, my good woman?" asked he.

"Judith Gardenier."

"And your father's name?"

"Ah, poor man, Rip Van Winkle was his name, but it's twenty years since he went away from home with his gun, and never has been heard of since—his dog came home without him; but whether he shot himself or was carried away by the Indians, nobody can tell. I was then but a little girl."

Rip had but one question more to ask; but he put it with a faltering voice: "Where's your mother?"

"Oh, she too had died but a short time since; she broke a blood vessel in a fit of passion at a New-England peddler."

There was a drop of comfort, at least, in this intelligence. The honest man could contain himself no longer. He caught his daughter and her child in his arms. "I am your father!" cried he "Young Rip Van Winkle once—old Rip Van Winkle now! Does nobody know poor Rip Van Winkle?"

All stood amazed, until an old woman, tottering out from among the crowd, put her hand to her brow, and peering under it in his face for a moment, exclaimed, "Sure enough! it is Rip Van Winkle—it is himself! Welcome home again, old neighbor. Why, where have you been these twenty long years?"

Rip's story was soon told, for the whole twenty years had been to him but as one night.

The company broke up and returned to the more important concerns of the election. Rip's daughter took him home to live with her. She had a snug, well-furnished house, and a stout cheery farmer for a husband, whom Rip recollected for one of the urchins that used to climb upon his back. As to Rip's son and heir, who was the ditto of himself, seen leaning against the tree, he was employed to work on the farm; but evinced an hereditary disposition to attend to any thing else but his business.

For many years thereafter, Rip Van Winkle (the elder) could be found lounging about outside the new village inn, under the sign of George Washington, retelling the story of his strange travel into the mountains, and the odd fellows he met there, playing nine-pins that echoed like thunder.

— *The End* —

78. Little Red Riding Hood

READER TIP: Here is another fine story to play around with voices. Children especially love it when the wolf pretends to be Grandma.

Once upon a time there lived a little girl named Red Riding Hood. She was called "Little Red Riding Hood" because she always wore a red hood that her grandmother had made for her.

Little Red Riding Hood was a very happy girl. She lived on one side of the great forest with her mother and father. Her grandmother lived on the other side of the forest, and Little Red Riding Hood and her parents often visited her.

One day, Little Red Riding Hood's mother came up to her and said, "Little Red Riding Hood, your grandmother is feeling poorly. I think we should make a basket of goodies for you to take to her."

"Sounds like a great idea," Little Red Riding Hood said.

So Little Red Riding Hood and her mother began to bake and cook. They baked chocolate chip cookies and a chocolate cake and a chocolate cream pie. Chocolate, if you haven't already guessed, was her grandmother's absolute favorite. They also made her a big container of chicken soup so that she would feel better.

"Little Red Riding Hood," said Little Red Riding Hood's mother, "Why don't you go out and pick some flowers for your grandmother. You know how much she likes flowers."

So, Little Red Riding Hood went outside and picked all kinds of beautiful flowers to take to her grandmother. When she was finished, she came back inside and said, "I'm ready. Let's to go to Grandmother's house."

"I can't come with you today," said Little Red Riding Hood's mother. "I have to do some work on the Internet. But you're a big girl now, you can go through the woods by yourself. Just make sure that you stay on the path and don't talk with any strangers."

So, Little Red Riding Hood tied on her hood, picked up the basket and the pretty bouquet of flowers, and skipped off down the path to Grandmother's house.

Soon, she was deep in the forest, and she began to grow afraid. She had gone this way many, many times with her mother and her father, but she had never walked the whole path to her grandmother's house all by herself.

"I shouldn't be afraid," thought Little Red Riding Hood. "I'm a big girl now. I can take care of myself."

She began to sing, and as soon as she started to sing, she felt better.

But, not far from the path lived a wicked wolf. He heard the singing and thought, "Hmm, sounds like a little girl. I wonder if I can eat her for dinner."

The Wicked Wolf sneaked out of his lair and peered through the woods. There he saw Little Red Riding Hood skipping along the path, singing sweetly to the trees and the birds.

"Yes, indeed," the Wicked Wolf thought. "A yummy little girl. Hmm, I wonder where she's going."

The Wicked Wolf loped ahead and stepped out in front of Little Red Riding Hood.

"Hello there little girl," said the Wicked Wolf. "What is your name and where are you going?"

"My name is Little Red Riding Hood," said the young girl. "I'm going through the forest to visit my grandmother. She's feeling poorly, so I'm bringing her this basket of goodies filled with chocolate chip cookies and a chocolate cake and a chocolate cream pie, and chicken soup to help her feel better."

"Sounds yummy," said the Wicked Wolf, licking his lips. He was feeling very hungry. "Can I walk along with you?"

The wolf, you see, didn't dare attack Little Red Riding Hood on the path, but he thought he might convince her to stray, and then he'd get her!

"No thank you," said Little Red Riding Hood politely. "My mother told me not to talk with strangers. Good day to you."

"And good day to you," said the Wicked Wolf. He made a great bow and allowed Little Red Riding Hood to skip on past.

Now, the wolf had a plan. He waited until Little Red Riding Hood was well out of sight, and then he ran for a shortcut that he knew through the forest. He ran all the way to grandmother's house and got there well ahead of Little Red Riding Hood.

He knocked on the door.

"Who is it?" Little Red Riding Hood's grandmother asked.

The wolf coughed twice, and then cleared his throat. Then, in the sweetest voice he could possibly muster, the wolf said, "It is I, Little Red Riding Hood. I have brought you a basket of goodies, filled with chocolate chip cookies and a chocolate cake and a chocolate cream pie, and chicken soup to help you feel better."

"Mmm," said the old lady. "Chocolate is my favorite!"

She opened the door and was quite surprised to see the Wicked Wolf standing on the steps, licking his lips.

Before Little Red Riding Hood's grandmother even had a chance to scream, the hungry wicked wolf opened his mouth and swallowed her whole.

"Now," he said to himself, "let's see if I can get the little girl and the basket of goodies as well."

He put on one of Little Red Riding Hood's grandmother's night shirts and night caps, pulled down all the window shades, and crawled into the bed.

In a little while, there was a knock at the door.

The wolf coughed twice and then cleared his throat. Then, in his best little old lady voice he said, "Who is it?"

"It is I, Little Red Riding Hood," came the young girl's voice. "I have brought you a basket of goodies, filled with chocolate chip cookies and a chocolate cake and a chocolate cream pie, and chicken soup to help you feel better."

"Mmm," said the Wicked Wolf. "Come in!"

Little Red Riding Hood opened the door and was surprised to find her grandmother in bed and all the window shades pulled down.

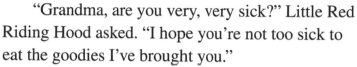

"Grandma, are you very, very sick?" Little Red Riding Hood asked. "I hope you're not too sick to eat the goodies I've brought you."

"Nonsense," said the Wolf in his old lady voice. "I'm very hungry. Come closer child."

"Why Grandma," said Little Red Riding Hood, "What big ears you have."

"The better to hear you with," said the Wolf.

"And Grandma," said Little Red Riding Hood, "What big eyes you have."

"The better to see you with," said the Wicked Wolf.

"But Grandma," said Little Red Riding Hood, "What a big nose you have."

"The better to smell you with, my sweet child. Come a little closer."

"Why Grandma," said the innocent Little Red Riding Hood, "What a big mouth you have, and what sharp pointy teeth."

"The better to eat you with!" cried the wolf. He lept out of bed and ate Little Red Riding Hood whole.

The wolf was so tired from all his eating that he immediately fell fast asleep.

Now, that would have been the end of Little Red Riding Hood and her grandmother, except for a fortunate coincidence.

At just that moment, a brave hunter was walking past Grandmother's house, and he happened to wonder why the shades were drawn in the middle of the day. He had heard that there was a wicked wolf in the neighborhood, and he wanted to warn the old lady to be careful.

The brave hunter knocked on the door, but there was no answer.

"Grandmother?" he said, opening the door just a crack. "Are you all right?"

When the light of the door fell on the wolf lying in the old woman's bed, wearing the old woman's bonnet and night shirt, the hunter knew exactly what he had to do.

He dragged the wolf outside, killed him, and cut open his stomach.

There, inside, safe and sound, very much alive, although very, very frightened, he found Little Red Riding Hood and her grandmother.

They cheered when they saw the hunter, and felt very relieved when they saw the body of the dead wolf.

Then, after a quick bath, Little Red Riding Hood, her grandmother, and the Brave Hunter sat down to a fine dinner of chocolate chip cookies and a chocolate cake and a chocolate cream pie, and chicken soup.

From then on, Little Red Riding Hood was very careful never to talk with strangers as she walked through the forest.

— The End —

79. The Tale of Ali Baba and the Forty Thieves

From the Arabian Nights

*L*ong ago in Persia there were two brothers, one named Kasim and the other Ali Baba.

Kasim was a rich man and quite miserly. He surrounded himself with gold and silks, ate nothing but the finest food, and slept on the softest pillows.

Ali Baba, however, was quite poor. He worked hard, but could not seem to earn more than just enough to live. He and his wife were frequently hungry and wore clothing so old that even the holes had holes.

One day when Ali Baba was cutting wood in the forest he heard the thunder of hoof beats approaching. Not knowing why so many horses should be traveling through the forest in such a hurry, Ali Baba hid himself behind some boulders.

In a little while, a band of armed robbers rode into the small clearing. Ali Baba could tell that they were thieves because each wore a wicked face and carried a sharp dagger.

Ali Baba shook in terror, afraid that the thieves would see him or even hear him breathing. To quiet himself, he began to count, and was even more terrified when he realized that there were forty thieves standing in the clearing not fifteen yards from where he hid.

The leader of the band of forty thieves climbed off his horse and stood in front of the largest boulder in the clearing.

"Open, Sesame!" he shouted.

There was a rumbling, and lo, the giant boulder rolled to one side, revealing a dark opening in the hill behind it.

The leader mounted his horse, and all forty thieves rode inside the cave, and then the rock rolled shut behind them.

Ali Baba did not dare to stir from his hiding place, because he had no idea when the thieves would return. So he waited and prayed that he would not be discovered.

A short time later the boulder opened up, and robbers rode out of the cave. The rock shut itself, and soon the robbers had vanished from sight and sound.

When at last he was sure they were gone, Ali Baba crept from his hiding place and stood in front of the giant boulder.

"I wonder if the magic words will work for me," he said. Ali Baba turned to the great rock and said, "Open, Sesame!"

Even though the two words were spoken quietly, the boulder rolled aside. Ordinarily, Ali Baba would have turned and fled, but his curiosity got the better of him. He quietly crept inside the cave.

As soon as he stepped inside, the boulder rolled back into place, and for a moment Ali Baba was certain that he was doomed.

"But I remember the magic formula to open it again," he said, and he proceeded deep into the cave.

Fully expecting to see nothing more than the bed rolls and camp-fires of the forty thieves, Ali Baba was surprised when he saw the great treasure piled about. From floor to ceiling were rich rugs, great chests filled with gold and silver, piles of gold, heaps of jewels. He had to be careful where he stepped for fear of slipping on diamonds or silk.

Ali Baba emptied the food out of his back pack, and filled it full with gold dinars. Then he loaded as many sacks as his mule could carry and dragged them to the mouth of the cave.

"Open, Sesame!" he cried. Again the great rock opened, and Ali Baba emerged into daylight a very rich man.

When Ali Baba arrived back home, his wife was surprised by the riches that her husband spilled onto the table.

"We must bury these," she said. "If people discover that we are suddenly wealthy they will ask where it came from and the thieves will certainly find out and kill us."

Ali Baba agreed, and he sent his wife next door to his brother's house for a measure, so that he could know how much treasure he had.

"Take care not to tell them what it is you are measuring," he warned. Even though he loved his brother, Ali Baba knew that Kasim was frequently heartless and cruel.

Ali Baba's wife went next door and asked Kasim's wife for a measure, but refused to say what purpose it would serve.

Kasim's wife knew that Ali Baba was poor and wondered what they could possibly want to measure. She poured a layer of honey in the bottom of the measure, knowing that whatever was measured, some would stick to the bottom.

The next morning when Ali Baba's wife returned the measure, Kasim's wife looked into the bottom and saw a gold piece stuck in the honey.

She immediately brought it to her husband, saying, "What riches your brother has that he must count his gold with a measure! You must find out where it has come from."

Kasim immediately went next door and asked Ali Baba where his new fortune came from. At first Ali Baba refused to tell, but Kasim threatened to turn his brother over to the authorities, so he told the story of the thieves, the boulder, and the two magic words.

When he was finished Kasim urged Ali Baba to give him detailed instructions on how to find the thieves' lair.

"But, Brother, I will share half of what I bring out with you," Ali Baba said.

"And what if something should happen to you?" Kasim warned. "Then your knowledge would be lost."

At last, with a heavy heart, Ali Baba told Kasim where to find the boulder.

The next morning, Kasim took a caravan of pack horses with him into the forest, and at length he made his way to the great boulder his brother had described.

He stood in front of the boulder and cried, "Open Sesame!"

As promised, the great stone rolled aside, and Kasim ran inside with a large blanket, which he intended to fill with treasure.

The size of the thieves' horde dazzled Kasim's eyes. Never had he, even in his wildest dreams, imagined such wealth. He began piling the blanket full of treasure, grabbing this and that until there was a great heap in the middle. Then he dragged it to the cave's mouth.

But the boulder had closed behind him, and Kasim had been so dazzled by the wealth that he had forgotten the magic words.

"Open Rye!" he cried. "Open Barley. Open, Oats!"

The rock did not budge.

"Open Millet! Open Rice! Open Buckwheat!"

He stood behind the closed door, shivering in terror as he listed every cereal and grain he could remember, save the one true password that would cause the door to open.

At last, just as he was beginning to give up all hope, the door opened.

Kasim grabbed the great blanket filled with treasure and tugged.

Then, into me cave, rode the forty thieves. In an instant they had captured Kasim. Trying to save his life, Kasim told them that it was not he, but his brother, Ali Baba who had first penetrated the secret of the cave.

The captain of the thieves nodded, and then ordered the cowardly brother put to the sword.

So ended the life of the wicked brother Kasim.

The captain ordered his lieutenant to go into town, find the house of Ali Baba, and mark its door. That evening the entire band would descend upon the house and kill everyone who lived within.

Now, when Kasim did not quickly return, Ali Baba worried that something had happened to him. He warned his wife and all his household to be wary.

It happened that Ali Baba had an intelligent slave girl named Morgiana. She was returning home from the market when she saw a suspicious-looking man marking the door to her master's home with a white piece of chalk. "Surely," she thought, "this can mean my master no good."

So, Morgiana took a piece of white chalk and marked the door to every house in the neighborhood.

That evening when the band of forty thieves rode into town they found that every door was marked and each house looked the same.

They rode from the town, even more determined to kill Ali Baba the next night.

This time, the captain of the thieves ordered his men to hide in great empty oil jars. These he strapped onto mules, so that soon he led a great caravan with forty jars. Thirty-nine jars held robbers, and the last was filled with oil.

Pretending to be a merchant, the captain of the thieves made his way into town and asked to be shown to Ali Baba's house. When he arrived there, he begged Ali Baba to offer him a place to sleep for the night.

Ali Baba, who was a kind soul and did not recognize the thieves' captain, invited the stranger inside.

They ate and talked late into the night, and the lamps began to burn low. Morgiana, knowing that the merchant sold oil went outside to replenish the lamps' supply.

Imagine her surprise when she heard a whisper from one oil jar, "Is it time yet?"

"No," the smart girl said, "not yet." So she went to every jar and told the thief waiting within. "Not time yet."

At last, she took the jar that truly was filled with oil and brought it into the kitchen. There she heated the oil to boiling, and then with great stealth, she crept back into the courtyard and smothered each of the thieves in the jars where they were hidden.

But, she knew that inside the house was the captain, the greatest thief of all.

She asked her master if she might perform the dance of the knives, an exotic dance that she had learned in a faraway land.

Ali Baba thought this would be wonderful entertainment and Morgiana began her dance.

Closer and closer to the dinner guest she danced, until at last she took one of her knives and plunged it into the thief's heart.

"Morgiana," cried Ali Baba, "what have you done?"

"Master," said the slave, "this is no merchant, but the captain of the thieves. He had brought his whole band hidden in the oil jars to kill you."

She led Ali Baba outside and showed him the dead thieves in the jars.

Ali Baba was touched by his slave's loyalty.

"Morgiana, today I free you from your bonds," he said. "And I give you my son to be your husband. You have saved my family and my life, and now you will become part of my family."

And so, O Auspicious King, Ali Baba and his family lived happily and in great wealth for many many years to come.

— The End —

80. Puss in Boots

Many years ago, in a land far far from here, a miller had three sons. His eldest two sons were lazy and spendthrift. They preferred to spend their days lounging about the house while the third son helped his father in the mill.

One day, the miller died, and he left behind only three things. To the oldest son he left his mill. To the second son he left a donkey. But to the youngest son he left only a cat.

The eldest son sold the mill and went off to seek his fortune. The second son rode away on his donkey to seek his fortune.

The youngest son stared at the cat and said, "What am I ever going to do with a cat?"

The cat heard the youngest son's words, stood up on its hind paws, and said, "Don't worry young master, I will take care of everything."

"A talking cat?" said the young boy. "I must be dreaming."

"Nonsense," said the cat, and to prove it he did a little jig. "If you will give me a cloth sack, a pair of boots and a nice cloak and a hat with a feather in it, I will bring you fame and fortune."

Well, thought the youngest son, what do I have to lose?

So he gave the cat a cloth sack, and stitched together a wonderful cloak and a hat for the cat, and made him two tiny boots.

The cat put on the clothing and danced about in joy.

"Now, don't worry," said Puss in Boots, "I will be back in a while."
Off he went down the road.

In a short time, the cat caught a fat rabbit and popped it into his sack. Then off he ran to the castle of the King.

"What do you want?" said the guards.

"My master, the Marquis of Carabas has a gift for the King."

"Oh," said the Guards, marveling at the strange cat. "Come right in."

The cat was escorted into the King's throne room. He bowed low.

"Sire, my master, the Marquis of Carabas would like to give you this fine, fat rabbit."

"A rabbit," said the King. "Send your master my thanks."

"So I will," said the cat. "Until tomorrow." And then he bowed very low.

The next day, Puss in Boots caught half a dozen plump partridges and popped them into his bag.

When he arrived at the castle, he told the king, "Here is another present from my master, the Marquis of Carabas."

"Tasty partridges," said the King. "Send your master my thanks."

"So I will," said the cat. "Until tomorrow." And then he bowed very low.

"This Marquis of Carabas is a very thoughtful man," said the Princess after the cat had gone.

Every day for the next two weeks, Puss in Boots visited the castle and brought a gift of one kind or another. One day it was a hawk, the next an owl, the day after that more rabbits, and so on. Each day he gave the gifts to the king in the name of his master, the Marquis of Carabas.

Everyone in the palace had wonderful things to say about the Marquis of Carabas.

"He is very loyal to the king," said one. "A fantastic hunter," said another. "Where does he live?" asked a third. "I've never heard of him."

The Princess especially was curious about the thoughtful man who sent these gifts.

"What is your master like?" she asked the cat.

"He is young and handsome," replied Puss. "And rich as well. Would you and the King like to meet him at his castle?"

"Of course," said the Princess.

"Of course," said the King.

"Then I will make the arrangements," said Puss in Boots.

The young miller's son was shocked when his cat returned home and told him that the King and the Princess would soon come and visit them.

"They'll see that I'm a poor miller's son," said the boy. "Then they'll know it was all a fraud."

"Leave everything to me," said the Puss. "My plan is masterful."

The next day the King and Princess rode forth from their castle in their carriage attended by their footmen and guards.

The cat saw them leave the palace and hurried on ahead.

"Quickly, master, quickly!" shouted the cat. "Take off your clothes and jump in the river."

"But I can't swim," said the young boy.

"Trust me," answered Puss in Boots. "All will be well."

Still, the youngster hesitated. At last, just before the king's carriage rounded the bend in the road, the cat shoved his master into the water.

SPLASH!

"Glub," said the young boy. "Glub!" His arms and legs flailed about.

"Help!" shouted the Puss. "My master, the Marquis of Carabas, is drowning."

When the King and Princess heard the cat, they sent their guards diving into the river to rescue the boy.

When they dragged him ashore, the Princess was embarrassed to see that he was wearing not a stitch of clothing.

"Thieves came and stole everything," said Puss in Boots.

The King ordered new clothes to be immediately brought to the Marquis of Carabas.

"He is indeed a very handsome man," said the Princess to her father.

"You cannot marry beneath your station," said the King, although if truth be told, he had taken an immediate liking to the bedraggled boy.

"My master is very, very rich," said Puss in Boots. "He owns all this land, and our castle is not far up ahead. Come, follow me there."

Then Puss ran off so fast that the horses were hard put to keep up.

Every time Puss came across a peasant or shop-keeper he told them, "If anyone asks you who your master is, tell him 'The Marquis of Carabas.' Otherwise terrible things may happen."

Well, the peasants saw no harm in humoring a talking walking cat, so as the King's carriage pulled past, they all told him that their master was the famous Marquis of Carabas.

Now, the castle wasn't exactly empty. It was occupied by a gigantic and mean ogre. The ogre was more than just a giant monster, he was also a magician of great and terrible power.

"I'll outfox him," thought Puss, as he knocked on the gate.

"What do you want?" said the giant ogre, staring down at the tiny cat.

"My goodness, it can't possibly be true," said Puss in Boots, bowing low and removing his feathered hat.

"What can't be true?" asked the Ogre.

"I heard from someone that you have magical powers."

"I do have magical powers," the ogre bellowed.

"I've heard that you can change yourself into a tiger or a bear," said the crafty cat.

"Of course I can change myself into a tiger or a bear," said the Ogre. "Just watch."

The Ogre said a magic spell and POOF, it turned itself first into a fierce white tiger, and then POOF, it turned into a ferocious black bear.

"But you couldn't possibly turn yourself into anything tiny," asked Puss.

"The tinier the better," growled the Ogre.

"As tiny as a mouse?" asked Puss.

"Just watch," said the Ogre. He said a magic spell and POOF, he turned himself into a tiny white mouse.

In an instant, Puss jumped on the mouse and ate him in one big bite.

Then he ran to open the castle gates for the king's carriage.

With a great flourishing, Puss in Boots bowed low. "Welcome, your majesty to the home and castle of my master, the Marquis of Carabas!"

The boy, who was quite dumbfounded said not a word, which was fortunate, because dressed as he was in the King's finest robes, and standing as he was in the hallway of the great castle, he did indeed seem like a Marquis.

"This is quite a castle," said the King. "And you do have quite a bit of land. How, if I may ask, is your wife?"

"Alas," said the boy, finally catching on, "I am not yet married, but I would like to be."

The Princess blushed, and the boy blushed back.

They smiled at each other.

"Then it shall be so," exclaimed the King.

"You see, master," whispered Puss in Boots. "I told you that all would end well."

And that is how the Marquis of Carabas, who was once a miller's son came to be the Princess's husband and later in his life King of the entire land. And always at his side was his wisest and finest advisor, a small black and white cat who wore boots and a red hat.

Together they all lived happily ever after.

— *The End* —

81. I've Been Working on the Railroad

I've been working on the railroad
All the live-long day
I've been working on the railroad
Just to pass the time away
Can't you hear the whistle blowing,
"Rise up so early in the morn'"
Can't you hear the Captain shouting,
"Dinah blow your horn!"

Dinah won't you blow
Dinah won't you blow
Dinah won't you blow your hor-r-rn
Dinah won't you blow
Dinah won't you blow
Dinah won't you blow your horn

Someone's in the kitchen with Dinah
Someone's in the kitchen I know-oh-
oh-oh
Someone's in the kitchen with Dinah
Strumming on the old banjo

Singing
Fee-Fie Fidle-i-oh
Fee-Fie Fidle-i-oh-oh-oh-oh
Fee-Fie Fidle-i-oh
Strumming on the old banjo
Bum bum

— *The End* —

262

82. She'll Be Coming Round the Mountain

READER TIP: Of course half the fun in this story-poem are the hand movements that accompany the sounds. Pulling the whistle (Toot toot!), yanking back on the reins (Whoa back!), waving (Hi, Babe!), a chopping motion (Hack hack), tummy rubbing (Yum yum), making a pillow with the hands (snores), and scratching.

She'll be coming round the mountain when she comes (Toot toot!)
She'll be coming round the mountain when she comes (Toot toot!)
She'll be coming round the mountain
She'll be coming round the mountain
She'll be coming round the mountain when she comes. (Toot toot!)

She'll be driving six white horses when she comes (Whoa back!)
She'll be driving six white horses when she comes (Whoa back!)
She'll be driving six white horses
She'll be driving six white horses
She'll be driving six white horses
*   when she comes.*
(Whoa back! Toot toot!)

And we'll all go out to meet her when
*   she comes. (Hi, Babe!)*
Yes, we'll all go out to meet her when
*   she comes. (Hi, Babe!)*
We'll all go out to meet her

We'll all go out to meet her
We'll all go out to meet her when she comes.
(Hi, Babe! Whoa back! Toot toot!)

We will kill the old red rooster when she comes (Hack hack)
We'll kill the old red rooster when she comes (Hack hack)
We'll kill the old red rooster
We'll kill the old red rooster
We'll kill the old red rooster when she comes.
(Hack hack. Hi, Babe! Whoa back! Toot toot!)

And we'll all have chicken and dumplings when she comes. (Yum yum)
Yes, we'll all have chicken and dumplings when she comes. (Yum yum)
We'll all have chicken and dumplings
We'll all have chicken and dumplings
We'll all have chicken and dumplings when she comes.
(Yum yum. Hack hack. Hi, Babe! Whoa back! Toot toot!)

She'll have to sleep with grandma when she comes (Snore snore)
She'll have to sleep with grandma when she comes (Snore snore)
She'll have to sleep with grandma
She'll have to sleep with grandma
She'll have to sleep with grandma when she comes.
(Snore snore. Yum yum. Hack hack. Hi, Babe! Whoa back! Toot toot!)

She'll be wearing red pajamas when she comes (Scratch scratch)
She'll be wearing red pajamas when she comes (Scratch scratch)
She'll be wearing red pajamas
She'll be wearing red pajamas
She'll be wearing red pajamas when she comes.
(Scratch scratch. Snore snore. Yum yum. Hack hack. Hi, Babe! Whoa
    back! Toot toot!)

— *The End* —

83. Casey at the Bat—A Baseball Legend in Verse

Ernest Thayer

The outlook wasn't brilliant for the Mudville nine that day;
The score stood four to two with but one inning more to play.
And then when Cooney died at first, and Barrows did the same,
A sickly silence fell upon the patrons of the game.

A straggling few got up to go in deep despair. The rest
Clung to that hope which springs eternal in the human breast;
They thought if only Casey could but get a whack at that—
We'd put up even money now with Casey at the bat.

But Flynn preceded Casey, as did also Jimmy Blake,
And the former was a lulu and the latter was a cake;
So upon that stricken multitude grim melancholy sat,
For there seemed but little chance of Casey's getting to the bat.

But Flynn let drive a single, to the wonderment of all,
And Blake, the much despised, tore the cover of the ball;
And when the dust had lifted, and the men saw
    what had occurred,
There was Johnnie safe at second and Flynn
    a-hugging third.

Then from 5,000 throats and more there rose a lusty yell;
It rumbled through the valley, it rattled in the dell;
It knocked upon the mountain and recoiled upon the flat,
For Casey, mighty Casey, was advancing to the bat.

There was ease in Casey's manner as he stepped into his place;
There was pride in Casey's bearing and a smile on Casey's face.
And when, responding to the cheers, he lightly doffed his hat,
No stranger in the crowd could doubt 'twas Casey at the bat.

Ten thousand eyes were on him as he rubbed his hands
    with dirt;
Five thousand tongues applauded when he wiped
    them on his shirt.
Then while the writhing pitcher ground the ball into
    his hip,
Defiance gleamed in Casey's eye, a sneer curled
    Casey's lip.

And now the leather-covered sphere came hurtling
    through the air,
And Casey stood a-watching it in haughty
    grandeur there.
Close by the sturdy batsman the ball
    unheeded sped—
"That ain't my style," said Casey. "Strike
    one," the umpire said.

From the benches black with people, there went up a muffled roar,
Like the beating of the storm-waves on a stern and distant shore.
"Kill him! Kill the umpire!" shouted someone on the stand;
And it's likely they'd have killed him had not Casey raised his
     hand.

With a smile of Christian charity great Casey's visage shone;
He stilled the rising tumult; he bade the game go on;
He signaled to the pitcher, and once more the spheroid flew;
But Casey still ignored it, and the umpire said, "Strike two."

"Fraud!" cried the maddened thousands, and echo answered
     fraud;
But one scornful look from Casey and the audience was awed.
They saw his face grow stern and cold, they saw his muscles strain,
And they knew that Casey wouldn't let that ball go by again.

The sneer is gone from Casey's lip, his teeth are clenched in hate;
He pounds with cruel violence his bat upon the plate.
And now the pitcher holds the ball, and now he lets it go,
And now the air is shattered by the force of Casey's blow.

Oh, somewhere in this favored land the sun is shining bright;
The band is playing somewhere, and somewhere hearts are light,
And somewhere men are laughing, and somewhere children shout;
But there is no joy in Mudville—mighty Casey has struck out.

— *The End* —

84. How Thor Was Nearly Married

Adults may remember Thor from the comic books, but well before Marvel he was the Norse God of Thunder. In fact, the day "Thursday" is named after him (Thor's day). Pronunciation of the word "Mjollnir" is entirely in your hands. This Norwegian version of Red Riding Hood is based on the original myth, but has been embellished with a bit of poetic license.

Thor, the God of Thunder, awoke with a start. His hammer, the mighty Mjollnir was stolen from his bedside. He leaped out of bed and roared, "Who has stolen Mjollnir? Who dares take the property of Thor?"

But the bedroom was silent, with only the winter's wind whispering in through the window.

Thor raced into the main hall and sounded the great anvil that summoned all the Aesir. They gathered in the sleepy morning's cold, and Odin, chief of all the gods sat on his throne.

"Why do you summon us at this unearthly hour?" he demanded of Thor.

"Mjollnir, my mighty hammer is missing!" Thor bellowed. "Someone has stolen it."

A murmur rippled among the gods. They knew that the great battle with the giants would soon be approaching, and without Thor and his mighty war hammer Mjollnir, Asgard, the land of the Gods would surely fall.

"We must find it," cried Balder.

"But where shall we look?" demanded Odin.

"I have an idea," said Loki, the fox, the trickster. He borrowed beautiful Freya's falcon wings, and flew off across the wide world in search of Mjollnir.

A short time later, Loki returned.

"I have found mighty Mjollnir," Loki panted, catching his breath. "It has been stolen by Thrym, king of the frost giants."

Thor's eyes turned ruby red and his face bulged with rage. "Let us reclaim my property," he said to Loki.

"Perhaps you should take a deep breath, Thor," Loki suggested. Thor's bad temper was known throughout the world. "If Thrym sees you coming, he may hide or worse destroy Mjollnir."

So, Loki traveled again to Jotunheim, the land of the frost giants and asked, "Good afternoon, friend Thrym, I was wondering if you happened to have seen Thor's hammer, Mjollnir, lying about."

Thrym, the wicked frost giant, grinned. "I have the hammer," the giant laughed. "I have hidden it in a secret place eight miles under the earth. All the gods could search for centuries and never find it."

"I know that Thor would like it returned," Loki said.

"He will never see it again," answered Thrym, "unless I am given Freya's hand in marriage."

"Freya is indeed the most beautiful of the gods," Loki said. "I will ask her if she will consent to the wedding."

Loki returned to Asgard and put the matter before Freya. "So, good Freya, you see that you must. . . ."

"Never!" Freya roared cutting him off. "I will not!"

At this all hope fled Asgard. When the giants came, as they surely would when they heard of Mjollnir's theft, their walls would be left without Thor's power and their land was doomed.

But a light glinted in Loki, the trickster's eyes. "I think I have an idea."

"Speak," Odin commanded.

"Perhaps if Thor himself put on the bride's dress," Loki began. "We could fool Thrym into thinking that his bride has come."

All the gods looked at Thor the Thunder God, and imagined him wearing a dress. Thor was broad and burly. His arms were heavily muscled and his face red with rage. His red hair flowed down his back, and his red beard bristled at the suggestion.

"I?" Thor bellowed. "Would you have me play the fool?"

"Do you have any better ideas?" Loki asked. "If it makes you feel any better, I will come along as your maid servant." This, thought Loki, will be too good to miss.

At last Thor agreed, and word was sent to Thrym that Freya would come to him in a week's time.

Finally, the day came when Thor and Loki left Asgard dressed in women's clothes. Loki led the way, as befit a maid servant, and Thor followed along behind, sullen and glum in his white gown and veil.

"When we get to Jotunheim," Loki said, "let me do all the talking. If you open your mouth, you're liable to roar."

Thor agreed and cast his eyes upon the path.

Thrym opened his house gladly at the arrival of the two "women."

"Welcome to Jotunheim," he said. "I have prepared the bridal feast for my fair Freya."

He led his fair Freya to the high seat at the table and sat at her side.

Thor was so hungry that he immediately devoured an entire ox, a dozen salmon, and the entire banquet of fine set out for all the women. Not only that, he drank five casks of mead and wiped his face with two fine linen tablecloths!

"I have never seen a woman eat so much!" Thrym exclaimed.

"Freya is hungry," Loki quickly answered, "She was so excited about the wedding that she has not eaten for the past week."

"Ah," said Thrym. "I should like to kiss my bride." Then the repulsive frost giant leaned forward, and peeked under the bridal veil.

"Her eyes are so red!" Thrym cried, dropping the veil quickly. "They burn like two hot coals. I have never seen a woman with such fierce eyes."

"Well," crafty Loki said, "Freya was so excited about the wedding that she has not slept for the past week. Her eyes burn with passion for you."

The frost giant was pleased with this answer, and he again resolved to kiss his bride. He lifted the veil, and then dropped it again.

"Her face is covered with hair as red as a man's beard," Thrym said. "I have never seen a woman with a beard."

"Ah," Loki the fox answered, "that is the latest fashion in Asgard. She has been so excited about the wedding that she spent all week working on her hairdo. Is it not attractive?"

"Attractive?" wondered Thrym. "Strange. . . ."

Perceiving that the frost giant was growing too curious, Loki said, "Freya would like to see Mjollnir before the wedding begins. Can you bring it to her?"

"Immediately!" Thrym answered. "Bring Freya the hammer!" He ordered ten of his minions to fetch Thor's hammer (so heavy was the hammer that it took the strength of ten Frost giants to lift it).

In a short time, Mjollnir was brought into the great hall, and the ten frost giants set it on Freya's lap.

At that moment, Thor tore away his veil and stood revealed. His eyes glowed fiercely red, his red beard flowed, and his arms rippled with strength.

"Thank you for returning my hammer, Thrym," Thor said. "I don't think we'll be getting married today."

Thrym, king of the frost giants, backed away in terror.

Thor lifted the great hammer, Mjollnir, and began to swing it.

When he was finished, the frost giants were all dead, and not a stone remained of the great palace in Jotunheim.

At last, Thor stood among the rubble, his hammer restored. Beside him Loki stood, observing the destruction.

"Loki," Thor warned, "tell no one in Asgard what has occurred."

Loki, however, only grinned.

— *The End* —

85. Thor Finds a Servant

*I*nspired by his victory against the frost giants, Thor decided to travel to Utgard, stronghold of the giants, to survey their holdings.

"Giants are tricky," Loki said to Thor. "You'll need someone with brains."

"Brains," Thor agreed.

"And your brains are as sharp as your hammer," Loki winked. "I recommend that you bring me along."

"We leave tomorrow," Thor answered, gruffly.

The next day, Thor hitched his two goats to his golden chariot, and off they rode. After traveling all day, they came to a small farm house.

"This looks like a good place to rest," Loki said.

"I'm a bit hungry," Thor said. He knocked on the door and a farmer answered. "We are traveling to Utgard," Thor said. "We require food and shelter."

"We'll be happy to give you a place to sleep tonight," the farmer answered, his voice quivering in terror. "But we have very little food. A few potatoes and carrots, but no meat."

"Very well," Thor said. "We will kill my goats and eat them."

Thor killed the goats and spread their skins on the ground. "As you eat, be sure to throw my goat's bones onto their skins. Be careful. Don't break or lose any bones."

The farmer built a roaring fire, and soon the goats were roasting. When they were cooked, all began to eat.

Thialfi, the farmer's son, had not eaten meat in so long that he ate far too quickly, and accidentally broke one of the goat's bones. He didn't mention this, but threw the bone onto the skins anyway.

When the meal was done, Thor wrapped the goat skins into a bundle. Then he waved his hammer Mjollnir over the skins and pronounced a spell.

"Goats eaten outside in
Bones go back into your skin."

In an instant the two goats jumped up completely restored and began nibbling on grass outside the house.

The next morning, Thor hitched the two goats to his golden chariot, and realized that one of the goats had gone lame.

"Who dared disobey me?" he roared. "One of my goat's thighbones has been injured!"

The farmer and his wife wept because they were certain that their lives upon this earth were about to come to an end.

At last, Thialfi stepped forward and admitted that he had been careless.

Thor raised his hammer, high to strike down the boy, but the farmer jumped in front of his son.

"Please, please, have mercy," the farmer begged. "Take my farm. Take everything I own, but spare my son. Spare my family."

Thor was impressed by the farmer's bravery, and he lowered his hammer. His rage had disappeared as quickly as it had appeared. "You, Thialfi," Thor said, "will come with me as my servant."

Thialfi immediately agreed. What an adventure, he thought, to travel with the great Thor and Loki!

He bade his mother and father good-bye.

Then, all three leaped into the golden chariot and rode away in the direction of Utgard.

— *The End* —

86. Thor Meets the Giant Skrymir

*N*ot long after Thor and Loki and Thialfi left Thialfi's father's farm, they came to the edge of the land of Utgard. They left Thor's goats and golden chariot behind and traveled ahead on foot.

At last, night fell and they came to a great hall. It held one vast main chamber and five smaller chambers each the size of a large building.

"This place is as big as the hall of Odin," Thor marveled.

"It will make a good spot to rest," Loki agreed.

The trio lay down to sleep but found that the hall was not such a fine place to rest. Every time their heads touched a pillow, the ground shook and thunder roared.

"How can I sleep in this din?" Thor roared.

"Surely something terrible will happen," Thialfi cried.

So the night passed restlessly.

In the morning, when the three arose they found their bones stiff and their clothing as wet as if they had slept on the grass. When, they stepped outside the great hall, they were surprised to find an immense giant, lying asleep in front of its door. Thor and Loki had seen many giants in their days, but never one as big as this.

"Who are you?" Thor asked.

The giant opened his eyes. "Skrymir," the giant said. His words were so loud that they echoed through the woods. "The big one."

"You can say that again," Loki agreed.

"Have you been keeping my glove warm?" Skrymir asked. He picked up the great hall that the travelers had been sleeping in and slipped it onto his hand.

Amazing, Thialfi thought, wondering if he would ever return home to his family, the entire hall with its five smaller rooms was only the glove of a single giant.

"I know who you are," Skrymir said. "Where are you going?"

"To Utgard," Thor said.

"Ah," replied the giant, "I'm traveling in that direction myself. May I travel with you?"

"If we pool our resources," answered Loki, thinking that the giant would certainly have enough food to feed the three of them.

"Agreed," Skrymir said. And off they went.

In the afternoon, Skrymir said, "I am becoming tired. I think I should like to take a nap. Eat whatever you want from my bag." He threw Thor a large food sack, and then he lay down and began to snore.

The sack of food was so heavy that even Thor himself had a hard time moving it. He began to work on the draw strings and quickly found that he could not untie them. Then Loki, who was well known as a locksmith, tried his hand, but he too found opening the bag impossible.

So enraged was Thor that he picked up his hammer Mjollnir and brought it down with a crash on the sleeping giant's forehead.

"Hum hmm," the giant stirred. "Only a gnat." And he swept Thor from his brow. In an instant the giant was asleep, snoring.

Not to be paused so easily, Thor ran forward and lowered Mjollnir with another crash.

"Hum hmm," the giant mumbled. "A bird nibbling at my hair." With his fist he again swept Thor from his brow. In an instant the giant was again asleep, snoring.

Incensed, Thor leaped up and brought Mjollnir down with a furious crash. The earth shook for miles, but again the giant only blinked.

"Hum hmm," he said. "An acorn has fallen on my head." He yawned and Thor flew from his perch.

Then the giant, Skrymir stood. "Thor," he said, "what are you doing over there?"

"I am just waking up myself," Thor said. "Shall we continue our journey?"

"Our paths diverge here," Skrymir said. "In Utgard you will surely see giants larger than I. A bit of advice, though. When you meet Utgardloki, keep your mouths shut and don't brag. There's nothing Utgardloki hates more than boastful braggarts."

Thor's eyes reddened in anger, but he remembered his three great blows had struck the giant without harm, and he stayed silent.

When at last Skrymir had vanished in the distance, Loki said, "I for one am glad he is gone and would be quite pleased never to meet him again."

For once, even Thor agreed with Loki.

— *The End* —

87. Thor's Challenges

Thor and Loki and Thialfi traveled quickly through Utgard, the land of the giants. Off in the distance, they frequently saw giants taller than any pine tree, but they kept their distance.

At last, they came to a castle with a gate so large it seemed to overwhelm the world. Thor tried to shake the gates and tugged at its lock. But the gates only rattled a little and did not bulge.

"The giants are very big," the boy, Thialfi, said. "Are you not worried? Perhaps we should return home."

"The bigger they are," Thor answered, "the harder they will fall." But even Thor was worried, because he had struck Skrymir three times on the skull without even making the giant dizzy.

"Strength is all very well and good," Loki said, "but here wits may be to our advantage. I, of course, will provide as much in the way of brains as my friend Thor will in brawn."

Then, with a sly smile, Loki turned himself sideways and slid in between the gate's bars. With a laugh, Thialfi followed Loki.

Thor, however, got stuck in between the bars, and only with much tugging by Thialfi and Loki did he finally gain entrance into the great castle.

They made their way into the great hall and saw a giant sitting on a throne at the other end of the hall.

"That must be Utgardloki," Thialfi said. "He is even bigger than Skrymir!"

The three travelers approached and announced their names.

The giant king ignored them completely.

Again, the three travelers introduced themselves, and again they were ignored.

Loki yawned, and Thor opened his mouth to shout, "I AM THE GREAT . . ."

The giant Utgardloki's eyes blinked. "I know who you are. You're that pip-squeak Thor and the two mice he calls friends."

Thor trembled with rage, but he noticed that there were far too many giant guards to do battle with safely.

"You're supposed to be strong," Utgardloki said. "But have you any really useful skills? No one is allowed to stay in Utgard unless they possess some unusual skill or craft."

"Well," Loki said, "It's not much, but I can eat faster than anyone else. I bet there's no one in Utgard who can eat as fast as I can."

The giant king rubbed his chin. "All right. Let's find out. Logi, come here. We're having an eating contest."

A small giant, not even as tall as Loki, stepped forward. A long table was brought out filled with lambs and hams, sides of beef and fish.

At one end of the table sat Loki, and at the other hunched Logi. "Ready," Utgardloki said. "Begin!"

They munched and crunched and chewed and swallowed. Loki ate so fast that his head hummed. He pulled food into his mouth and practically climbed onto the table for more.

No sooner had they begun than the meal was finished. "There!" Loki said, "I have won."

"Not so," said Utgardloki. "You've only eaten the food. Logi has eaten all the plates and the table as well."

Loki looked down and saw that he had been defeated.

"What can the boy do?" Utgardloki asked.

"I am a fair runner," Thialfi said. "What about a race?"

"Hugi," the giant king bellowed. A short fat giant with stubby legs stepped forward. "Are you ready?"

A tree was picked off in the distance. Hugi and Thialfi stood at the starting line.

"Begin!" Utgardloki said.

Off they ran, legs pumping as fast as they could. Hugi was so fast that he had rounded the tree before Thialfi had finished even a quarter of the distance. "Hello," Hugi said to Thialfi as he passed. And then he was back at the finish line.

"Well," Utgardloki said. "Not bad for a human."

Thialfi's face fell, and he stared at his feet in shame.

"Thor," Utgardloki said, "I hear you're a real bragger. You're always going on about how wonderful you are doing this and that. Is any of it true?"

Thor stifled his anger and answered quietly. "I'm a pretty good drinker," he said.

"Excellent," Utgardloki said. He brought forth a small drinking horn. "Most giants can finish this in a single gulp, but if you can do it in two I'd say that was fair enough."

Thor put the horn to his lips and drank long. When he was done, Utgardloki looked inside. "Barely touched," the giant king said. "Try again."

Again Thor raised the horn, and again he drank long. When he was done, Utgardloki looked inside. "A little lower," the giant king said. "Try once more."

This time Thor held the drinking horn high and raised it to his lips. He drank and drank until his face turned blue and it seemed he would die from lack of breath. At last he stopped.

Utgardloki looked inside. "Ah well," he said. "I suppose you'll say you weren't really thirsty."

The horn was still completely full. Thor looked disgusted with himself.

"Well," Utgardloki said. "What else can you do?"

"I am strong," Thor said.

"Ah," the giant king said. "Many of the young giants like to train themselves by lifting my cat." He inclined his head toward an orange and yellow tom cat lying near the fire.

Thor laughed, stepped forward, and tried to lift the cat. He found it far heavier than it looked. It budged not an inch. Then, Thor wrapped his arms around the cat, bent his knees, and hoisted with all his strength.

The orange Tom cat only arched its back a little and yawned.

"I suppose," Utgardloki said, "that the cat is a bit bigger than you expected. Perhaps you're allergic."

Thor only scowled. "Say whatever you want. I will wrestle with any giant here and prove to you how strong I am!"

"Very well," Utgardloki said. "Call Elli, the old woman."

A few moments later, a stooped and tired-looking old crone stepped into the great hall.

"Surely this is no contest," Thor said.

"Afraid of an old woman?" Utgardloki said. "The mighty Thor?"

Thor shrugged the insult off and began to wrestle with the old woman.

The moment they touched, Thor knew that she was far stronger than she appeared. In an instant she picked him up and threw him on the ground. Thor leaped up and grabbed her tightly, but a moment later she tossed him aside. Again Thor bounded to his feet and grabbed the old woman in a furious lock. She shrugged her shoulders and raised her arms, and the mighty thunder god fell to one knee, panting with exhaustion.

"Well, well," Utgardloki said. "I suppose you're going to say that you didn't want to hurt an old woman and that you're tired from your journey. Perhaps you should sleep a while and we'll talk again in the morning.

The shamed trio bid their good nights and went to bed, tired and sullen.

The next day, Utgardloki himself stood and escorted them from the castle.

"Here we say good-bye," Utgardloki said once they stood outside the gates.

"Thank you for your hospitality," Loki said.

Thor stared up at the great giant king. "I am ashamed that we three came in second place in every contest you gave us."

"Thor," said Utgardloki, "since we have left Utgard, I am going to tell you the truth. You will never be able to enter Utgard again."

Thor looked puzzled.

"If I'd realized how powerful you were, I never would have let you in in the first place. You nearly destroyed us all!

"In addition to being a giant, I am a wizard. I used my spells to trick you. I pretended to be the giant Skrymir. The hall that I pretended was my glove was just an illusion, you really slept on the ground. My bag of food was tied with iron wire, you could never have untied it. And any one of your three blows would have killed me had they really struck my head. Look." Utgardloki pointed his finger. "See those three canyons. With the last of those blows, you nearly split the world in two!"

"What about the contests?" Thor asked, his temper beginning to show.

"Illusions," Utgardloki said, "Spells. Loki ate very quickly, but his opponent, Logi, was fire. No one can eat as fast as fire. It burned the table and plates as well as all the food. When Thialfi ran against Hugi he ran very quickly. But Hugi was thought, and nothing can run as fast as human thought.

"As for you," Utgardloki turned to Thor, "the horn you drank from was connected to the oceans. You drank so deeply that you have created the low tides! The cat you tried to lift was the Midgard serpent, which encircles the world and bites its own tail. You actually managed to lift it a bit off the floor, which no one has ever done before. Finally, the old woman, Elli, is old age. No one, not even the great Thor can withstand old age, but you fought well against her.

"So, you see," the giant king said. "I will never see you again, and I will never permit you to enter Utgard. You are quite dangerous."

At that, Thor's anger blossomed, and he grabbed the mighty hammer Mjollnir and swung at Utgardloki in a blind rage.

But the giant king had vanished.

Thor turned and swung his hammer at the walls of the great castle, but it too vanished. The forest on all sides vanished as well, and a moment later, Thor and Loki and Thialfi stood on an empty plain, with only the three vast gorges in the distance for company.

"Well," Loki said at last. "I wonder if anyone will believe this story."

At last his anger subsided, and Thor shrugged.

— *The End* —

88. Cinderella

Once upon a time, a well-to-do merchant decided he wanted to remarry. His first wife had been lovely, intelligent, and kind, and had born him a lovely, intelligent, and kind daughter named Cinderella. Unfortunately, Cinderella's mother died when the girl was quite young. Her father, the Merchant, came under the spell of the proudest and most arrogant woman in the village. A short time later they were married, and the woman (who was a widow herself) and her two daughters moved into the Merchant's house.

As soon as the wedding was over, the new mother-in-law began to complain and nag. The house was too small and dirty, and the girl, Cinderella was far too cheerful.

So, the stepmother put Cinderella to work. She gave her all the menial chores.

Cinderella had to do all the laundry, all the dishes, all the cleaning and scrubbing and mending and washing. Not only did she have to take care of her stepmother, but she was also responsible for every mess her stepsisters made. They took away her clothing and made her wear old rags. Still worse, the two stepsisters moved Cinderella out of her own bedroom, which had a lovely view of the garden, and made her sleep on a bed of straw up in the attic on the top floor of the house.

Poor Cinderella felt quite sad, sitting crouched on her bed, darning her stepsisters' socks, while downstairs the three women drank hot tea and ate cakes. Still, she did not dare to tell her father, because his new wife already had the poor man terrified. All the stepmother had to do was to open her mouth and cough, and her husband was standing at her side, begging her pardon and asking what he might do next.

Despite all this hard work, hardship, and heartache, and even in the ragged dress she was forced to wear, Cinderella was still more beautiful, kind, and intelligent than her two stepsisters put together.

Now, it happened that the King decided to give a ball in honor of his son, the Prince. Invitations were sent out to all the best houses, and of course the merchant's three daughters were all invited.

Immediately, the Stepmother began purchasing gowns and linens and silks and shoes to dress up her daughters for their appearance before the prince.

"If you look well and act well," the Stepmother advised, "then the Prince will fall in love, and our future will be assured."

Cinderella, of course, was put to work sewing the gowns, taking up the hems, and letting out the waists. The dresses really were quite beautiful. The eldest sister's was made of red velvet from France, and the youngest wore a diamond petticoat from Italy.

Cinderella helped them with their choices and even braided their hair in beautiful plaits.

"Oh, Cinderella," teased the eldest, "wouldn't you like to come to the ball."

"Hush," taunted the younger stepsister. "You know that someone as dirty as she would never be admitted."

"Still," Cinderella agreed, "it would be lovely to see."

Both stepsisters looked at each other and laughed merrily at the thought of their dirty servant standing in rags at the ball.

At last the stepsisters were ready, and their carriage pulled up before the front door. Cinderella waved and watched the carriage roll down the street until it was completely out of sight.

Then the poor girl burst into tears.

"Why are you crying, child?" said a voice.

"Who's there?" said Cinderella.

"I am," said the voice.

Cinderella looked down and saw standing on the table a tiny woman no larger than a tea cup. "Who are you?" the teary-eyed girl asked.

"I am your fairy godmother," said the woman in a sparkly voice. "Why are you so sad?"

"I wish . . . I wish . . ." Cinderella began, but every time she tried to finish, her words were choked off by her tears.

"You wish you could go to the ball?" The Fairy Godmother finally asked.

"Yes," wept Cinderella. "But I am too poor and too ugly, and everyone would laugh."

"Nonsense," laughed the Fairy. "You are beautiful and kind and quite rich. I'll just give you a little help. Shall I?"

"Oh, please," Cinderella said.

"Run into the garden and bring me a pumpkin," said the Fairy.

Cinderella hurried to the garden and brought back the biggest and finest pumpkin she could find.

The Fairy Godmother scooped out the insides, and then touched the pumpkin with her wand. Instantly it was transformed into a golden coach

Then she sent Cinderella to the mousetrap for the six mice that were caught there, and with another wave the mice became six fine horses of a beautiful mouse-colored dapple grey. In the rat trap they found three rats who became two coachmen and one coach driver with a fine long beard of white rat whiskers. Two lizards from the garden became two footmen in green silk.

"Now," said the Fairy Godmother, "you have your carriage, we must see to your gown."

"I have nothing but this to wear," Cinderella said, and she began to cry.

"Oh, tush," said the Fairy. She touched Cinderella with her wand, and instantly the raggedy dress was transformed into a beautiful white gown of silk, with beads and pearls and diamonds glittering here and there. Even her slippers, which were worn and torn and dirty transformed into a pair of glass slippers, the most beautiful shoes the world has ever seen.

"Now, go to the ball," said the Fairy Godmother. "But be sure to leave before midnight, because at the last stroke of midnight, the coach will be a pumpkin again, the horses will become mice, the coachmen rats, and the footmen will be lizards. And, of course, your gown will resume its old form."

Cinderella nodded eagerly, promised her Fairy Godmother that she would be home by midnight, and kissed the tiny woman softly on the top of the head.

"Now, hurry, child," said the Fairy.

The footmen opened the door, Cinderella hopped into the coach, and away they rode to the palace.

Now, the ball had been a little bit tiresome, but when the Prince heard that a beautiful princess had arrived in a golden carriage drawn by six marvelous grey horses, he hurried out to greet her. He gave her his hand as she stepped from the coach and led her into the great hall.

As soon as the two made their entrance, the assembly fell silent. The people stopped talking, and even the musicians ceased their playing. So beautiful a pair were the Prince and the strange girl that no one could say a word.

At last, at a signal from the Prince, the musicians picked up their instruments and began to play a waltz. He took Cinderella into his arms, and together they began to dance.

"What a fine dancer she is," said the Stepmother, not recognizing the young girl.

"Her dress is more lovely than mine," complained the oldest stepsister.

"Her shoes are more lovely than mine," echoed the younger one.

"Quiet, you two," hissed the Stepmother, as Cinderella and the Prince waltzed by. All three women smiled and waved at the Prince, but he had eyes only for Cinderella.

The hours passed like minutes. Cinderella danced and ate and talked with the Prince and danced some more.

Then she heard the clock sound the hour of twelve. She thought it was only eleven, but a glance at the clock showed her that doom was near. Terrified that she might be discovered, she had time only to kiss the Prince softly on his cheek and hurry from the Palace. She rushed down the steps, hopped into her coach, and was gone in an instant.

So quickly did Cinderella run away that one of her slippers fell off, and it was picked up by the Prince who had turned to follow the girl whose name he hadn't even learned.

Just as they were out of sight from the palace, at the last stroke of midnight, the pumpkin and rats and mice and lizards all returned to their original selves, quite confused I might add. Even though her clothing was once again rags, Cinderella did not feel sad. All that was left of her wonderful gown was the second glass slipper, which she put into her pocket. She remembered the warmth of the Prince's cheek against hers, walked all the way home, and went up to her attic bed of straw, quite happy and content.

The next morning, her stepsisters told her all about the ball, that the most beautiful princess had appeared and stolen the Prince's heart.

That afternoon, a proclamation was declared in the town square that the Prince himself would be visiting every house in the town to find the owner of the missing glass slipper.

The Prince tried the slipper on all the other princesses and duchesses in the court, but none of their feet fit.

The two stepsisters knew that he would soon come to their house. They fluttered about all excited.

"Calm down," said the Stepmother. "If the shoe fits, then surely he will make you his wife." The doorbell rang. "Open the door for the Prince."

"Welcome, your Highness," said the first Stepsister. Her face turned as red as a mottled turnip.

"Hi," waved the second Stepsister, giggling.

The Prince frowned, but asked the two girls to remove their shoes.

The Stepsisters tried to make the shoe fit. They shoved and pried and pushed and squeezed, but it refused to take hold on their large and ugly feet.

At last, Cinderella peeked her head around a corner.

"May I try?" she asked meekly.

"You?" said the Stepmother.

"That's just the cleaning girl," said the oldest Stepsister.

"She's a nobody," said the second Stepsister.

"Let her try," said the Prince.

Cinderella sat down in the chair and the Prince lifted the slipper to her foot.

It fit beautifully.

"Are you my Princess?" the Prince asked.

"I am," Cinderella whispered, shyly.

"She can't be!" said the Stepmother.

"Impossible!" shouted the two Stepsisters.

From her pocket, Cinderella pulled the other glass slipper and slipped it onto her other foot.

Just then, her fairy godmother came in and touched her with her magic wand. In an instant, Cinderella was clothed in a gown even more beautiful than the one she had worn to the ball.

When they saw the transformation, her two sisters and stepmother threw themselves at her feet. "Please forgive us," they begged. "We had no idea."

"I forgive you," Cinderella said kindly. She hugged the three women to her, and some say that at that moment their wicked hearts melted and they became kind.

Then the Prince took Cinderella's hand and led her off to the palace, where they were married in splendor and lived happily ever after.

— *The End* —

89. Jack and the Beanstalk

Many years ago, in the reign of Good King Alfred, lived a widow who had a young son named Jack. Jack was a nice enough boy, although he tended to be extravagant, careless, and a little bit lazy. He didn't do a lick of work on the farm, and soon all the money was gone. All that was left was the old cow, Bessie, and even she stopped producing milk.

One day, Jack's mother, with tears in her eyes said to Jack, "Son, we have nothing left but our old cow, Bessie. Take her into town and sell her that we may buy a bit of bread and some beans for our soup."

Jack, who had never been to town by himself, was eager to make the journey. He looped a rope around Bessie's neck and set off on his way.

At the crossroads half way to town, Jack met a man sitting off to the side of the road among the weeds.

"Hello, Jack," said the man.

"Hello, Sir," said Jack. "Why are you waiting so by the side of the road?"

"I've been waiting for you," said the fellow lazily. "You've got a cow to sell, don't you."

"Why, yes," said Jack. "Would you like to buy it?"

"How much?" said the fellow, without even standing.

"Five gold pieces," Jack replied boldly.

The man frowned. "I don't have that on me, but I do have something even better."

"Better than five gold pieces?" Jack said. "I'll have to see that."

Slowly the fellow stood up. He reached into his pocket and withdrew a small pouch. From the pouch he shook out four small multicolored beans.

"What are those?" Jack asked.

"Magic beans," said the fellow. "They will bring you fame and great fortune. Shall we trade?"

Jack thought for a moment and then agreed. He gave the man the rope, and patted Bessie good-bye. Then he put the beans in his pocket and lay down for a nap by the side of the road.

Just before sunset, Jack woke up with a start. "I'd better be heading home," he said. "Mother will be expecting me." And off he went.

When Jack arrived back at home, his mother greeted him eagerly.

"Well, Jack, I see you're back from the market," she said. "What did you get for our cow Bessie? One gold piece? Two?"

"Something even better than gold," Jack said.

"What could be better than gold?" said the poor woman, eagerly.

"Look," Jack said. He pulled out the pouch and spilled the beans on the kitchen table.

"Four beans?" his mother asked.

"They're magic beans," Jack said. "The man at the crossroads said so."

"Jack, you fool!" his mother cried. "You've been swindled. These beans are worthless. They'll hardly make a bite for dinner."

With that, the old lady picked up the beans and threw them out the kitchen window, where they landed in the garden.

Then both Jack and his mother went to bed without any supper.

That night it rained and thundered. Jack tossed and turned, barely able to sleep through the din.

The next morning, Jack woke and as was his custom, fetched the water bucket from the kitchen. He would fill the bucket with water from the well and make a cup of tea for his mother.

Imagine his surprise when instead of finding the garden empty, he saw a wonderful woven beanstalk that was thick and strong and tall, reaching right up into the sky.

Jack looked up the beanstalk and realized that he felt a little dizzy.

"I'm going to climb the beanstalk," he told his mother.

The old woman tried to persuade her son to stay home, but Jack would not listen. At last, she gave him a kiss for luck.

"Be careful, Jack," she said.

So, Jack climbed. He climbed and climbed and climbed. And then he climbed some more. He climbed until his arms were tired and his legs could barely lift. Finally, he took a little rest. Far below he saw his house, and it looked like a little speck. "Well," said Jack to himself, "I've come all this way, it would be a shame to stop before I reach the top." Then he started climbing again.

At long last, he reached the top of the beanstalk, which just poked through a particularly dark cloud. Jack stuck his head up through the cloud, and was surprised to discover a beautiful field of grass. Way off in the distance, he saw a huge castle.

"This is very strange," said Jack. "Let's have a look." He jumped off the beanstalk onto the grass, and began walking to the castle. It took quite some time to get there, and by then he was very very hungry. (Remember, he hadn't had any dinner, breakfast, or lunch.)

At last Jack reached the gigantic castle. But how was he to get in? The door was as big as a mountain (or at least a very, very high hill). Still, he knocked anyway, and soon the door opened.

"Who's there?" said a loud booming woman's voice.

"Just a hungry boy," Jack shouted back. He looked everywhere, but didn't see anyone, until he looked up and saw a giant's wife looking back down at him.

"You're very small for a boy," said the woman, "but I don't suppose you'll eat much. You can come in, but my husband will be home soon, and if he does, you'll have to hide in the cupboard."

The Giant's wife picked Jack up and carried him into the kitchen where she gave him a crumb of bread the size of a boulder and a morsel of cheese the size of a piano. Jack ate and ate until he was quite full.

Then he heard a distant rumble growing closer.

"My husband!" shouted the Giantess. "Quick, into the cupboard."

The rumbles shook the house, and soon a gigantic giant burst into the kitchen. He had feet the size of horses, legs as tall as tree trunks, a head the size of a house, and one eye blinking in the middle of his particularly ugly face.

"Fee, Fi, Fo, Fum," roared the giant. "I smell the blood of an Englishman. Be he alive, or be he dead, I'll grind his bones to make my bread."

The Giant began sniffing and snuffing and looking in all the corners of the kitchen.

Well, Jack quivered and quaked, certain that the Giant's wife would give him away and he'd be eaten by the Giant.

Fortunately, just then, the Giantess brought her husband his dinner, and so hungry was the Giant that he quite forgot all about finding Jack.

When the Giant had finished eating his dinner, he barked, "Wife, bring my golden hen!"

The Giant's wife hurried from the kitchen and was back in the minute with an ordinary-looking golden hen that looked surprisingly tiny in her hands.

"Hen, lay!" the giant ordered.

The hen clucked three times, and then sat down and laid a golden egg! The giant picked the egg up, squinted at it, and then put the egg in his pocket. Then he fell asleep at the table, his beard dribbling into his soup.

Well, Jack saw his opportunity. He jumped from the cupboard onto the table and snatched up the golden hen. Then he ran as fast as he could out of the castle, across the great green field, and began climbing down the beanstalk.

It was nearly midnight by the time Jack returned home, and his mother was quite frantic.

"Jack," she said, "where have you been?"

"Winning riches," said the young boy. He reached into his shirt, and brought out the golden hen, which had fallen asleep while he had climbed down.

"A chicken for dinner!" cried his mother, snatching up a kitchen knife. "Good lad!"

"No!" Jack raised his hand. "Watch this. Hen, lay!"

And the hen clucked three times, and then sat down and laid a golden egg.

Jack plucked the egg from underneath the hen and showed it to his mother. She tapped it against a skillet, and was a little disappointed when it didn't crack and make a nice omelet. Then Jack pointed out that eggs made of solid gold would be much more valuable than the ordinary white or brown kind.

The two of them danced and talked until dawn. Then the old lady went into town and sold the golden egg for enough money to feed a family of fifty for a month. From that day on, Jack and his mother lived well and happily, taking the eggs that the golden hen laid and selling them for whatever they needed.

In ordinary circumstances, that would be the end of our story, but Jack was not an ordinary boy. Soon, he found his mind wandering back to the marvelous land high up in the sky.

One morning he called to his mother, "I'm going to climb the beanstalk."

The old woman tried to persuade her son to stay home, but Jack would not listen. At last, she gave him a kiss for luck. "Be careful, Jack," she said.

Jack climbed and climbed and climbed. And then he climbed some more. He climbed until his arms were tired and his legs could barely lift. This time, however, he didn't take a break until he had reached the very top and could see the field of tall green grass and the Giant's castle off in the distance. When he'd recovered his breath, he ran across the field, and again knocked on the door.

Once again, the Giant's wife opened the door and asked who was there.

"A hungry little boy," Jack said, smiling and waving.

"Go away," said the Giant's wife. "The last time a little boy came, he stole away my husband's golden hen."

"But I've come such a long way," said Jack, and "I'm very hungry."

"Very well," the Giantess said. Even though her husband was a man eater, she had a soft spot in her heart for tiny boys. "I'll give you a quick bite, but if my husband comes home early, I'll have to hide you in the cupboard."

The Giantess carried Jack into the kitchen and gave him some crumbs of bread and cheese. Jack ate, and waited for the thunder in the distance that signaled the coming of the Giant.

"My husband is coming!" said the Giantess. "Quick, into the cupboard with you."

A moment later the kitchen door burst open and in came the giant.

"Fee, Fi, Fo, Fum," roared the giant. "I smell the blood of an Englishman. Be he alive, or be he dead, I'll grind his bones to make my bread."

The giant began sniffing and snuffing and looking in all the corners of the kitchen.

Seeing the giant's immense size and his fearsome face for a second time, Jack wondered if coming back to the castle was such a good idea. Still, it was too late to complain, and too early to run away.

Fortunately, the Giant's wife once again distracted her husband with dinner. After the Giant had eaten his fill, he ordered, "Wife, bring my harp."

The Giant's wife scurried out, and then hurried back with a perfectly ordinary-size harp, which she set on the table in front of her husband.

"Harp, play!" the Giant roared.

Immediately the tiny (for a giant) harp began playing the most beautiful tunes. It even sang accompaniment!

"Now that is something that I could make my name with," thought Jack. He waited until the Giant had fallen asleep with his mustache in the gravy, and then he leaped from the cabinet onto the kitchen table.

He snatched up the harp and began to run.

This time, Jack's escape was not so simple. As soon as Jack touched the harp, it began to shout, "Master! Master! A thief! A thief!"

The Giant woke with a roar, and Jack ran as fast as he could out of the Giant's castle and across the great field. He didn't look back once. But, when he reached the beanstalk, he saw that he was only a little bit ahead of the Giant. Jack jumped onto the beanstalk and began sliding down it as fast as he could for dear life.

The Giant paused a moment, considered the strange bean plant, and then followed, climbing down slowly and carefully. (Giants, if you can believe it, are frequently afraid of heights.)

Meanwhile, Jack had reached the bottom of the beanstalk.

"Mother, mother, bring an ax!" Jack shouted.

"Oh, there you are," his mother said. "I was just beginning to. . . ."

"An ax! Hurry!"

The old woman ran to the wood pile, while Jack caught his breath. She handed him the ax, and he began hacking away at the beanstalks.

Chop, chop, chop. By now they could just see the Giant's feet high up in the sky. Chop Chop. Closer and closer.

And then, with a sudden "crack!" the beanstalk snapped and fell.

The Giant fell headlong into the side of a hill and was instantly killed.

After that, things were quiet for quite some time. The Giant's wife became the leader of the land in the sky, which grew rich and prosperous.

Jack himself became well known as a famous giant killer and had many adventures with his magic harp. But from that day on, he was quite careful to make sure that his mother was well taken care of.

And they all lived happily ever after.

— *The End* —

90. Chicken Licken

One day, Chicken Licken was walking through the woods and plink! An acorn fell from a tall oak tree on her head.

"Oh my goodness!" said Chicken Licken. "The sky is falling! The sky is falling. I must go and tell the President."

So, Chicken Licken ran back down the road, and on the way she met Ducky Lucky.

"Chicken Licken, where are you going in such a hurry?" asked Ducky Lucky.

"I was walking in the forest and a piece of the sky fell on my head. I am going to tell the President."

"Oh my goodness," said Ducky Lucky. "The sky is falling! The sky is falling!"

The two of them ran into the farmyard where they found Goosey Loosey.

"Chicken Licken and Ducky Lucky, where are you going in such a hurry?" asked Goosey Loosey.

"I met Chicken Licken, who was walking in the forest," said Ducky Lucky, "when a piece of the sky fell on her head."

"We're going to tell the President," said Chicken Licken.

"Oh my goodness," said Goosey Loosey. "The sky is falling! The sky is falling!"

The three of them hurried into the garden where they saw Doggy Loggy.

"Where are you three going in such a hurry?" asked Doggy Loggy.

"I met Ducky Lucky who met Chicken Licken, who was walking in the forest," said Goosey Loosey.

"When a piece of sky fell on her head," added Ducky Lucky.

"And we are going to tell the President," said Chicken Licken.

"Oh my goodness," barked Doggy Loggy. "The sky is falling! The sky is falling. I will come with you."

The four of them hurried into the barn where they saw Horsey Lorsey.

"Where are the four of you going in such a hurry?" asked Horsey Lorsey.

"I met Goosey Loosey who met Ducky Lucky who met Chicken Licken, who was walking in the forest," said Doggy Loggy.

"When a piece of sky fell on her head," added Ducky Lucky.

"And we are going to tell the President," said Chicken Licken.

"Oh my goodness," barked Horsey Lorsey. "The sky is falling! The sky is falling. I will give you a ride."

So, Chicken Licken and Ducky Lucky and Goosey Loosey and Doggy Loggy all hopped on Horsey Lorsey's back, and off they rode toward the capital.

On the way, they met Turkey Lurkey.

"Where are you five going in such a hurry?" asked Turkey Lurkey.

"I met Doggy Loggy who met Goosey Loosey who met Ducky Lucky who met Chicken Licken, who was walking in the forest," said Horsey Lorsey.

"When a piece of sky fell on her head," added Ducky Lucky.

"And we are going to tell the President," said Chicken Licken.

"The sky is falling," said Horsey Lorsey.

"The sky is falling!" barked Doggy Loggy.

"The sky is falling," clucked Turkey Lurkey. "Can I come along with you?"

"I will give you a ride," said Horsey Lorsey.

And off they all trotted toward the capital.

Now, it happened that as they were going, they met Foxy Loxy.

"Where are you six going in such a hurry?" asked Foxy Loxy.

Turkey Lurkey took a deep breath and said, "I met Horsey Lorsey who met Doggy Loggy who met Goosey Loosey who met Ducky Lucky who met Chicken Licken, who was walking in the forest."

"When a piece of sky fell on her head," added Ducky Lucky.

"And we are going to tell the President," said Chicken Licken.

"The sky is falling," said Horsey Lorsey.

"The sky is falling!" barked Doggy Loggy.

"Well, well, well," said the sly Foxy Loxy. "I think I can show you a shortcut."

So all the animals followed Foxy Loxy into the forest.

Now, Foxy Loxy planned on capturing all the animals and eating them up, but as soon as he tried to bite them, Doggy Loggy began to bark, Turkey Lurkey began to gobble, Goosey Loosey began to honk, Ducky Lucky began to quack, and Chicken Licken pecked Foxy Loxy right on the nose. Then Horsey Lorsey reared back, and they all rode away safe and sound back to the barnyard.

In the barnyard they met Kitten Litten. "Where are you six coming from in such a hurry?" asked Kitten Litten.

"Well," said Chicken Licken, "I was walking through the forest and I met Ducky Lucky who met Goosey Loosey who met Doggy Loggy who met Horsey Lorsey who met Turkey Lurkey, and then we all met Foxy Loxy and barely escaped with our lives."

"That's quite some adventure," said Kitten Litten.

"Yes it was," said Chicken Licken. "We were going to go somewhere, but we've quite forgotten where. So instead, I think we'll all go to sleep."

One by one all the animals fell asleep, and they never told the President that the sky was falling.

— The End —

91. The Ugly Little Duckling

After Hans Christian Andersen

*O*nce upon a time in early spring, Mother Duck was waddling by the lake, when she found a strange-looking egg.

"Hmm," said Mother Duck, "I must have misplaced one of my eggs."

So, using her wide bill, she pushed the egg back to her nest, where she sat on it and its five brother and sister eggs for many, many days.

At last, one by one the eggs began to hatch, and out popped six little ducklings. All the ducklings were cute and cuddly, all except for one. The one duckling who had popped out of the strange-looking egg was the ugliest duckling Mother Duck had ever seen.

"What a strange-looking fellow you are," said Mother Duck. "Well, you're one of my babies, and I will love you very very much anyway."

The Ugly Duckling loved his Mother Duck and all his little brother and sister ducklings, and they loved him back.

But the other ducks on the pond were not very nice.

"What an ugly duckling," said one duck.

"He really isn't very pretty," said another.

"Ug-ly, ug-ly," teased a third.

The Ugly Duckling's brothers and sisters tried to protect him from the teasing, but it wasn't easy. Wherever they paddled on the pond, the other ducks would turn their tails, or laugh, or point, or call out "Ug-ly! Ug-ly!"

At last, the Ugly Duckling was so ashamed that he swam away from the pond, and hid himself away. He felt very lonely, and missed his mother and brothers and sisters, but it was still better to live alone than to be tormented and teased.

Summer passed and autumn came. The Ugly Duckling noticed some new birds swimming on the pond. They were much larger than ducks and had long white necks and beautiful thin beaks.

"How lovely they are," thought the Ugly Duckling. "But I am so ugly, I can't let them see me." So the Ugly Duckling stayed hidden in the rushes and paddled by himself.

Then, one day, the Ugly Duckling heard a girl's voice say, "Hello, handsome."

He turned around and was surprised to see one of the beautiful white birds, with the long necks talking to him.

"Are you making fun of me?" asked the Ugly Duckling.

"Oh no," said the white bird. "I think you're very handsome."

The Ugly Duckling frowned. The bird seemed to be telling the truth.

"What are you?" the Ugly Duckling asked.

"I am a swan, silly. Just like you. Only I'm a girl swan, and you're a boy swan."

"Me? A swan?" said the Ugly Duckling. "I'm just an ugly duckling."

"Nonsense," said the swan. "Come here."

The Ugly Duckling followed the swan into the middle of the pond and looked down into the water at his reflection.

Many many months had passed, and the Ugly Duckling had grown into a beautiful swan!

He fell in love with the girl swan, and they were married. Imagine the surprise Mother Duck and all the Duck brothers and sisters felt when the Ugly Duckling came home with his beautiful bride.

"Why, you're quite grown up," said Mother Duck. "I always knew you were a handsome boy."

And they all lived happily ever after.

— *The End* —

92. The Princess and the Pea

After Hans Christian Andersen

Once upon a time, there was a prince who thought he should marry a princess. He was a very picky prince, and his parents were very picky as well. They wanted to make sure that the princess the prince married was a real princess.

"She should be beautiful," said the Prince.

"And kind," said the Queen.

"And sensitive," said the King.

"And delicate," said the Prince.

"And intelligent," said the Queen.

"Well, I'll go out and find one," said the Prince.

So, he traveled all over the globe looking for his princess. He met many princesses. Some of them were beautiful, and some were kind. Some were both kind and beautiful but weren't very sensitive. One princess was kind and sensitive and delicate and intelligent but not very beautiful, and the prince (who was a fairly superficial guy) gave her the thumbs down.

At last, the Prince had traveled the entire world without finding a princess who suited his list of requirements.

He came home and felt very sad. "I'm afraid I'll grow old and die all alone," he said to his father.

"Don't worry," said the King. "We'll find you a princess."

That evening, there was a great thunderstorm. It rained buckets, and lightning flashed through the sky.

The Queen hid under the royal bed, and even the King sitting on the throne was afraid.

Then they heard a knocking at the door.

"Don't answer it," said the Queen, wailing in terror.

"It's probably an ogre," agreed the King.

"I'll just go see," said the Prince. He drew his sword and opened the door.

What do you think he found but the most beautiful princess he had ever seen. She wore a beautiful white gown and a small diamond tiara, and she was completely and utterly soaking wet.

"Come in," said the Prince. "Come in."

"Thank you," said the Princess, curtsying.

Well, the King and Queen came into the hallway to see who their son had let into the castle, and they were very surprised to find this bedraggled girl dripping puddles of water all over their nice new carpeting.

"Are you a princess?" said the Prince, who had already fallen in love.

"Yes," said the girl. "I am. I was on my way to visit a Prince who I heard was looking for a wife, but I'm afraid I got lost in the rain."

"I am . . ." the Prince began, but the Queen clapped a firm hand over her son's mouth.

"He's pleased to meet you," said the Queen. She wanted to make sure that this girl really was a princess before letting her son get too attached. "Come, you must be quite tired. I'll have the servants find a towel, and we'll prepare you a nice soft bed."

"That would be wonderful," said the Princess.

"mfff," said the Prince.

The servants came and led the Princess out.

"What are you doing?" said the Prince to his mother.

"Yes, dear," said the King. "She seems to fit the bill."

"Yes, she's good-looking," said the Queen. "And she seems kind and intelligent, but how sensitive is she? Is she really a princess? We'll soon find out."

The Queen went into the guest bedroom and lifted the mattress. Underneath the mattress she placed a tiny pea. Then on top of the mattress she piled twenty more mattresses and twenty goose down comforters.

"This is your bedroom," said the Queen, escorting the Princess in. "Sleep well."

The Princess was puzzled by the odd tall pile of bedding, but she climbed to the top and lay down.

The next morning at breakfast, when the Princess came downstairs, the Queen was all smiles and cheer. The Prince, of course, could do nothing but stare, and the King was busy reading his newspaper.

"How did you sleep," asked the Queen.

"Oh, very badly," said the Princess. "I could scarcely close my eyes. I tossed and turned all night. I don't know what was in that bed, but it was something very hard. I'm black and blue all over."

The Queen was amazed, because she didn't imagine anyone in the world could pass her difficult test.

"There," said the Prince. "No one but a true princess could be as sensitive as you. Will you marry me?"

"Of course," said the Princess. "Only I must have a very soft and comfortable bed."

So, the Prince and the Princess were married, and they lived happily ever after.

— The End —

93. Foolish Jack

After Hans Christian Andersen

In a land far far from here lived a merchant with three sons, Bob, Hank, and Jack. The two oldest, Bob and Hank, were known as the smartest lads in the whole county. They could add and subtract, multiply and divide, read and write. Now, Jack could do all those things, too, but he wasn't quite as quick as his brothers to brag about his accomplishments. In fact, he was known throughout the county as Foolish Jack, because he did nothing but lounge about all day and look at the sky.

One day word came that the king's daughter was looking for a husband. She declared a contest, that the smartest man in the entire country would be her husband. Whoever could talk sweetly and convince her that he was the brightest would be her prince.

Well, Bob and Hank were excited by the challenge. They asked their father for horses to ride to the city, and he gave them each a tall black horse. They packed books and plays and poems up in their saddle bags, because each one wanted to prove to the princess that he was the smartest.

"Hi there," said Foolish Jack, "Where are you two going?"

"We are going to win the Princess's hearts with our fine words," said Bob.

"At least I am," said Hank.

"So you think," said Bob. "But I will prevail."

"Hey, I think I'll give it a try myself," said Foolish Jack.

"You?" laughed the two older brothers. "Why you're just a fool. You don't even have a horse to ride."

"No," said Foolish Jack, "but I have my old billy goat. Wait for me. He'll do quite well."

Off rode the two brothers, laughing at the Foolish one's ideas.

Well, Foolish Jack wasn't one to hang about and sulk. He found an old saddle and put it on his old billy goat. The goat bucked and kicked, and when Foolish Jack hopped on, it took off like a shot.

"Ya-hoo!" Jack shouted. "This is some ride!"

Soon he passed his two brothers as if they were standing still.

A little later, Bob and Hank caught up with Foolish Jack.

"Hi, Foolish Jack," said Bob. "What have you there?"

"I've found a dead turkey in the road," said Foolish Jack.

"Ah, a dead turkey," said Hank. "What will you do with it?"

"I will give it to the Princess and win her heart," said Jack. He put the dead turkey in his backpack.

"What a fool," laughed the brothers, and off they rode.

A little while later, Jack's angry billy goat passed them at full tilt, and then a time after that, they found Jack again standing in the road.

"Hi, Foolish Jack," said Bob. "What have you there?"

"I've found an old pie plate in the road," said Foolish Jack.

"An old pie plate," said Hank. "It's battered and has a hole in the middle. What will you do with it?"

"I will give it to the Princess and win her heart," said Jack. He put the old pie plate in his pocket.

"What a fool," laughed the brothers, and off they rode.

A little while later, Jack's angry billy goat passed them at full tilt, and then a time after that, they found Jack again standing in the road.

"Hi, Foolish Jack," said Bob. "What have you this time?"

"Look at this mud," said Foolish Jack. "It's so slippery and pretty."

"Mud," said Hank. "Think of that. What will you do with it?"

"I will give it to the Princess and win her heart," said Jack. He picked up a few handfuls of mud and put it into his pocket.

"What a fool," laughed the brothers, and off they rode.

At last the three brothers arrived at the city. There they found that more than two hundred men had arrived to show their intelligence to the beautiful princess. They were all given numbers and told to wait their turn.

While they waited, Hank and Bob studied their books and prepared their speeches.

While he waited, Foolish Jack watched the other contestants. Every single one of them rose, walked toward the princess, and bowed very low. Then, they looked up and saw the King's face frowning down at them. Then they turned and saw the television cameras and newspaper reporters waiting to write down every word they said. Then the wisest and smartest and wittiest men in the entire country sputtered and stuttered and found themselves completely tongue tied.

The King looked angry. Every so often he poked at the stove with a stick, and the fire flared up brightly. The Princess looked bored. Only the reporters seemed interested at so many young men making fools of themselves.

At last it was Bob's turn. He rose, walked toward the Princess, and bowed. Then he saw the King. Then he saw the reporters. Then his face turned bright red and he said, "Hot in here, isn't it?"

"Yes, it is," the Princess said.

"Hmm, hum," said Bob. And then he ran from the room in tears.

Then it was Hank's turn. Hank rose, walked toward the Princess, and bowed. Then he saw the King. Then he saw the reporters. Then his face turned bright red and Hank said, "It's really hot in here, isn't it?"

"Yes, it is," the Princess said.

"Hmm, hum," said Hank. And then he too ran from the room in tears.

At last it was Foolish Jack's turn.

He rose, and walked toward the Princess. Along the way, he tripped, and he heard her giggle softly. Then he stood up and looked the King right in the eye. The King glared back, and Foolish Jack winked slyly. The Princess giggled again. Then Jack turned and looked at the reporters. He stuck his tongue out, and even the King smirked a little.

"Well, what have you to say," the King said at last.

"It sure is hot in here," Foolish Jack said.

"Yes, yes," said the Princess, the little hope she'd felt began to die.

"Would you mind if I cooked my turkey on the stove?" Foolish Jack said. He pulled the turkey from his backpack.

"No," said the Princess, delighted. "You're welcome to, but we don't have any pots or pans handy."

"That's all right," said Foolish Jack. "I have this old pie plate." He brought out the old pie plate, held it up to his face, and winked through the hole at the Princess.

She smiled broadly. "What about sauce? You can't have a turkey without sauce."

"Hmm," said Foolish Jack. "I've got some sauce in my pockets." He reached into his pockets and began smearing the turkey with the mud.

By now the Princess was laughing quite merrily, as was the King.

"Aren't you afraid of the reporters?" asked the King. "They're writing down every word you say."

"Well," said Jack, "I've got enough sauce for them too."

And he threw handfuls of mud at the reporters and television crews until they all ran away.

The turkey went onto the stove, and cooked until it was quite tasty. That evening Foolish Jack and the Princess were married. And they lived happily ever after. Although I must admit that the reports from the newspapers were quite muddy on the details.

— *The End* —

94. The World's Best Jumper

After Hans Christian Andersen

A Flea, a Grasshopper, and a Frog decided to have a contest to see who could jump highest. They invited the whole world, and surprisingly the King and his court accepted their invitation.

On the day of the contest, the three famous jumpers gathered in the King's throne room. People from all over the world crowded around to see the amazing sight.

"I will give my daughter to the one who jumps the highest," said the King.

The Flea stepped up first. He had very fine manners. He smiled nicely, and bowed in all directions. Fleas, as you know, have a habit of drinking blood from young girls and boys, and so this flea felt he had quite a lot in common with human beings. He was very proud of himself, and very confident.

Next came the Grasshopper. He was much bigger than the flea, and he seemed very handsome. He wore a bright green uniform and claimed that his family was as old as the hills. He could trace his family line all the way back to the land of Egypt, where, he said, his kind were worshipped almost as gods.

Both the Flea and the Grasshopper took their time, bowing and smiling, and announcing their names and their lineage, and that they thought they would be very good matches for the Princess.

The Frog said nothing. Instead of babbling on and on, he sat quietly, and it was up to the King's Dog to tell the King that the Frog had been a good friend to him. The King's Dog also said that the Frog had the gift of prophecy and could tell whether the winter coming was going to be harsh or mild.

"Come now," said the King. "Enough talking. Prepare to jump."

First leaped the Flea. The Flea jumped so high and so fast that no one could see him. Everyone in the court said that it looked as if he hadn't jumped at all. Even though he had, and the judgment was rather cruel, the King shrugged and agreed that the flea hadn't gone anywhere.

Next was the Grasshopper's turn. He considered the lesson of the Flea and decided to jump only half as high as he could. But the Grasshopper miscalculated, and he jumped right up into the King's face. The King scowled and swatted him away.

"That was quite rude," the King said, disqualifying the Grasshopper's jump.

For a long time, the Frog stood and thought. Some people began to whisper that he could not jump at all.

"I hope he isn't sick," said the King's Dog. "It would be a shame to lose by forfeit."

The King's Dog sniffed forward and then said, "Yip!"

The Frog leaped with surprise straight into the lap of the Princess, who sat nearby on her golden throne.

"The highest, bravest, and smartest jump," said the King, "was taken by the Frog, who jumped directly into my daughter's lap. Anyone can jump high, but one who can jump with intelligence is rare. The Frog has shown that he is quite smart."

The flea jumped onto the King's Dog, who scratched horribly from that day on. The Grasshopper hopped back into the fields and cried, "I coulda won! I coulda won!"

And the Frog married the Princess, and they lived happily ever after.

— The End —

95. Androcles and the Lion

In the ancient land of Greece lived a brave young shepherd named Androcles. Every day he brought his large flock of sheep out from the town into the fields, where he played his harp and watched over the sheep. If any sheep wandered, Androcles went searching for it. If a sheep was hurt, he bound its foot. He kept the wolves away by throwing stones. In the evening, he gathered his flock and brought them back to his home.

For many months, Androcles had heard rumors of a lion in the area. Sometimes at night, it seemed that he could hear it roar far off in the distance. Other shepherds told him that they'd seen the lion, and that some of their sheep had been stolen. They began to go into the fields in groups rather than alone.

But Androcles wasn't worried. He was a good man and knew how to throw a stone straight and true. Every morning he brought his sheep out to pasture, and every afternoon they returned home unscathed.

Then, one day, Androcles took his sheep to a far field and lay down for a nice nap under a tree. When he woke, he thought he heard some creature snuffling. It didn't sound like a sheep, but whatever kind of animal it was, it sounded hurt. He followed the whimpering to a small hollow in a hill, and there he found the lion.

The lion opened his mouth, as if to issue a hearty and terrifying roar, but then he shut it again, and resumed his whimpering.

Androcles was puzzled. He never met anyone who had come this close to a lion and lived to tell the story.

He stepped forward, and the lion raised its paw as if to strike.

Androcles stepped back, frightened. Then he noticed that the lion was still holding its paw up in the air. He looked closer and saw a large thorn sticking out of the lion's paw.

"You stepped on a thorn, didn't you?" Androcles said in his most soothing voice. "If I take it out, do you promise not to hurt me?"

The lion didn't answer, but it seemed to nod its head, yes.

Androcles wasn't sure whether or not the lion understood him, but he was a good man, and he decided to help the lion.

He approached slowly and cautiously. When he touched the lion's paw, it drew back in surprise and roared. Androcles was patient. "This is going to hurt a little bit," he said. At last, the lion gave him his paw.

Slowly and carefully Androcles drew the thorn from the lion's paw. Then he took a little water and washed the hole clean. "Be careful walking," Androcles said, just as if he was a real doctor. "But after a few days I imagine you'll be right as new."

The lion leaped to his feet, bowed his head slightly, and bounded past Androcles back into the forest.

Some time later, Androcles was accused of stealing another man's sheep. It wasn't at all true, but the other man was rich and had bribed the judges. All Androcles's sheep were forfeited to the other man, and Androcles himself was sentenced to death.

"Cast him to the lions!" the judge ruled.

The poor shepherd prayed all night that some miracle would save him, but the next morning the guards came to lead him into the lion's den.

He raised his head and bravely followed.

When the lion was released from his cage, he recognized Androcles as the man who had helped him. He bounded forward, and instead of attacking and killing him, placed his head upon Androcles's lap.

When the King heard this tale, he ordered the Lion to be set free again in the forest. The liar who had accused Androcles and the judge were both punished. And Androcles was returned to his flock.

They all lived happily ever after.

— *The End* —

96. Whatever the Old Man Does Is Right

After Hans Christian Andersen

In a strange country not far from here lived an old man and his old wife. Now, these two were quite poor, having only the farm house above their heads, a poor barren garden, and an old farm horse.

"Old man," said the Old Woman, "take the horse and sell it for a good price. Then we'll have something good to eat."

"Aye," said the Old Man, cheerfully. His wife gave him a sweet and lovely kiss. He gave his wife a peck on the cheek and headed off into the world.

Not long after, he came to a farmer leading a cow.

"That's a fine-looking cow," said the Old Man.

"And that's a fine-looking horse," said the Farmer.

"I imagine that she gives milk," said the Old Man.

"That she does," said the Farmer.

"Would you like to trade?" said the Old Man. "My horse won't give milk, but she's quite good at pulling this and that."

"A fair trade," said the Farmer.

So the two swapped animals, and off went the Farmer leading his new horse, and off the Old Man went, leading his new cow toward the town. He whistled happily. "My wife," he thought "has always wanted a cow."

A little while longer, he came upon a shepherd leading a fine fat sheep well covered with wool.

"That's a fine-looking sheep," said the Old Man.

"And that's a fine-looking cow," said the Shepherd.

"I imagine that her wool would make a nice warm coat," said the Old Man. "My cow won't make a wool coat, but she'll give milk. Would you like to trade?"

"A fair trade," said the Shepherd.

So the two swapped animals, and off went the Shepherd leading his new cow, and off the Old Man went, leading his new sheep toward the town. He whistled happily. "My wife," he thought "has always wanted a sheep."

A little while later, the old man came across a woman carrying a big goose under her arm.

"Excuse me, Ma'am," said the Old Man, "that's a fine-looking goose."

"And that's a fine-looking sheep," said the Woman.

"My wife has always wanted a goose," said the Old Man. "The feathers and down will make a nice blanket to keep us warm in winter."

"So they will," said the Woman.

"This sheep won't make a warm pillow, but it can give you wool," said the Old Man. "Would you like to trade?"

"A fair trade," said the Woman.

So the two swapped animals, and off went the Woman leading her new sheep, and off the Old Man went, carrying his new goose toward the town. He whistled happily. "My wife," he thought "has always wanted a goose."

A little later, the Old Man came across a young fellow carrying a plump red hen.

"That's a fine-looking hen," said the Old Man.

"And that's a fine-looking goose," said the Young Fellow.

"A hen like that can lay many eggs," said the Old Man. "My goose will only make a pillow or a blanket with her feathers. Perhaps you'd like to trade?"

"A fair trade," said the Young Fellow.

So the two swapped animals, and off went the Young Fellow carrying his new goose, and off the Old Man went, leading his new hen toward the town. He whistled happily. "My wife," he thought "has always wanted a chicken. She will enjoy eating its eggs."

A little ways later, the Old Man came across a poor fellow carrying a sack on his shoulders.

"Why what have you there?" asked the Old Man.

"A sack full of rotten apples," said the Pauper glumly. "Barely fit for feeding the pigs."

"What a waste!" said the Old Man. "Last year our apple tree bore only a single apple, and it was quite rotten. Here you have an entire sack of rotten apples. This is something that my wife would definitely like. Would you like to trade."

"Are you sure?" said the Pauper.

"Well, my chicken is not nearly as heavy as your apples," said the Old Man, "but I think it might be a fair trade."

So the two swapped, and off went the Pauper carrying his new chicken, and off the Old Man went carrying his sack of rotten apples toward the town. He whistled happily. "My wife," he thought "will be so pleased to see so many rotten apples!"

Well, by the time the Old Man got into town, it was getting quite late. The Old Man stopped at an inn. He dropped his sack next to the stove, and took off his coat.

Now, it happened that there were two merchants resting at the inn. They were quite rich and had been spending the evening making bets about anything at all. Silly bets, like how many times the serving girl would drop the tray or how many flies the cat had buzzing around its ears.

In a few minutes, they smelled the warm sweet stink of the Old Man's rotten apples which were roasting next to the stove.

"What is that smell?" said one Merchant.

"Ah, that's my prize!" said the Old Man. He told them how he had traded his horse for a cow, traded the cow for a sheep, the sheep for a goose, the goose for a hen, and the hen for the sack of old rotten apples.

"You're kidding?" said one Merchant.

"I bet your wife will be furious!" said the other Merchant.

"Of course not," said the Old Man. "When I get home and show her what I've brought, she'll give me a sweet and lovely kiss, and say, 'Whatever the Old Man does is right.'"

"That sounds like a bet," said the first Merchant. "I'll wager a ton of gold that she'll box your ears."

"And I will wager another ton!" said the second Merchant.

"No, no, no," said the Old Man. "It wouldn't be fair to you. Let's just make it a sack full of gold. After all, I can only wager my sack full of apples against it."

"Done!" said the Merchants.

The trio set off from town to the Old Man's house. They got there just after sunset, and the Old Woman was pleased to see her husband had returned.

"Hallo, Old Woman!"

"Hallo, Old Man! What did you get in exchange for the horse?"

"Well," said the Old Man, "I got a cow!"

"Wonderful!" said the Old Woman. "Now we can have milk and butter and cheese."

"Then I traded the cow for a sheep"

"Perfect," said the Old Woman. "Our lawn needs trimming, and we can use the sheep's wool for clothing. Perhaps it too will give milk. You are quite a genius."

"After that," said the Old Man, "I swapped the sheep for a goose."

"Lovely," said the Old Woman. "I have always wanted to have a goose for a pet. I can lead her around on a string. And we can have goose down pillows, and maybe a roast goose for our New Year's dinner."

"Of course I had to change the goose for a hen."

"Fantastic!" said the Old Woman. "We can have eggs for breakfast and then hatch a few and we'll have more hens. Then soon we'll have hens for dinner and be able to sell more hens. That's exactly what I want."

"And at last," said the Old Man. "I traded the hen for this sack full of rotten apples."

"My goodness," said the Old Woman. "You have outdone yourself this time. This morning after you left I was talking to our neighbor, and she said that we were so poor that we didn't even have a rotten apple to our name. Now I can go next door and show her that we have a whole sack of rotten apples. She will be so envious! Husband, I am so happy!"

Then the Old Man's wife leaned forward and gave him a sweet and lovely kiss. "Whatever the Old Man does," she said, "is right."

The two Merchant's looked at each other and shrugged. They paid a whole sack full of gold to the Old Man and set off about their business no wiser and quite a bit poorer.

"Well, well, well," said the Old Woman, "whatever the Old Man does is right."

Then she kissed her husband again.

— The End —

97. The Tinder Box

After Hans Christian Andersen

A soldier came marching down the road. "Left, right. Left, right." He had been a long time at the wars and was glad at last to be returning home.

"Hi there," said a voice.

The soldier turned and saw a witch.

"You look like a strong fellow," said the witch. "You have a big knapsack. How would you like to earn a fortune for a few minute's work?"

"Perhaps," said the soldier cautiously.

"Do you see that oak tree," said the witch, pointing to a tree by the side of the road. "It is hollow inside. If you climb to the top, you'll see a hole. Then you can climb all the way down the hollow to the bottom. We'll tie a rope around your waist, and I'll pull you out when you're done."

"Why?" asked the soldier. "What would I want at the bottom of the tree?"

"Money," said the witch. "As much as you can carry. At the bottom of the tree, you'll find yourself in a long cave tunnel lit by lamps. Follow the tunnel down into the ground and you will come to three doors. Behind the first door is a big chest, and on the chest sits a dog with eyes as big as coffee cups. Don't be afraid of the dog. Pick him up and set him on my apron, which you will take along. You can fill your backpack with as much money as you want from the chest because it is full of coppers.

"If it's silver you want, go to the next room. Inside you will see a large chest, and on the chest sits a dog with eyes as big as truck tires. Don't be afraid of the dog. Pick him up and set him on my apron, which you will take along. You can fill your backpack with as much money as you want from the chest because it is full of silver coins.

"Then, if you want gold, go to the next room. Inside you will see a large chest, and on the chest sits a dog with eyes as big as merry-go-rounds. They spin and whirl, but don't be afraid of the dog. Pick him up and set him on my apron, which you will take along. You can fill your backpack with as much money as you want from the chest because it is full of gold coins."

"That sounds like an interesting adventure," said the soldier. "But what do you want, old witch? Surely, you're not doing this out of the goodness of your heart."

"I don't want a single penny," said the witch. "Just bring me the old tinder-box my grandmother left behind down there. It is a family heirloom, and I would like it to remember her by."

"All right," said the soldier. "I'll get it for you. Tie the rope around my body, and let's go."

"Here," said the witch. "Don't forget my blue checked apron."

The soldier tied the rope tightly around his waist, climbed up the tree, and lowered himself down into the hole. He was amazed to find the

tunnel just as the witch told him, lit by the light of hundreds of lamps. Soon he came to the first door and opened it.

Inside, sitting on top of a great big chest was a dog with eyes as big as coffee cups.

"My goodness," said the soldier. "You do have big eyes."

He lay down the witch's blue checked apron and set it on the floor. Then he put the dog on the apron and opened the box. It was, as she had promised, full of copper coins!

The soldier filled his backpack and wondered whether the rest of the witch's story was true. He put the dog back on the chest, picked up the apron, went to the second door, and opened it.

Inside, sitting on another trunk, he saw dog with eyes as big as truck tires. "Good boy," said the soldier. He lay down the witch's blue checked apron and set it on the floor. Then he put the dog on the apron and opened the box. It was, as she had promised, full of silver coins!

Well, the soldier dumped out all the copper coins and filled his backpack with silver coins. Then he wondered whether the rest of the witch's story was true. He put the dog back on the chest, picked up the apron, went to the third door, and opened it.

In this room, on a third trunk, sat a dog with eyes as big as merry-go-rounds. The dog's eyes spun and whirled, but the soldier wasn't afraid. "If you keep looking at me like that," said the soldier, "your eyes will cross." He lay down the witch's blue checked apron and set it on the floor. Then he put the dog on the apron and opened the box. It was, as she had promised, full of gold coins!

The soldier quickly dumped out all the silver coins and filled his backpack and his pockets with gold coins. He put the dog back on the chest, picked up the apron, and walked back to the bottom of the tree.

"I'm done," he shouted. "Pull me back up."

"Do you have my granny's tinder box?"

"Ah," said the soldier. "I knew I forgot something. I'll go get it."

He hiked back down the tunnel and quickly found the tinder box. It looked quite ordinary, but the witch wanted it, so he put it in his pocket.

"I've got it now," he shouted. And the witch hauled it out.

"Give me the tinder box," the witch demanded as soon as the soldier's feet touched the ground.

"What do you want it for?"

"What difference does it make to you?" she asked. "I've kept my end of the bargain, now you keep yours."

"I have," said the soldier. "I've brought it to you as promised. But if you don't tell me what it's for, I'll cut your head off."

"No," said the witch.

So, the soldier drew his sword and cut the witch's head off. He knew that it doesn't pay to trust witches. Then he put the tinder box in his pocket and marched off to town.

When he arrived, he found the finest hotel and lived in the grandest suite. He bought himself new clothes and ate wonderful meals. He had more money than he knew what to do with, so he spent his time at the race track, and at the theater, and eating out with the many new friends that he found suddenly hanging on his every word.

One friend in particular told him that he hadn't seen anything until he saw the Princess, who was the most beautiful woman in the land.

"Take me to her," commanded the soldier.

"You can't," said the friend. "The King and Queen are very jealous of her and keep her locked up in an iron castle. You see there was a prophesy that she would marry a common soldier, and they didn't want that."

"Ah well," sighed the soldier. "What good is beauty if no one can see it."

Then he went back to his task, which was to live well and expensively.

Unfortunately, although the soldier knew how to spend money, he did not know how to earn more. He went back down the road, but couldn't remember which tree the witch had sent him down. At last, all his money was spent, and he found himself turned out of his fine hotel room. All his new friends faded away. At last, he was left alone in a small hut at the end of town, wearing nothing but his old uniform.

One evening, sitting in the dark and gloomy hut, the soldier wished for a bit of light to cheer him, but he didn't even have enough money to afford a candle. Then he remembered that there was a small piece of candle in the tinderbox he had taken from the witch.

He opened the tinderbox, took out the candle, and struck the flint once against its hard steel edge.

In an instant, there was a woosh and a bark, and there standing before him was the dog with eyes as big as coffee cups.

"What do you wish, my master?" said the dog.

"Wow!" said the soldier. "This is some tinder box. Dog, bring me a sack full of money, please."

Whoosh! The dog vanished. Woof! It returned with a bag of copper coins in its mouth.

"Thank you," said the soldier, petting the dog before it vanished again with another whoosh.

After experimenting a little, the soldier found that if he struck the tinderbox twice, the dog with eyes as big as truck tires appeared; he had it bring him silver coins. He struck it three times, and the dog with eyes as big as merry-go-rounds appeared; he had it bring him gold coins.

The next day he went back to his fine hotel room and found that all his old friends returned.

The soldier lived well for a short time longer, but he felt dissatisfied. "It is all very well to have money and friends, but I would much rather have someone dear to share it with. I would like to see the beautiful princess who is locked in the iron castle."

Then he thought for a moment. "Hmm, perhaps I can!"

He struck his tinderbox once and the dog with eyes as big as coffee cups appeared. "I know it is late at night, but could you please bring me the beautiful princess, right away?"

Whoosh! The dog vanished. Woof! It returned carrying the beautiful princess on its back. The princess was fast asleep, and since the soldier was a kind man, he did not wake her. He only leaned forward and gave her a soft kiss on the cheek. Then he told the dog to send her back to the castle.

The next morning, when the Princess woke up she told her mother, the Queen, that she had the strangest dream.

"I dreamed that a big dog carried me off," she said. "And that a handsome soldier kissed me on the cheek. And then the dog brought me back home."

The Queen was immediately suspicious. She ordered one of the Princess's attendants to watch over the Princess.

That night, the soldier once again ordered the dog to go and fetch the Princess. The attendant saw the dog go flying out the window with the Princess on its back and put on a pair of seven-league boots. She ran after the dog and arrived just in time to see it emerge from the soldier's room with the Princess on its back.

Thinking quickly, the attendant took a piece of white chalk and marked a large X on the door to the soldier's room. Now they would be able to tell where the Princess had been.

The dog, however, noticed the attendant, and when she had gone back to the castle, the dog took chalk and made a large X on every door in the hotel.

The next day, the King sent guards to arrest the soldier, but when they found every door in the hotel marked by an X they didn't know whom to arrest.

That night, the Queen fastened a bag with white talcum powder to the Princess's night gown. She poked a small hole in the bag.

When the dog came back that evening and took the Princess on his back, the talcum powder leaked out of the bag and made a clear white trail leading straight to the soldier's door.

The next morning, the King's guards followed the trail and arrested the soldier.

"You'll hang tomorrow," said one of the guards.

That news didn't cheer the soldier. He had been taken so quickly from his apartment that he had left the tinder box behind. He saw that everyone in town was gathering to watch the hanging.

Just then, a shoe-maker happened to pass by the jailhouse window.

"Hi, you," said the soldier. "Slow down. If you'll do me a favor, I'll give you a gold coin."

"What can I do for you?" asked the shoe-maker, eager to make a quick fortune.

"Go to my hotel room and bring me my tinder box," the soldier said. "If you go quickly, I'll give you two gold coins."

The shoe-maker hurried off and was quickly back. He threw the tinder box up to the soldier, and the soldier threw down three gold coins to the happy fellow.

Just then, the guards came and led the soldier off to the scaffold.

The whole town was there to watch. The King and Queen looked quite pleased, but the Princess looked rather sad.

"Do you have anything to say for yourself?" the King asked.

"I wished only to see your beautiful daughter," said the soldier. "I did not harm a hair on her head. I wonder if as my last request, I might smoke a pipe before you hang me."

The King waved his hand, "You may."

The soldier struck his tinder box six times and Woof! Woof! Woof! all three dogs appeared.

"Quickly, help me!" he shouted. "They're going to hang me!"

One of the dogs knocked over the soldiers. Another broke down the scaffold. The third dog, with eyes as big as merry-go-rounds, sat on the King and the Queen.

"I wonder, your highness," asked the soldier politely, "if I might have your permission to marry your daughter?"

"Yes," gasped the King.

"If she agrees," wheezed the Queen.

"I do," said the Princess, because the soldier was quite handsome and had been kind to her.

And so they were married. The royal wedding feast lasted for seven days. And at the wedding table sat three dogs, one with eyes as big as coffee cups, another with eyes as big as truck tires, and the third with eyes as big as merry-go-rounds, spinning merrily.

— *The End* —

98. Aladdin and the Magic Lamp

Part One: How Aladdin Gets the Lamp

*I*n the far off city of Baghdad lived a boy named Aladdin who lived alone with his mother. His father had died many years earlier and had left Aladdin and his mother impoverished.

One day, a tall man with a dark beard came up to the boy and asked, "Excuse me, kind sir, but is your name Aladdin?"

Aladdin had been taught never to talk with strangers, but this man was so polite that he had to answer.

"Why yes, it is. How did you know?" Aladdin said.

"Because I am your long-lost uncle!" the man said. He clapped the boy up into a great hug. "You look just like your father did when he was a boy."

"How do I know you are my uncle?" Aladdin asked, suspiciously.

"See here," said the man. He drew a large gold ring with a bright red ruby from his finger and gave it to Aladdin. "This ring was your father's, was it not? Put it on your finger, and remember your father."

Aladdin slipped the ring on his finger, and thought back many years. At last he remembered that the ring was indeed worn by his father.

"How did you get this ring?" Aladdin demanded.

"Your father gave it to me just before he died," the man said. "He asked that I bring it to you and help you to find a great treasure. I have kept my first promise and would like to fulfill my second promise."

Now Aladdin had never heard that he had an uncle, and with good cause. The man who was even now smiling and laughing was in fact a wicked magician. Whether he had met Aladdin's father before the poor man's untimely death or found the ring afterward is something that we shall never know.

"Would you like to help me on an adventure?" the magician asked. "It could be quite profitable."

"Of course!" Aladdin said. "My mother and I are very poor, and we could certainly use some money."

"Well, well, well," said the so-called uncle, grinning. "Come with me."

The magician led Aladdin to a huge pile of rocks and pointed to a small crack in the middle of the pile. "Squeeze your way through that opening," said the magician, "and follow my instructions. I would do it myself, but as you can see, I'm much too large."

Aladdin scrambled up the rocks and easily slid in between the boulders. He dropped down a few feet, but landed unharmed. Inside, he was surprised to find a flight of stairs leading down. He followed the stairs and soon found himself in a great chamber dimly lit by the flame of an old oil lamp.

When Aladdin's eyes became accustomed to the dark gloom of the chamber, he was amazed to see that he was standing in an underground forest. Some of the trees hung with the succulent and delicious fruit while other trees dripped with strands of pearls. In one corner was a pile of chests which were overflowing with gold and silver coins. Another corner was heaped high with jewels: emeralds, rubies, diamonds, sapphires, and opals. On a small pillar in the middle of the chamber was the lamp, old and tarnished, flickering faintly.

"Put out the lamp," said the wicked magician's voice echoing from above. "Slip the lamp into your pocket, and bring it to me. Then we'll go back and get the rest of the treasure."

"But if I bring out the lamp," Aladdin said, "then how will I be able to see the rest of the treasure?"

"Do what I say, Boy," the magician said. "Or you'll regret the day you were born. Now bring out the lamp."

Aladdin grew suspicious. If this man was his uncle, why was he being so rude and unkind. Still, he was a good and dutiful son of his father, and he felt that his uncle deserved the benefit of the doubt. Aladdin extinguished the lamp, and slid it into his pocket.

"Give me a hand up," Aladdin said, as he began to climb the boulders.

"Give me the lamp first," said the magician.

"Please, Uncle," Aladdin said. "I don't want to fall. Help me up, and then I will give you the lamp."

"Give me the lamp first."

"No," Aladdin said, firmly. "I can't reach it without letting go."

"Foolish boy!" cried the magician. He waved his hands in a magic pass, and instantly the boulders sealed shut. Aladdin fell, not far perhaps, but far enough to knock the wind from his lungs.

When he came to his senses, he realized that he was all alone in the dark. Poor Aladdin realized now that the man was certainly not his uncle, and that he had wanted nothing more than a gullible boy to do his bidding.

Aladdin stumbled back down the stairs, feeling his way in the dark. When he reached the bottom, he sat down and began to cry. He had all the treasure a man could possibly want, but what use was it to a boy buried alive?

Aladdin cried for quite some time, and at last his tears dried, but still he felt his heart filled with worry. While he was thinking, trying to devise a way out of this terrible trap, he found himself absently turning the ring the magician had given him.

As soon as the boy turned the ring, there was a great roaring, and a moment later a Genie with red glowing eyes stood before Aladdin. (Many years earlier, the magician had heard of the great cave filled with treasure in a book. He also knew that the only person who could bring the magic lamp from the cave was a boy named Aladdin, which was why he had sought out the boy in the first place. What the magician did not know was that the Aladdin's father's ring was magical.)

"I am the Genie of the ring," said the Genie. "Your wish is my command. What would you like, Master? What would you like?"

As frightened as Aladdin was of this terrible apparition, he kept his head. "Please, good Genie of the Ring," Aladdin said, "release me from this cave."

As soon as Aladdin spoke, the ceiling above shivered and rumbled open, and Aladdin found himself standing alone on the hilltop not far from where he had entered the cave.

He quickly hurried home to his mother and told her the whole story.

"Truly that was not your uncle," said his mother. "My husband never did have a brother. I am only thankful that you are alive."

Aladdin hugged his mother close, and soon fell asleep in her arms.

And they lived happily ever after until. . . .

— *The End*—

99. Aladdin and the Magic Lamp

Part Two: How Aladdin Becomes Rich and Marries

The next morning, when Aladdin awoke he felt both refreshed and saddened. If only he had thought to fill his pockets with pieces of gold, then both he and his mother could have lived happily for many many years. Then he remembered the lamp and brought it out of his pocket.

"Mother," said Aladdin. "Perhaps you can take this lamp into the market and sell it. It will surely bring enough for us to eat a good meal."

Aladdin's mother looked at the lamp and scowled. "But it is so old and beaten and tarnished," she said. "Who would pay for that?"

"Perhaps I can polish it up a bit," Aladdin said. He took the edge of his shirt sleeve and rubbed the lamp.

There was a great roaring, and a moment later a Genie with red glowing eyes stood before Aladdin.

"I am the Genie of the lamp," said the Genie. "Your wish is my command. What will you have, Master? What will you have?"

Aladdin's mother was terrified, and she cowered in the corner, but Aladdin recognized the Genie as the cousin of the Genie of the ring.

"We are hungry," Aladdin said. "Bring us some food."

In an instant the Genie was gone, and in an instant the Genie returned with a large silver tray filled with fruits and meats and delicacies of all kinds. As soon as the tray touched the ground, the Genie vanished, and Aladdin began to eat.

"Come, Mother," he smiled. "Tell no one the secret of this marvelous lamp, and we will never again be hungry."

Aladdin's mother hesitated, but at last hunger drove her to taste the food the Genie had brought. "This is delicious," she said. "How wonderful."

"Even more wonderful, look at the platter," Aladdin said.

Aladdin's mother looked at the silver platter and realized that it would bring a small fortune in the market. "Truly we are blessed," she said.

So, every day Aladdin asked the Genie to bring him breakfast, and every afternoon the boy sold the platter for a half dozen gold pieces. In a short time he was both wealthy and well-known as a merchant of fine silver.

Several years passed happily, and then one day while striding through the marketplace, Aladdin happened to catch a glimpse of the Sultan's daughter. The Princess Badir was known as the most beautiful girl in the land, and Aladdin was immediately captivated by her beauty.

He stumbled home and immediately went to his bed.

"What is the matter?" his mother asked. "Are you ill?"

"I am sick," Aladdin smiled, "sick with love."

"Whom do you love?"

"The Sultan's daughter, the Princess Badir," Aladdin said.

"Hush," said his mother, clapping her hand over the boy's mouth. "We may be rich today, but not long ago we were but peasants. If the Sultan hears that you covet his daughter, he may have us both killed."

Aladdin would not listen to his mother, and the more he thought about the Princess, the more he became determined to marry her.

At last, he came to a decision. He summoned the Genie of the Lamp and commanded him to bring a bowl filled with jewels. When the bowl arrived, overflowing with the most perfect jewels the world has ever seen, Aladdin told his mother: "Take these to the Sultan as a present. If he asks whom they are from, tell him nothing, simply say, 'They are a gift.'"

Terrified though she was, Aladdin's mother agreed. She carried the heavy bowl to the palace and was soon admitted to the Sultan's presence.

"Whom are these jewels from?" the Sultan asked.

"They are a gift," answered Aladdin's mother. "I can say no more."

With a shrug, the Sultan dismissed the old woman.

The next day she returned with an even larger bowl filled with jewels.

"Whom are these jewels from?" the Sultan asked.

"They are a gift," answered Aladdin's mother. "I can say no more."

With a frown, the Sultan dismissed the old woman.

The next day, Aladdin sent his mother again, telling her, "This time, if the Sultan asks, tell him that you are my mother, and that I seek the hand of his daughter Badir in marriage."

When Aladdin's mother arrived at the palace, she was immediately shown into the royal presence.

"These jewels are even more magnificent than the last," said the Sultan. "Whom are they from? What does he want?"

At last, Aladdin's mother spoke. "Please, oh great one, spare my son's life. He has an unworthy request, but. . . ."

"Speak," ordered the Sultan. "His life is already spared."

"He wishes to marry your daughter, Badir," said the old woman, her eyes filled with tears.

The Sultan stepped down and handed her his own silk handkerchief. "Lady, your son has brought me the finest jewels I have ever seen," he said. "Why should I not give him my finest and most precious jewel? Send for him at once. They will be married today."

Aladdin's mother hurried home and told her son the good news.

With a great smile, Aladdin hugged and kissed his mother. "Now, we must get ready for the wedding," he said.

"But I have nothing to wear," said the old lady.

Aladdin only laughed and rubbed his magic lamp.

There was a great roaring, and a moment later the Genie with red glowing eyes stood before Aladdin.

"I am the Genie of the lamp," said the Genie. "Your wish is my command. What will you have, Master? What will you have?"

"Dress my mother in the finest gown," Aladdin ordered. "Bring me the finest horses. Assemble a brigade of soldiers, and each should carry a chest of treasure finer than the next one."

Soon, the long and marvelous parade of soldiers made its way to the palace. The doors were opened, and the Sultan's eyes widened as one by one the soldiers deposited chests filled with precious treasure at his feet.

At last arrived Aladdin and his mother, both richly dressed, riding two of the finest horses the world has ever seen.

Aladdin leaped from his horse and helped his old mother down.

The Sultan brought forth his daughter Badir, and at last the two met face to face. Their love for each other was instant.

That evening they were married, and that night the nightingale sang sweetly in the palace courtyard.

And they lived happily ever after, until. . . .

— *The End* —

100. Aladdin and the Magic Lamp

Part Three: Aladdin Loses and Regains All

*M*any years had gone by since Aladdin had married the Princess Badir, and together the two lived happily. With the help of the Genie of the Lamp, Aladdin built a huge palace for his bride and another for his mother just down the street. The kingdom prospered, and all would have been well for them, except. . . .

In a far off land, the evil magician who had sent Aladdin into the cave to fetch the lamp happened to think about the misadventure. The boy had surely died, he thought, but what had ever become of the lamp? He peered into a magic crystal ball and saw that the lamp was missing from its pillar in the chamber under the ground.

"The boy escaped!" the magician raged. "He has stolen my lamp."

Eventually the evil magician calmed himself and began to search the world for the treasure he thought was rightfully his. At last he found it.

The next day, a strange merchant set up a shop beneath the palace window. "New lamps for old!" he cried. "New lamps for old."

Now, the Princess Badir knew that her husband Aladdin kept an old lamp on the table in his library, but he had never told her the reason why.

"Aladdin is traveling with my father," she thought. "It will be a wonderful present for him, if I exchange that old and battered lamp for a wonderful new one."

So, she fetched the lamp and sent a servant girl to take it to the merchant and exchange it for a new one.

"Sir," said the girl, "my mistress would like to exchange this old lamp for a new one."

The merchant, who was really the magician in disguise, saw the old lamp and recognized it immediately. He began to shiver with delight.

"Is something wrong?" asked the servant girl. "Is this lamp too old?"

"Oh, no," said the magician. "Pick out any lamp you like. Take them all, if you will."

The servant girl blushed, thinking that the merchant was just being kind. She gave him the old lamp, and began searching for a new one.

The instant the magician held the old lamp in his hand, he rubbed it.

There was a great roaring, and a moment later a Genie with red glowing eyes stood before him.

"I am the Genie of the lamp," said the Genie. "Your wish is my command. What will you have, Master? What will you have?"

"Take Aladdin's palace, and everyone inside, and transport them all to an oasis in the middle of the desert," the Magician ordered. "Bring me with it also."

"It will be done," said the Genie, clapping its hands. An instant later, the entire palace, and the magician himself vanished from the city of Baghdad.

When Aladdin and the Sultan returned home from their travels, they were astonished to find Aladdin's palace missing.

"Where is my daughter?" the Sultan demanded. "What have you done with her?"

"I do not know," Aladdin cried.

"Then into the dungeon with you!" the Sultan ordered. "If you do not return my daughter by tomorrow morning, then I will have your head." In an instant, Aladdin was seized by guards and taken to the dungeon beneath the Sultan's old palace.

As soon as he was thrown into his cell, Aladdin began to cry. He cried not only for himself, but for his lost Princess, who he feared was dead. He wept and wept, and even the guards turned their heads away, because they had grown rather fond of the young prince.

When at last all his tears had gone dry, Aladdin found himself absently turning the old ring of his father.

There was a great roaring as soon as the young man turned the ring, and a moment later a Genie with red glowing eyes stood before Aladdin.

"I am the Genie of the ring," said the Genie. "Your wish is my command. What would you like, Master? What would you like?"

Aladdin smiled, "Please, good Genie of the Ring, bring back my castle and my princess."

The Genie frowned and said, "I am only the Genie of the Ring. I can not undo the work of the Genie of the Lamp."

"In that case," Aladdin said, "bring me to the palace, and take me to my wife, the Princess Badir."

"It will be done," said the Genie, clapping its hands. An instant later, Aladdin stood in his Palace, which now resided in an oasis in the middle of the desert. Standing before him, amazed at her husband's sudden appearance, was the Princess Badir.

"Beware, my husband," she said. "A wicked magician has stolen us away from Baghdad. He is not here now, but may return soon."

Aladdin hugged his wife close. "Tell me, Badir, what has become of the old lamp that I kept on my desk in my library?"

The Princess Badir's eyes filled with tears as she told Aladdin how she had wanted to exchange the lamp as a gift for her husband.

So, she had sent her servant to the market, and the next moment she was face to face with a wicked magician. The magician had told the Princess that she had married an impostor. He was determined to take her as his bride.

When her story was done, Aladdin comforted her. "You did nothing wrong, my sweetness. If I had told you my secret, then all would yet be well."

Then, Aladdin told his wife that it was true. He had been born a pauper and had come by his riches through magic. The Princess Badir blinked not an eye.

"Your manners have never been as refined as I might have expected from a prince," she said. "And yet I love you."

"We must find the lamp," Aladdin said.

"The magician keeps it in his pocket," said Princess Badir. "He is never without it."

"I have an idea," Aladdin said. He summoned forth the Genie of the Ring, and asked for a sleeping potion, which the Genie immediately brought. "Tonight when the magician asks you to marry him, tell him yes."

"But. . . ." Badir cried.

"Hush!" Aladdin said. "You will ask him to drink a toast. Give him a glass with this sleeping potion. When he falls asleep, we will take the lamp from him and all will be well."

Aladdin hid himself in a closet and waited until nightfall.

That evening, the evil magician came into the Princess Badir's bed chamber.

"Now that you've had time to think," the magician said, "will you give up that impostor and marry a true magician."

"I have given it much thought," Princess Badir said. "I agree. Now we must drink a toast to our future together."

The Princess poured the magician a glass of the sleeping potion. Their glasses clinked in a toast. The magician greedily drank the potion down and immediately fell to the ground fast asleep.

Aladdin rushed from his hiding place and hugged his Princess. Then he searched the magician's pockets until he found the old and battered lamp.

He rubbed the lamp. There was a great roaring, and a moment later a Genie with red glowing eyes stood before him.

"I am the Genie of the lamp," said the Genie. "Your wish is my command. What will you have, Master? What will you have?"

"Take this palace and all in it, and return it to Baghdad," Aladdin said. "But this magician, send him to a remote part of China where no one speaks a word of his language."

"It will be done," said the Genie, clapping its hands. An instant later, the palace stood in its original place in Baghdad, and the Magician found himself fast asleep far away in a forgotten province of China.

When the news of the palace's return reached the Sultan, he hurried to Aladdin's palace, and demanded to see his daughter.

Hand in hand, Aladdin and the Princess Badir went to greet the Sultan.

And from that day until the end of their days, they lived happily and in peace.

— *The End* —

We Have
EVERYTHING!

Available wherever books are sold!

Everything® **After College Book**
$12.95, 1-55850-847-3

Everything® **Astrology Book**
$12.95, 1-58062-062-0

Everything® **Baby Names Book**
$12.95, 1-55850-655-1

Everything® **Baby Shower Book**
$12.95, 1-58062-305-0

Everything® **Barbeque Cookbook**
$12.95, 1-58062-316-6

Everything® **Bartender's Book**
$9.95, 1-55850-536-9

Everything® **Bedtime Story Book**
$12.95, 1-58062-147-3

Everything® **Beer Book**
$12.95, 1-55850-843-0

Everything® **Bicycle Book**
$12.95, 1-55850-706-X

Everything® **Build Your Own Home Page**
$12.95, 1-58062-339-5

Everything® **Casino Gambling Book**
$12.95, 1-55850-762-0

Everything® **Cat Book**
$12.95, 1-55850-710-8

Everything® **Christmas Book**
$15.00, 1-55850-697-7

Everything® **College Survival Book**
$12.95, 1-55850-720-5

Everything® **Cover Letter Book**
$12.95, 1-58062-312-3

Everything® **Crossword and Puzzle Book**
$12.95, 1-55850-764-7

Everything® **Dating Book**
$12.95, 1-58062-185-6

Everything® **Dessert Book**
$12.95, 1-55850-717-5

Everything® **Dog Book**
$12.95, 1-58062-144-9

Everything® **Dreams Book**
$12.95, 1-55850-806-6

Everything® **Etiquette Book**
$12.95, 1-55850-807-4

Everything® **Family Tree Book**
$12.95, 1-55850-763-9

Everything® **Fly-Fishing Book**
$12.95, 1-58062-148-1

Everything® **Games Book**
$12.95, 1-55850-643-8

Everything® **Get-a-Job Book**
$12.95, 1-58062-223-2

The ultimate reference for couples planning their wedding!

- Scheduling, budgeting, etiquette, hiring caterers, florists, and photographers
- Ceremony & reception ideas
- Over 100 forms and checklists
- And much, much more!

$12.95, 384 pages, 8" x 9¼"

Personal finance made easy—and fun!

- Create a budget you can live with
- Manage your credit cards
- Set up investment plans
- Money-saving tax strategies
- And much, much more!

$12.95, 288 pages, 8" x 9¼"

For more information, or to order, call 800-872-5627
or visit everything.com

Adams Media Corporation, 260 Center Street, Holbrook, MA 02343

OVER TWO MILLION EVERYTHING BOOKS SOLD

Web Site Links for All the Tools You Need!

THE **EVERYTHING** BUILD YOUR OWN **HOME PAGE BOOK**
Create a site you'll be proud of, without becoming a programmer
Mark Binder and Beth Helman

$12.95, 304 pages, 8" x 9¼"

Your friends and family will be amazed with what you can do!

- Tutorials on the most popular programs
- Simple instructions to get your home page started
- Maintenance routines to keep your site fresh
- And much, much more!

THE **EVERYTHING PREGNANCY BOOK**
Your body, your baby, and much more
What every woman needs to know—month-by-month, to insure a worry-free pregnancy
Maryann Brinley
with Stephanie Goldstein, M.D.

$12.95, 320 pages, 8" x 9¼"

A pregnancy book that really does have everything!

- Extensive medical evaluation of what's happening to your body
- Exercise and diet tips
- 40-week pregnancy calendar
- And much, much more!

EVERYTHING KIDS'®

Now Available!
Only $9.95 each

THE EVERYTHING KIDS' PUZZLE BOOK

THE EVERYTHING KIDS' MONEY BOOK

THE EVERYTHING KIDS' NATURE BOOK

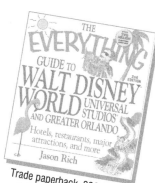